A HOUSE IN CHICAGO

HARRIET CONVERSE TILDEN
(Aged seventeen)

By OLIVIA HOWARD DUNBAR

A HOUSE
IN CHICAGO

THE UNIVERSITY OF CHICAGO PRESS
CHICAGO · ILLINOIS

THE UNIVERSITY OF CHICAGO PRESS, CHICAGO 37

Cambridge University Press, London, N.W. 1, England
W. J. Gage & Company, Limited, Toronto 2B, Canada

TO
THE MEMORY OF
MY MOTHER AND FATHER

CONTENTS

PART I

PART II

ACKNOWLEDGMENTS

INDEX

PART I

CHAPTER I

REBIRTH

THERE are certain springtimes when the natural world seems in an inexplicable hurry. Gardens burgeon incoherently, and the seasons become telescoped. Chronological spacing, ordinarily congenial both to man and nature, is defeated by a wild and lawless ecstasy of growth.

Something of the sort seems to have happened in the field of American letters in a period beginning about the year 1912. And though several of the more significant names in this interesting composite birth were, after all, those of easterners, still this is the moment when the Middle West entered into a new and exciting consciousness and when Chicago took its place as the center of momentous happenings. This city was already acknowledged to be a habitable spot for the fine arts in general. Poetry was now to feel especially at home there.

Just how all this came to happen the literary historian will no doubt determine. But it may meanwhile be pointed out that the silence of the middle western region had been broken by William Vaughn Moody, dead in 1910 with half his life unlived. Not that Moody was a "regional" poet. But he was a native of Indiana, had lived much in Chicago, taught at its university. He had created an audience. Who would there be to follow him?

By way of answer to this question an actual chorus began to be heard within a few years of his death. Those who did not live in the Chicago region appeared in the pages of Chicago's magazine, *Poetry*, and many of them came to the newly awakened city, returning again and again. From all quarters of the country they came, as well as from across the seas. And the lives of such men as Robinson and Lindsay, as well as of John Masefield and

3

Rabindranath Tagore, came to be linked together, not so much, astonishingly enough, by being contemporaries and fellow-artists as by their common relationship—a matter with which these pages have chiefly to do—to one perceptive, generous, and forceful woman, a woman whose contribution to her time comes more and more to seem of memorable importance. This woman was the poet's widow, Harriet Converse (Tilden) Moody.

Now the notable persons who paused in Chicago during these years were in most ways dissimilar. But they were alike in discovering in Harriet Moody a woman of intellectual power, arresting personality, and diverse gifts, chief among these being the gift of friendship—a statement to be understood in no sentimental sense. Among the wide range of her friendships the most remarkable are naturally those in which writers, as well as other artists, figured; and, happily, these come alive again in Mrs. Moody's correspondence.

So intimately allied was she, in fact, with the production of that fertile period that it would be natural to attempt to claim too much for her. Thus, it is wiser to claim nothing whatever and to limit one's self to suggesting just what did happen during the fifteen or more surprising years when so many reputations were made and during which she formed and developed her most memorable associations.

At the start, however, it cannot be made too clear that Mrs. Moody was very far from being a deliberate collector of celebrities. If her hospitality had had the slightest taint of self-interest, these relationships of hers would, of course, not be worth chronicling. But, disinterested to an extreme degree, it was she, always, who was the lavish giver, and it was first of all herself that she gave. Did she actually fertilize the productivity of the younger ones among the writers who surrounded her? That would, no doubt, be too much to say. But any writer, of any age, would have admitted that there was reinforcement in the mere fact of association with a woman so largehearted and discerning. Beyond this, poets, indeed artists in any field who were fortunate enough to know her, soon found the machinery of their communication with the public deftly oiled, the problems of their private lives simplified, and conditions actually provided for their creative work. On her part, such services as these were an everyday matter. They were always imaginatively conceived, delicately offered, and carried through with quietly efficient generalship. Perhaps the artists themselves, at least the younger ones, scarcely understood what was being done for them. At Mrs. Moody's most vital period the MacDowell Colony, which for many years was happy in sheltering Edwin Arlington Robinson and other writers, was still to become widely known, and other retreats designed to smooth the artist's pathway were not yet in operation. Fellowships and "grants" from rich foundations were far rarer phenomena than now. Most poets at least, as perhaps must always be the case, were all too dismally familiar with the practical difficulties of existence.

An outsider might readily take it for granted that the life led by Mrs. Moody after 1910 was simply an expression of devotion to the memory of her husband. This view may be held only with reservations. In developing her friendships with writers, painters, and others, in playing toward them the complex role of sibyl, counselor, friend, she was obeying her own native urge. That was the charm of it—and of her. Her action was, however, partly directed and her outlook partly colored by her loyalty to the poet with whom she had had such close understanding. Her Massachusetts "farm," as she called it, at West Cummington, in the Berkshires—to which she took delight in transferring the William Cullen Bryant birthplace and which was conducted only nominally as a farm but actually as a summer retreat for musicians, painters, or poets in need of country seclusion—was acquired solely because Moody had wished to own just such a place. The fact that it was so many hundreds of miles from Chicago and that she herself was greatly restricted in her physical movement counted for little to a woman who regarded distance as lightly as youth regards it in an age of the airplane. The flat in Waverly Place, New York, a few steps away from Washington Square, she retained for many years because Moody had lived and worked there. She had, indeed, vainly

5

dreamed of acquiring the entire building and of converting it into a permanent headquarters for poets, as a memorial to her husband. But even as it was, the rooms were occupied successively by Percy MacKaye, Padraic Colum, and Ridgely Torrence, while Robert Frost, Vachel Lindsay, and a score of others lodged there more or less briefly.

Moody's name was constantly on her lips, and she proselyted for him to the end of her days.

But those who knew neither of them should realize that this woman's personality must have made itself felt much as it did, so powerful were its interior forces, had she never known Moody at all.

It was in line with her own strong preferences that outside the limits of her wide personal acquaintance Mrs. Moody was almost unknown. Her life was, in fact, strictly a private one. Except in the single instance of her marriage to Moody, which fulfilled the conditions of a newspaper romance, she didn't do the things that attract popular attention. And, in particular, never could she have publicly promoted the cause of poetry. She did not see poetry as a cause or as a thing to hold meetings about or form associations for. If you were a poet, you withdrew to your closet, as Moody had done, and wrote your poems, which was nobody's business but your own, and, later, your readers'. She knew very well, none better, that a writer has often another need, that of a helping friend; but that was a private matter, too. It was her way of thinking and feeling about these things that explains why men of exceptional gifts, indeed men of genius, paused content, once under her roof, and exchanged with her pledges of permanent friendship.

CHAPTER II

2970 GROVELAND AVENUE

IT WAS often by a rather casual route that during the years, roughly speaking, from 1913 to 1928 so many followers of the arts, of greater and lesser stature, found their way to a three-story red brick house on a street then called Groveland (later Ellis) Avenue in an unfashionable part of Chicago.

Let us suppose, for instance, that you were, at that time, a personable young American poet somewhere on the hither side of general recognition. In which case it is more than likely that some older or more fortunate friend, perhaps finding you bound for the West, would, memorably for you, have taken you in hand. You were to stop off in Chicago, he would have told you. You were to be the guest of Mrs. William Vaughn Moody. He himself would make the arrangements, and no decision on your part was necessary.

This is, in fact, precisely what happened in who shall say how many cases.

Or, if you had been an English poet temporarily on the wing because of lectures or readings in this country, the preliminaries might have been even more airily arranged. It seemed at that time necessary for an English writer only to cross the Atlantic in order sooner or later to find himself Mrs. Moody's guest.

In either case, to you, as to many others, the spell of Moody's poetry was still immediate. The shock of his early death was widely felt, and you shared in it.

Then, you had been told something of the remarkable woman who would be your hostess and of the unique character of her hospitality. To you, since you were young and unknown, such a visit doubtless seemed somewhat like admission to a club formed of the experienced and the arrived. Yet with masculine

7

self-protectiveness you may have had your moment of hesitation. Keeping open house for poets, on the part of a poet's widow, might be all that it sounded. But what, on the other hand, would be expected of you, you cautiously asked yourself. Just what part were you to play?

You exchanged notes with your prospective hostess, and you wired your time of arrival.

It was she, however busy she may have been, who met you at the Chicago station. She was scrupulous about such matters. Also, she was tirelessly alert for fresh adventure, adventure of the mind, such as even this very meeting, however unfledged you were, might chance to yield. So, as you left the train, Anton, her chauffeur for so many years, would skilfully detach you from the crowd and lead you to the car. Here an impressive woman of middle age, her face that of a wearied Buddha, waited to greet you. If at first you were a little disconcerted by her rather regal presence, you would shortly have sensed that you couldn't be in better hands. And if you began, rather nervously, to talk about yourself at considerable length, that was, after all, what was expected of you, and your companion gave you ample rein. Her full blue eyes unwaveringly bent on you; she was deliberately forming her impression.

By the time you reached Groveland Avenue, you may have felt like a strayed child reassuringly held in the lap of a protecting stranger.

Entering the house, you were aware of considerable space and of an agreeable bareness. At the right was the drawing-room in which stood a piano and some pieces of sculpture, including Alfeo Faggi's bust of the Japanese poet Yone Noguchi. There were water-color paintings, obviously contemporary. In the room across the hall there was a fireplace and a massive swing, upholstered in black velvet and hung by chains from the ceiling. This latter arrangement was the accustomed seat of the hostess, who, you would have noticed by this time, was slightly lame. The paintings here were Moody's work, including his pleasantly romantic self-portrait. In this, as in most of the other rooms in the house, were shelves crowded with books—enough to supply a reader for a lifetime, Frank Swinnerton,[1] who must have noted their quality, has reported.

At the rear, through wide doors, you entered the dining-room. Here hung Moody's portrait of "Harriet," in oils. The bay window in this room supplied an alcove which was large enough for a flat-topped desk and chair and which constituted Mrs. Moody's study and workroom during the hours she spent at home.

Almost a masculine interior, you would have thought it, on the whole, in its absence of clutter, intentional or otherwise, and in its absence, indeed, of any domestic atmosphere. Certainly not the house of a woman who gave time or thought to details of embellishment. More like a stage it was, perhaps, which might at any moment be set for the production of some unexpected drama. It was a house where things happened.

A moment more and you were being introduced to the quiet feminine presences that moved through the rooms, members of the household. And somebody would have led you to a large light room on the floor above, where, you were told, your breakfast would be brought in the morning. Tonight, at dinner, there would be other guests. At teatime Mrs. Moody would be glad to see you downstairs by the fire.

It is a considerable departure from realism to assume that you would have been the only house guest, for it was during these years that Rabindranath Tagore, with his son and daughter-in-law, spent long periods in this house. And it would have been strange indeed if Padraic and Mary Colum hadn't happened to be staying there, or Vachel Lindsay, or James Stephens, or any one of a great number of painters, sculptors, or musicians. But since the episode we are now following is a synthetic one, it is simpler and at the same time more sharply illustrative to clear the house of these conjectural figures and to leave its hostess relatively free.

We may further take it for granted that no outsiders came in for tea. And evidently the other members of the household, still flitting about in a leisurely way, bent on their own affairs, didn't

[1] *Autobiography: Frank Swinnerton.* New York: Doubleday, Doran.

form a group at this hour. So, with scarcely any preamble, your hostess spoke of your poetry, which she may have read only the night before. But in no case would she have omitted to read it. You already knew the embarrassment of being flattered by women who made a cult of poets while knowing next to nothing about poetry itself. But your new friend did not flatter you. Perhaps in an instance or two she even taught you something about yourself which you were willingly surprised to learn.

Then, you wouldn't have spoken long together before she gently catechized you as to your knowledge of her husband's work. This you would have foreseen, and it is to be hoped that you had something adequate to say. She would have mentioned other names—those of Frost or Lindsay or Masefield, all friends and recent guests.

As long as you preserved the relationship thus far indicated, of respectful docility on your part and of sibylline authority on hers, you wouldn't have approached each other very closely. However, you were beginning to acknowledge your surrender to a personality. Your honest liking for her deepened. You hoped she was beginning to think well of you in return.

Suddenly you said something, perhaps by inadvertence, that amused her. In a flash, she retorted in kind. Here was a new conduit between your two minds. . . . . So, after all, you weren't merely an amiable young man of still undetermined gifts, an appropriate subject for her benevolent concern, but a human being of full stature. As for the very appearance of the woman you were talking with, that was now transformed. Her outlines rippled into something more yielding and more fluid. Her delightful laughter now had a note of youth, even of girlishness. To know that you were responsible for the melting of a rather impassive figure into a charmingly responsive and gaiety-loving woman, was exhilarating. As for you, though you had so recently been a tolerated stranger on your best behavior, you were now, in an hour, embarked on an actual intimacy. The truth was, of course, that, when Harriet Moody found human material that was to her liking, she lost no time in making it her own.

All this had not come about without interruption. Under

10

this roof the briefest talk wasn't possible without half-a-dozen surrenders to the insistency of the telephone. And an instrument stood always within easy reach of anyone occupying the swing. To the mistress of the house, however, the telephone was never an annoyance. It seemed rather as if she really enjoyed conferring with somebody at the ends of the earth at the same time that she was engaged in confab with an intimate circle.

Then, tea would scarcely be finished before you felt the stir of fresh preparation. If, as was usually the case, there were to be more guests than the round dining table would accommodate, the evening meal took the form of a buffet supper. So Milary, the Hindu butler,[2] would arrange small tables, each set for a single diner, in the room where you were sitting and would suitably place chairs and lights.

Guests began to arrive early—Ferdinand Schevill, perhaps, now known as a historian, then a professor at the University, close friend of both Will and Harriet Moody, and with him his

[2] Milary, who had a stately, frock-coated presence and rather a fantastic sense of form and ceremony, was a source of much amusement to Mrs. Moody's friends. On withdrawing from the household, at about ten in the evening, he would approach Mrs. Moody, making a low bow. "Good-night, Mamma," was his respectful formula. And, distinguishing Ferdinand Schevill from other men who came often to 2970 and who were all "Papas," he would address him as "Glasses-Papa," Vachel Lindsay being "Lecture-Papa."

On a winter morning, entering a guest's room to start an early fire in the grate, the briefest comment on the weather was enough to set Milary off. Striking a platform attitude, he would thrust his hand within his buttoned coat. "As to that," he would begin and then proceed to exhaust the subject.

He vaunted his own accomplishments as a cook, and, after demanding three days off for its preparation, would produce a curry whose excellence Mrs. Moody herself attested.

Milary was an entertaining character, in short, except for his emotional crises, one at least of which was induced, he said, by his excessive love for his employer. Shaken by loud sobs, unable to work, he one day declared to Mrs. Moody that what so violently moved him was having just signed a will in her favor. So deep was his love for her that he had bequeathed her "everything." Obligingly overlooking the fact that Milary was always extremely hard up, Mrs. Moody abandoned her own work and helped him to control himself.

There were at least four other Orientals, Pierre, José, Kim, and Yim, all young students of varying nationalities, whom Mrs. Moody benevolently sheltered and fed, supposedly in return for household services. On two of these she commented in a letter to Charlotte Moody: "José is back in the University. Yim is studying at the Art Institute. Both of these boys flurry in and do a little something about the house occasionally, Yim with his imperturbable gentleness, José with a proud efficiency that might break into indignation almost any moment but never does."

11

lovely wife, Clara, the musician. Carl Sandburg might come, to sing his latest find in folk songs, instinctively working out on the piano the inevitably right accompaniment. Edgar Lee Masters might appear with a new poem. Or Glenway Wescott, the novelist, then a charming and exceptionally promising youth. Edith Wyatt, able and versatile writer in various fields, might be there; or Harriet Monroe; or Alice Corbin, poet and coeditor of *Poetry*, with her husband, William Henderson, the painter. Perhaps half-a-dozen of the mere beginners.

With their air of being completely at home, all these comers must have been frequent guests. And the hostess was "Harriet" to everybody.

You noted that she did not move from her swing, which she may have seemed to occupy rather as a throne than as a concession—which, as a matter of fact, it really was—to her physical disability. This handicap of hers she had indeed combated with extraordinary courage and skill, though she never became reconciled to it, and for this and other reasons had a settled social policy of going out as little as possible and of having people come to her instead.

Somewhat dazed and probably still a little shy, you were privileged at first to look on, merely. But it didn't take long to feel one's self a part of an occasion that was so simply and naturally arranged. Years earlier, because a certain young poet, Will Moody, in whom she had become absorbingly interested, didn't care for needless ceremony, Harriet had deliberately reduced her social life to the plainest terms. And such it had remained—with the exception, always, of the material substance of her hospitality.

For the moment it is not necessary to elaborate this latter point, though no one who had ever been her guest would be content to have it ignored. It may merely be noted, now, that the dishes composing even an everyday repast were of incomparable distinction. Such gustatory memories as all her friends must share would have the effect of overstatement, however plainly one might set them down.

In the frame of mind thus induced, music would be acceptable. There would be more or less of it according to the character of the guests. Then you, the latest comer, might be asked to read from your poems. If, instead of yourself, you had been Robert Frost or Padraic Colum or Vachel Lindsay or any one of Harriet's favorite Englishmen, the evening would have been turned over to you without reserve. Or there would have been hours made memorable by Walter Hampden, the actor, or by Elly Ney, the pianist, or by the Kennedy-Frasers, mother and daughter, singers of Hebridean folk songs. In such case, Harriet would have assumed for the time being the role of prompter only. But tonight the poets who happened to be present might have alternated in reading or reciting their verses, and Harriet herself might have chosen to read something new and significant. Reading aloud was practiced more in her house than it is by most of us. But if you saw much of her, you fell into her ways.

Also, reading was a useful device for fusing the possibly divergent elements in a chance company and for holding it under benevolent control. Harriet appeared to distrust the formation of small groups among her guests, with their too likely outbreaks of irrelevance, even though her own good talk, which at her best was humorous, full of allusion, richly human, was oftenest heard in a group of three or four or five. Yet, when she had a large group to deal with, she instinctively knew how to bring about the complete harmony that she wished.

So you listened and watched and absorbed. . . . .

These dinner guests were all busy men and women. Considerably before midnight they were gone. And Harriet's life was as fully occupied as theirs. Before you, her guest, would sleepily approach your next morning's breakfast tray, she herself would have prepared her own coffee and worked for an hour or so at her desk, leaving the house at seven to begin her own workday. But of this she wasn't thinking now. Supremely uninterested in all hygienic regimen, nothing so much bored her as the human body's need of sleep.

So, as midnight approached, she bloomed, became radiant. Coffee must be brought, or tea, and something to eat. Liberated as she had now become, you saw that she was in the mood to talk, with a suitable companion, about the things that most interested her. That suitable companion you could scarcely call yourself. You were new and untried. But, in the absence of any other, it was just possible that you might serve. You protested your wakefulness.

The ensuing hours, three or four of them, may have been devoted to Robinson, or to Moody, or perhaps to Shakespeare, or to philosophizing of one lively sort or another. Certainly they included also, as the night waned, a confession on your part, wrung from you by Harriet, of your own circumstances, *in toto*. Your ambitions..... Your hope to sit at the feet of this or that poet..... Your desire to marry the girl you were in love with. Or perhaps you had married her, and there was a baby or two to be taken care of..... As she pressed you, you admitted your need of lecture engagements or perhaps of a job—any roof-supplying, grocer-paying job..... Not matters to be told a stranger, any of them. But you were no longer strangers, you and she. And somehow you could make these confidences without any loss of self-respect..... You knew as you staggered sleepily upstairs that you wouldn't have had these hours a moment shorter.

What you didn't know was that when the time came the next afternoon for a session with her secretary, the points made in your midnight talk would (now that she liked you and approved of you) be fruitfully re-covered. Letters would be written in your behalf and the first steps taken, whether toward securing engagements for you or toward arranging a summer shelter for you and your little family.

Your life had taken a new turn.

CHAPTER III

THE MIDDLE WEST IN FLOWER

AS IS the case with most richly endowed personalities, there is no satisfactory accounting for this quiet woman whose influence radiated so powerfully and so far. She was of those who create tradition, not of those who follow it. But it is worth while, before dealing with her most productive period, to glance briefly at her origin and to skim, however lightly, over her eventful personal history. Almost every circumstance in her life has something to yield for students of the American scene.

There may, to begin with, be significance in the fact that Harriet Tilden was a daughter of the midlands. Born in Ohio in 1857 and spending the greater part of her life in Chicago, she was a supreme creation of the Middle West, that is, of the newer America. As to the human roots she sprang from, a grandfather Tilden, interested in extending a line of stagecoaches, had migrated to Ohio from Randolph, Vermont. But it is the women in her ancestry, including her own mother, who stand out most sharply. Since Harriet herself had a strain of the pioneer in her, and the adventure-seeker,[1] she may have liked to recall her adventure-loving grandmother, Hannah Breck Parkman (the Parkmans were relatives of the historian), who, when still a girl, made the journey from the eastern coast on horseback, her brother for sole companion. Later, this young pioneer married John P. Converse—the Converses, originally of

[1] In August, 1929, beset by disasters and disappointments and with only a few years of life remaining to her, Harriet Moody proved her unconquerable resiliency by writing from Chicago to Ferdinand Schevill: "We took a little drive in the park this morning and tried to pretend there was some adventure in it, but . . . . I found it all tame to the last degree, and I am longing with heart and soul for adventure. Europe, or the Bad Lands, or the Black Hills, or the Canadian Rockies, or anything where there are heights to look out from, and where there is also a little danger."

15

French Huguenot stock, having also come recently from New England. As for her Tilden grandmother, this woman left so profound an impression upon her son William, Harriet's father, that forty years after her death he would hold long sessions with a younger half-brother, tenderly recalling their dark-haired mother's beauty and charm, her characteristic sayings, until both men were in tears.

From the fortunate blending of the Tilden and Converse strains, Harriet Tilden drew a magnificent endowment of health and vitality. Her happy, tomboyish childhood, which she always loved to look back upon, she spent in the lovely village of Parkman. Here, outside her own pleasant home, which was enlivened by the two younger brothers whom she always cherished with a half-maternal love, she had a recourse incomparably precious to any child in her daily access to the home of her indulgent Grandmother Converse. She herself has written of this delightful refuge:

"Did you have another home in your childhood to which you could run from your own? a grandmother's or an aunt's, where there was a sweet-smelling closet, and in it a jar filled with delicious cookies—old-fashioned soft ginger cookies with a little spice; or crisp ginger snaps? Did you and your playmates steal away to this closet, one watching while the others filled eager hands with these delicious trifles, put there to be hunted out by children, and generously allowed without comment?

"The way to my grandmother's house[2] was over a long gravel walk, up a terrace of many stone steps. On either side of this gravel walk were myriads of country flowers—French pinks, peonies, roses, tulips, trumpet flowers, sweet peas; and on the top of the terrace, more flowers, leading away to right and left from the path up the steps. The distance from my own home through this flowery garden, and up the terrace, was nearly as long as a summer's day, and was bewilderingly joyful because of the sweet smells and the beautiful colors of the flowers; and

[2] In 1922, Harriet Moody tried in vain to acquire this house, remembering with an acute nostalgia "the arrangement of the rooms, the carpets that my grandmother wove with her own hands, the flower beds that my aunt and mother tended."

16

because of certain sweet apples that fell over from a generous and heavy-laden tree, onto the garden walk, and could be caught up and eaten on the way to the cooky jar. This is one of the happiest memories of my childhood."[3]

Long afterward, revisiting Parkman, Harriet indicated to her companion a well-worn pathway between fields and village and lightly remarked that along this lane she had formerly led "the cow." This may have been jest and the cow thus evoked a purely symbolic one. Or it is probable that the Tilden family did own cows and that this suggested to the rather restless mind of William Mason Tilden that, while cattle didn't count for much in Parkman, they might—in Chicago, and in the mass—be made to count for a good deal.

At all events, when the little girl was about eleven years old, there came the first great change in her life. Her father took his wife, his daughter "Hattie," and Hattie's two younger brothers to live in Chicago.

William Tilden, it is remembered, was no countryman in type. "A handsome, urbane man," somebody has described him, to whom young Harriet bore close resemblance. As for his wife, she was a strong-fibered woman of dignity, reserve, and wit, interested chiefly in books and things of the mind, yet outwardly willing to follow her husband in the new life that he had chosen or that had chosen him—and, as it proved, to play her own impressive part in it. So, in a surprisingly short time, country simplicities were left far behind. William Tilden, shortly a member of the Chicago Board of Trade, was successful as a cattle baron, handled, acquired, spent—and eventually lost —great sums of money, and became a part of the flamboyant Chicago life of the seventies.

Before long the family was settled in a large house in a region then fashionable, Wabash Avenue and Thirteenth Street, the lake lapping the garden in the rear. Here shone forth all the outward signs of success. Daily a formally attired coachman, handling high-stepping horses, drove the financier to and from his office on La Salle Street. At the proper time each afternoon,

[3] *Mrs. William Vaughn Moody's Cookbook* (Scribner's, 1931), p. 302.

17

Mrs. Tilden, close-bonneted, wrapped in a silk dolman, holding above her head a tiny fringed parasol (you wouldn't have caught her faint skeptical smile at the frivolity of the parade she was a part of; neither would you have measured her satisfaction in the comfort of her own conveyance), was driven slowly, in the low-hung carriage built especially for her, along Michigan Boulevard. "Boul' Mich'," traveled Chicagoans liked to call it, thinking of their vast city as a newer Paris.

At home there was what was then considered a suitable background for the regal hospitality that competent Mrs. Tilden dispensed. Guests were shown into a drawing-room magnificently hung and upholstered in white satin, carpeted in white Axminster, with gilt furniture, gilt-framed pier mirrors and cornices—this perishable elegance brilliantly lighted by crystal chandeliers. On the south side of the house, opening out of the family sitting-room, was the conservatory and birdroom, where —Harriet's cousin, Mrs. Leila Kennedy Hutchens, remembered —"lived many varieties of gay-plumaged birds who throve in captivity, from parrots to canaries. They had the freedom of the living-room, came to Aunt Harriet's [Mrs. Tilden's] call, perched on her head and shoulders, ate from her lips."

By no means the least interesting fact in connection with these circumstances is that Harriet Tilden was so unaffected by them. Since she was at the same time the object of her father's excessive idolatry, she might easily have become a merely selfish and pleasure-loving creature. But you couldn't, it seems, turn a head so securely, let us say, so nobly, poised as hers. Her stern virtues were so integral a part of her that there was, after all, no real danger of their being smothered.

Meanwhile, there can be no doubt that the Parkman tomboy flowered early into a being lovely to look upon. Legends and photographs agree that she was a proud Amazonian figure, tall, well formed, and vigorous (Harriet was proud of the Tilden stature and admired height in women), blue-eyed and yellow-haired, challenging attention by her rather severe beauty—the last word being advisedly used. No less remarkable than her physique was her intelligence; but, as this was at least partly

18

camouflaged by her gaiety and companionableness, it probably did not cause her elders grave alarm. As she grew a little older, this unself-conscious young creature begins to seem to us like the heroine of a not too realistic novel of her very period. And, like many a novel heroine, drifting charmingly through the first untroubled chapters of her story, she seems to have had no plan for herself, no single directing urge. Her ego demanded little, then or later. Unharassed by any cares, deeply attached to her family, finding the world a wide and friendly playground, she must have drawn deep pleasure from the mere sense of her own unfolding.

However, education had to be considered. For a well-placed Chicago miss, an Eastern boarding school was taken for granted. The Tildens sent their daughter to the Howland School, a Quaker establishment in Union Springs, New York. Here she easily achieved, without giving a thought to it, that ambition of the typical adolescent, "popularity." Even after many decades the women who once were dazzled by their charming young companion recall her with the utmost tenderness,[4] one of them declaring that Harriet Tilden had once been her "ideal." Her sweetness of nature, which they speak of in particular, her charm, her intelligence, her capacity for both leadership and good-fellowship, her beauty combined with an utter lack of vanity—the very qualities, in fact, that were to be praised in her in the years to come—seem to have compelled the mass surrender of girls and teachers alike. And then there were her clothes—which her schoolmates admired without being envious and which, beautiful and costly as they were, seemed merely the fitting garments for this story-book young creature.

It is curious that a girl of this type, who was a leader in out-

<hr>

[4] Mrs. Theodore Sheldon (mother of Edward Sheldon, the playwright) remembers being a Freshman at Howland when "Harriet Tilden was an adored upper-classman," and her pride in being invited, since she was only thirteen, to a "midnight spread" (a device through which boarding-school girls of that day satisfied their sense of rebellion and desire for adventure) daringly engineered by Harriet, who procured pies from the school pantry, meeting (and eluding) a teacher on the way.

"What a woman!" Mrs. Sheldon exclaims. "What a caressing voice! It always made me feel like purring with sheer delight."

door games as well as in every other activity, should have suffered from a malady that oftenest attacks adolescents who believe themselves in some way inferior. But late in her life Harriet Moody wrote to a young correspondent:

"I don't know whether you have ever suffered from homesickness. I had a most terrible attack of it in my second year in boarding-school. Strangely enough, I got through the first year without experiencing it. But having had an attack of this kind, I personally deeply realize that there is nothing like it in the world in the way of suffering. It was almost a kind of mania during the month or two when I was trying to induce my people to let me go home. I thought I could not exist from hour to hour, although I was a strong athletic girl, with much participation in school pastimes, a hearty appetite, as a rule, and much independence. . . . ."

From the academic point of view the school must have been sound. In later years Harriet spoke gratefully of the grounding in German it had given her, a certain Madame du Long having been the capable instructor, so that she was always able to enjoy reading German. Her parents doubtless assumed that this school experience would complete both their daughter's education and her equipment for society.

But by the time she left Union Springs there was already talk of preparing the Tilden boys for Harvard. So far, these brothers had done nothing that Harriet at their age hadn't been able to do as well, from riding a horse to working out a problem in algebra. In fact, as a student she had far excelled them, though this disparity in the family attainments had never been stressed. So Harriet, within whom true intellectual curiosity was already burningly alive, decided that she herself would go to college.

Her announcement at home of this decision provoked a tremendous explosion from her father, which was no more than could have been expected. Harriet must have anticipated every word of it, for though there were then a few colleges that admitted women (Mr. Tilden must have said) only plain, spectacled girls, incipient schoolmarms, dreamed of going to them, whereas his beautiful, charming, and fortunate daughter needed only to stay at home with her parents, enjoy the happy life they offered her, and prepare herself for marriage.

But Harriet was patient and resolute and, as was usual in a tussle with her father, she won. As for her college, she chose Cornell. In this she was following the advice of no elder, the example of no familiar contemporary. Leaving Chicago for Ithaca the following autumn, she was embarked on her first bit of pioneering. There were to be others.

Meanwhile, her boarding-school life had had its suitable climax in a summer trip to Europe in the company of a group of school companions and a chaperon. This excursion naturally followed more or less the conventional pattern, though it diverged from this in giving the girls a brief glimpse of Ireland. Many years later Harriet recalled "one half day in my youth when I rode around in a jaunting car in Queenstown with a widower who was the father of a stairful of children, ten or twelve in number. We went . . . . in brilliant sunshine, through lanes bordered with bushy hedges and clung to the sides of the jaunting car like the greenhorns that we were. It is all very vivid to me still, and I have always meant to go back."

As a matter of course, the girls had somewhat more than a glimpse of the English countryside, which Harriet was not to see again until she went with Moody in 1909. (Later she was to go to England many times, but these periods were spent mostly in London.) At the last came Paris. Harriet was mature enough to absorb all that there was time for, both of the surface charm of Paris and of its encyclopedic treasure. She also dutifully followed instructions from home in equipping herself with a wardrobe that ravished the Cornell campus a few weeks later.

At Cornell they were no less aware of her than people continued to be aware of her throughout her life. For one thing, she completed the four years' course in two years and a half, which, if she hadn't been so noticeably good-looking, with so little in her of the objectionable character of a "grind," would doubtless have seemed to her male fellow-students presumptuous indeed. If the few straggling "coeds" of her day led rather a bleak social life, that was certainly not the case with Harriet. According to the legend, half the young men students admired her from a distance, the rest were more or less (though quite without encouragement) in love with her, while at least one member of the faculty is said to have relinquished his academic post in despair because he could not persuade lovely Miss Tilden to marry him. "The most beautiful woman who ever walked over the Ithaca hills," a contemporary of hers, Dr. Eugene Corson, Hiram Corson's son, is able, after many years, to say of her.[5] And eight-year-old Teresina Peck (later Mrs. Wilfred A. Rowell), whose father was professor of Latin, whose mother Harriet visited frequently and intimately, remembers of young Harriet Tilden "that her beauty and her general appearance made . . . . a sensation in Ithaca. . . . . I adored her."

Harriet herself admitted having been engaged to at least two young men during this period, but these early romantic affairs cannot have gone very deep with her. Probably she was not ready for them. Rather than being in love with any single person, it seems to have been life itself that she loved. As always, she was the serene center of her own social universe, knowing no other experience than to be warmly liked, if not actually courted, by everybody and to be free to pursue her own personal enthusiasms.

Then, at all seasons of the year, she had a thoroughly good time—skating, boating, hiking, dancing—with plenty of eager cavaliers to share these sports with her. And she was more than willing to comply—for she had a creative touch, always—when young Professor Björnsterne Björnson (by no means the only member of the faculty to "pay attention," as the phrase then went, to Harriet), noticing her charming clothes, implored her to help him dress the characters in the novels and stories he was writing.

[5] Dr. Corson speaks of her as "the divine Harriet—for to me she was always encased in a golden aura of divinity." And he adds that he dedicated to her "my book on Madame Blavatsky which she had suggested to me."

22

Altogether, she liked college very much.

The short vacations, when it seemed hardly worth while to go to Chicago, transit in those days being pretty time-consuming, the young student spent in Syracuse, with her half-cousins, the Kennedys. Leila Kennedy, later Mrs. Hutchens, recalled the delight with which these cousins, all younger than Harriet, awaited her coming. The visitor knew how to tell stories, long, fascinating ones, and she didn't have to be particularly coaxed to do it, so the Kennedys were utterly under her spell. To be sure, she wouldn't go to bed at a suitable time (then or later), and she somehow forgot to get up for breakfast; but "Aunt Betty," her uncle's wife, ordinarily punctilious about household discipline, waived these infractions of it because of her own complete surrender to the girl's sweetness and charm.

But all this was the pleasant froth of life. What really excited Harriet at Cornell was, of course, that she had been given a key to its treasure-house of learning. This was what she had come for, and she had by no means come in vain. The various distractions that have been noted did not prevent her from ranking as a brilliant student.

Now it may reasonably be urged that the essential value of college life lies not in achieving "grades" or in accumulating "credits," terms that didn't exist in Harriet's day, or yet in leaping the carefully constructed academic hurdles in less than the stipulated time; but rather in receiving an enkindling spark from some maturer but mysteriously kindred intelligence. If this happened to Harriet, the spark sprang from the lively mind of Professor Hiram Corson, in whose home she lived for a part of her college life and whose courses in English literature she profitably followed. Professor Corson, widely known at the time as an authority on Chaucer and lecturer on Browning, a learned if eccentric person,[6] taught Harriet much and stimulated her even more importantly. When she left college in 1876 with her Bachelor's degree, she was an eager and accomplished student

[6] He is described as a strange figure, with "a bowler hat, long sweeping beard and eyes that saw nothing." He forgot to keep lecture engagements but recited poetry aloud as he walked along the street, unaware that anyone heard him.

of English poetry; and this study, for the love of it, she pursued throughout her life. None of the young poets whom, much later on, she was able to understand and encourage will question that she put this knowledge of hers to sound uses.

But whatever Harriet may have owed to this teacher, the debt was by no means all on her side. Just before she came to Cornell, a young daughter of the Corsons', of Harriet's own age, had died. Overpoweringly stricken by this loss, the father spent hours at the girl's grave, mourning her. He turned also, and permanently, to spiritualism, becoming a devout exponent of the cult and believing firmly that he was thus enabled to commune with the dead daughter.

Harriet Tilden was not only a visible reminder of this daughter. For a time at least she seemed partly to replace her in the household and was held in great affection both for this reason and for her own qualities. At the same time Corson took great pride in her as a student and predicted for her a future as a writer. Years afterward, even, visiting the Kennedys in Syracuse, he became rhapsodical in extolling her.

A figure on whom, not unnaturally, Professor Corson centered a good deal of interest was the theosophist much talked of at that period and later—Madame Blavatsky. Long afterward (April 4, 1922), to a stranger who had sent her a letter of inquiry, Harriet wrote the following paragraphs of reminiscence:

"I can scarcely claim to have known Madame Blavatsky personally, for she had made her visit in Ithaca and left before my arrival there. But I lived in the house of Professor Corson for a time and was a constant student in his classes and heard him talk of Mme. Blavatsky, for whom he had a great admiration both as an intellectual and as a mystic. Professor Corson was himself a spiritualist. His philosophy was therefore not quite in accord with Mme. Blavatsky's, but he maintained a long correspondence with her. . . . .

"My own acquaintance with her was confined to a part of a day spent on an ocean liner where she was waiting for the time of departure of her boat and where my father left me to wait for friends who were taking the same boat and were doing some errands in the city.

"Mme. Blavatsky took my arm and walked up and down the steamer deck for several hours, talking to me about the theosophical society, then young in New York, and telling me a few of her own experiences. She pointed out to me the desirability of my giving my life to the service of the theosophical society, and as we walked and talked, she allowed me in the most friendly way to roll cigarettes for her. I was very young at that time, but I was deeply impressed by her quality and have carried with me always a profound impression of the hours I spent with her."

CHAPTER IV

EXPERIMENTS IN LIVING

NOW that Cornell was a finished chapter, a fresh conflict between father and daughter was inevitable, for Harriet had a new plan to announce, more startling and more untraditional than her decision to go to college. She wished to study medicine.

This project must have caused at least as great a shock in Ithaca, where she doubtless first made it known, as it did in Chicago. Professor Corson, who had watched his favorite pupil's intellectual blossoming, under his own guidance, with so much satisfaction, had quite other plans for her than this. It was clear to him that, with effort and desire on her own part, she could become a writer. Lesser talents were far more eager. Why was she not eager, too?

While her teacher could judge the authenticity of the girl's gift for expression, it was natural that he should have failed to understand her total lack of a motive for developing this gift. Though aware of her various abilities, she was without personal ambition—which does not at all mean that she was relaxed or indolent or that she did not place a value upon herself. But fame had no exciting message for her. On the other hand, she was powerfully impelled, even in her triumphant youth, by a desire paramount throughout her life—a desire to be of use to other people. It is difficult to make this clear without using cant phrases. Any study of her life, however, would convince one of its truth. And it was surely for this reason alone, since she had no marked scientific bent, that she chose the pursuit of medicine as affording close and fruitful contact with other human beings. A decade later it is barely possible that, instead of choosing the course she did, Harriet might have joined the idealistic young women who at that time went into settlement work—even though it was not her way to associate herself with groups, the impulse toward individual action having shown itself strong in her from childhood.

It is unlikely that she made the explanation that has been suggested to her parents or to anyone. Perhaps she made no explanation whatever.

William Tilden's father had been a physician. So the family had a certain proprietary interest in the profession. Yet this did not make the idea of a woman doctor any the less odious. The father's emotional recoil from the proposed association of his lovely daughter with the ugliness of disease was extreme. But he really stood no chance with her. Though he had the self-made man's overbelief in himself, and a strong will besides, Harriet had a strong will, too, and a better brain than her father. And his very adoration of her put him at a disadvantage. So she pursued her plan, passed the necessary examinations, and in the autumn after graduation from Cornell entered the Women's Medical College at Philadelphia.

However, the period that followed was to prove relatively unimportant in her life.

There is merely negative evidence, after these many years, to prove that in studying medicine Harriet found herself in the wrong boat, but such must, nevertheless, have been the case. It was an experience that she seldom referred to, though she spoke continually, and always with pleasure, of Cornell and in fact maintained with it a lifelong alliance that was not only agreeable to herself but useful to the university.[1] She might have made medicine a career, in which case she would certainly in her own individual way have made a human if not a strictly scientific success of it, if her family had not shortly decided to employ a none too subtle strategy.

The proposal made to Harriet the spring following was that, if she would consent to intermit her medical studies for a year

[1] For two successive five-year terms (1912–22) Mrs. Moody acted as trustee to Cornell University (the only woman then serving in that capacity). She was also one of a group that, when the time came to find a new president, chose President Livingston Farrand. And she was for many years an informal consultant of its School of Home Economics, conducted by Miss Flora Rose and Miss Martha Van Rensselaer.

27

and spend this time at home, making her début, already too long delayed, while supplying longed-for companionship to her parents, all objection would be removed as to her doing what she pleased after that.

This was a gamble on the parents' part, and Harriet, naturally, perceived it as such. The fact that she agreed to the proposal shows that she secretly didn't care whether or not the gamble was successful.

Then, of course, it was far from being the case that there was lack of sympathy between herself and her parents. Rather the contrary. Harriet had a good deal more than the ordinary share of family feeling. At different times in her life she proved her immense devotion to her father, her mother, and each of her brothers. And it was in no discontented mood that this happy-natured, thoroughly poised, almost abnormally warm-hearted young woman now contemplated returning home.

Back again with her parents on Wabash Avenue, a new stage of her life began, a safe and satisfactory stage, it naturally seemed to Mr. and Mrs. Tilden. They had rescued the lovely creature from the horrors of the dissection room and the dark menaces of the laboratory. They had made her countless flattering promises. Overlooking for the moment the fact that Harriet was no mere pretty puppet, they now complacently arranged to present their treasure to Chicago's social world.

It is sober compliance with facts, merely, that forces repeated reference to Harriet Tilden's beauty and personal charm. These are salient facts in her life that have to be dealt with, facts that are echoed by everybody who ever knew or even saw her.

And it is now that this girl was at the shining peak of her radiant youth. A Chicago acquaintance of the Tilden family—a sensitive woman of wide experience—who was at that time a child, still holds before her inner eyes the entrancing image of that young, proud, conquering Harriet. "I have never seen anything to equal her personal splendor," she testifies almost reverently—and the image seems to acquire actual substance.

Later on in her troubled life Harriet lost her external beauty, though never her distinction and impressiveness. Yet she did not and could not lose—what most women never possess—the memory of having once been beautiful. Now and then, in a detached, half-amused way, she spoke of it. . . . .

As agreed upon, the daughter of the prosperous Tildens played the social game.

In view of the sum of her attractions, being a success at balls and dinners was altogether too easy. Since she had never known anything else, Harriet could accept admiration with cool indifference. But the question of what to do with her surplus time and energy—here was something that hadn't been provided for. Though her mind needed springs to drink from, she had no urge to isolate herself for that reason. On the contrary, she wanted and needed people and more people—though this need wasn't met by the young men of her own age and social class, who seemed to her insipid and cut too much from a single pattern. Her situation therefore held dangers that nobody guessed.

The truth is that she was, in a superior sense, the most feminine of women, and this is one of the important things to be said of her. With her extraordinarily rich emotional nature, the fit thing for her, fundamentally, to whatever further use she might have put her talents and energies outside her home, was a woman's lot. As for careers, she could have driven them four abreast, and, later on, she did practically this. But happy marriage and happy motherhood she always idealized, to an extreme degree, as her letters touchingly prove; and it is deeply to be lamented that she did not have these early in life—that, in fact, she did not have them at all. Her brief, anxiety-ridden, tragically terminated marriage with Moody came late and, in spite of deep mutual devotion, was obviously no real fulfilment. With all the multiplicity and the intimacy of her associations, her profound hunger for the utmost that life could yield must have remained unassuaged to the end of her days.

Her parents couldn't, of course, have understood their daughter. Perhaps parents seldom do. It is easy to say now that the elder Tildens would have done well to bestir themselves sleeplessly until they had secured for a girl of this rare caliber an adequately princely mate. But the most adroit and farsighted of parents would have had difficulty, as the event proved, in guiding toward or away from matrimony a daughter who, though charmingly deferential in smaller matters, was immovable in crises.

So calamity descended.

Edwin Brainard, son of a Chicago physician of considerable eminence, Dr. Daniel Brainard, met and admired Harriet, wished to marry her, and pursued her to this end until he gained her consent—though not her parents'. Her father's opposition, in particular, was bitterly unyielding.

Perhaps Harriet fell in love with Brainard, as her Kennedy cousins, who saw her, and him, at the time of the marriage, believed—though this seems debatable. What is certain is that the young man, who had no career in view—although he had just returned from several years spent at European universities in company with his close friend Julian Hawthorne, son of the novelist—had gained at least superficial advantages that set him apart from Chicago young men of his own age. Here was a man Harriet could really talk with. As for his dissipations, she brushed that matter imperiously aside, for it must be recorded that this intelligent young woman actually believed, conscious as she naturally was of her personal power, that, since young Brainard was in love with her, she would have no difficulty in making him over. It is true that marrying a man in order to "reform" him was a familiar theme in the novels of that day, and a trickle of this superstition may have penetrated Harriet's able mind. "I was incredibly innocent," she said of herself, many years later. And, in spite of her pleasant flirtations at Cornell, she was doubtless still emotionally unawakened, in the serious sense.

Also, for a headstrong girl there was perhaps a perverse zest in combating the wishes of an overidolatrous parent. At all events, William Tilden's arguments, persuasions, and entreaties, reasonable as they were in this case, accomplished absolutely nothing. As a last resort, he tried the menace of disinheriting his daughter, which, of course, was of all measures the one least likely to sway her.

So the marriage took place, though not at the Tilden home. Earlier, Harriet had undergone a painful ordeal in the form of a parting with her father. At the close of it, he insisted on placing a hundred-dollar bill in her purse. "Keep this," he grimly advised her. "It may be of use to you when you decide to come back to us, as some day you surely will." Grief-stricken, Harriet clung to her father whom she genuinely loved, paying little attention to the money or to the prophecy. Later, she was to remember.

Meanwhile, on the wedding day, the bridegroom, whose family was more than well to do, is said to have settled one hundred thousand dollars on Harriet to make up for the dowry her father had withheld.

During the miserable time that Harriet remained Brainard's wife, she and her lonely father did not meet. Her mother she saw often, but secretly. These corrosive and humiliating years, spent in Chicago and on an estate in Waukegan, with scores of horses and dogs, and always with much entertaining, were far worse than merely wasted. Divorce, a word then hardly to be spoken aloud, would at any time have been possible, but in the eighties almost any ordeal seemed preferable to the suffering and scandal that—for a woman—it entailed. The time came, however, when she decided to be free.

On the very day that she achieved her divorce, Leila Kennedy and her mother passed through Chicago. Mr. Kennedy, Harriet's uncle, had just died.

"Dear Aunt Betty," she gently said to Mrs. Kennedy, and the others long remembered it, "there are things much worse than death." . . . .

First of all, now that Harriet was again an independent being, came reconciliation with her father, which brought intense satisfaction to both. Things hadn't gone well with the Tildens, either, in this unhappy decade. William Tilden had retired and invested the fortune he had made, but unsuccessfully, so that there was almost nothing left. His health had weakened; pride and spirit had deserted him. He cruelly needed his beloved daughter, and to this need Harriet, as always, abundantly and

31

joyfully responded. Remorseful at the suffering she had caused him, she gave him all she had to give, in love and care, during this last year of his life.

One's inclination is to follow the reticence Harriet herself observed in regard to the disastrous marriage that had consumed her youth. Yet because hers proved to be an important life and she a significant person, it cannot entirely be passed over.

The experience, direfully unhappy as it was, wasteful of her power as it was, left her no broken reed. She was a woman of uncommon strength, and her individuality couldn't well be seriously modified. Her enormous potentialities were indeed practically undrawn upon. Without attempting any amateur psychoanalysis, it may at least be suggested that she was permanently scarred. She may not herself have understood this. But, below the surface, you always felt that there was something baffling, unnaturally taut in her. It was as if, within her abounding warmth, there remained a core of ice. At times her very surfaces seemed frozen, too, so that it was by no means always apparent that she was, as nature had certainly intended her, a creature of buoyancy and joy. Underneath a lovely portrait of herself in her earliest youth Harriet once chose to write the words of Shakespeare's Beatrice: "A star danced, and under it was I born."

"My own nature seems to me gay," she wrote to the young painter, Vernon Hunter, at as late a period as January, 1928, "and on the surface light and trifling. I have the feeling that I do not disclose the deeper parts of my inner life at all, except in the rarest moments, but I think of myself always as young and as one who participates in the gayeties of youth with a fairly complete sharing of them. . . . . We don't know ourselves, of course."

CHAPTER V

TRIUMPH

REMEMBERING always that she was born to be a doer and an initiator, the creative period of Harriet's life will seem to have been long delayed. Now, at last, she was on the brink of it, and for her no trial term was necessary.

By the time that William Tilden died, the splendors of the Wabash Avenue house had become sadly tarnished. Gold and crystal were dimmed, white draperies gray and soiled, the conservatory untended, the servants fled, even the roof of the adjoining stable fallen in. There was no income to count upon.

In the midst of this melancholy disarray sat that enigmatic woman, William Tilden's widow. Conservative by nature, she had never sympathized with her husband's reckless methods of money-making; yet she had somehow managed to keep her eyes turned away from what was actually going on. And her husband had made this easy for her. "Don't tell your mother," he had one evening jovially confided to Harriet, in the days before her marriage, "but today I lost every cent I had in the world." It can only be assumed that on the following day fortune's wheel obligingly reversed itself.

Inevitably, Mrs. Tilden had become accustomed to the luxuries that a lordly income provided—even dependent on them. But she was neither frivolous nor stupid. She could, no doubt, have adapted herself to a life that henceforward, as it now seemed, would consist mainly of doing without, had it not been for her physical condition. A small woman, very much overweight, she was seriously crippled by arthritis. The confident chatelaine of the earlier period had become not only penniless but a permanent invalid.

33

Of the Tildens' two sons, the older, Will, now married and living in the East, had not so far been successful in the attempt to follow in his father's footsteps. He had the taste for speculation but hardly the right touch. His code demanded, according to the legend, that a lady should never ride in a public conveyance and that when in New York she should never venture below Twenty-third Street.

The younger son, Fred, at this time still a bachelor, was not established in business. Neither, therefore, was able to supply regularly the help that their mother needed.

There was, however, Harriet. And for Harriet this desperate family plight was merely an invitation to function naturally, as she had actually never had the opportunity to do before. (She herself was without resources, for, not having touched her hundred-thousand-dollar marriage settlement, she had been able to make the proud gesture of returning this on the day of her divorce.) Her feeling toward the suddenly dependent mother was, as it had always been, one of intense devotion. Harriet not only cherished her but deeply respected the opinions that Mrs. Tilden would express, often wittily, always in effectively tabloid form. In fact, to the quiet dominance of this small, calm, static person, who was not maternal in the sense of being either frankly emotional or fussily affectionate, Harriet, though herself a creature of tremendous latent power as well as of no small capacity for domination, offered no resistance whatever. Toward her mother, as one of her family has said, she was always "the tender, yielding child"—a child, however, with a powerfully protective instinct into which her mother's physical helplessness now completely dovetailed.

Here, then, might seem to be ideal material for one of those ingrowing mother-and-daughter relationships that tend progressively to shut out the rest of the world. The commonplace woman, in Harriet's situation, would have lent herself to an unventilated sort of emotionalism and would herself have shrunk within an anxious indoor life, occupied with petty economies. But for Harriet, preferring plenty of fresh air and magnificently declining to entertain either fears or regrets,

34

immediate purposeful action was both necessary and welcome. She decided to teach.

For such an individualist as Harriet the fact that teaching was at that time the preferred vocation for women would not in the least have recommended it. But she couldn't help knowing that her sympathetic understanding of youth would serve her superlatively, as in fact it did. And, too, she had grown homesick for those "countries of the mind" through which she was so well equipped to conduct authoritative expeditions. So she presented her Cornell record, made application, took examinations, and in January, 1889, was filling the post of instructor of English literature in the West Division High School. Later, she taught in two other of the city high schools.

There could have been no doubt but that this experiment would be of great advantage both to teacher and taught. Since, happily, she knew nothing of pedagogy, this teaching of Harriet's was purely inspirational, and it was a brilliant success. Not a moment was given to mechanical routine. Instinctively she knew how to communicate to these boys and girls her own soundly based enthusiasms and in so doing won over many of them as lifelong disciples and friends. Furthermore, she encouraged her students to write—stories, plays, and verse. She also, while teaching at the Hyde Park High School, installed a printing press in her own home, where four or five books of these student writings were struck off under the imprint, "The Windtryst Press."

Through sheer personality, as well, she impressed and stimulated her students. One of them, Mrs. Edith Foster Flint, afterward for many years professor of English at the University of Chicago, recalls that there was always a hush of expectation before Harriet entered the classroom and that, when she did come in, smiling, graceful, becomingly dressed, her class was as taut and eager as an audience keyed for the entrance of an Ellen Terry. Which is far from implying that Harriet made use of any theatrical methods or that she was even conscious of the effect she produced.

From the day that she began to teach, Harriet's real life, the life of multiple and rich associations, the life for which she is remembered, was under way. Strong of body, keen of mind, and overflowing with bountiful impulses, teaching supplied her with congenial and, indeed, necessary outlets.

It had, however, one serious drawback. Public schools do not pay salaries adequate to maintain such a mother as Harriet's, a woman who needed medical care and many comforts and who even, Harriet almost quixotically insisted, must have, as she had always had, her own carriage.

So more money must be forthcoming.

It may be taken for granted that the creative impulse, not fully absorbed by teaching, was at work in this surprising woman and that the inherited instincts of the adventurer and pioneer were alive and strong. So that she no doubt welcomed the excuse of her mother's requirements, as she interpreted them. But as her benevolences were always planned on a grand scale, she knew it was no trifling sum that she would need.

The reminder is perhaps pertinent at this point that when, years later, Harriet maintained a house in Chicago, a farm in the Berkshires, a flat in New York, and often a summer cottage; that when her Chicago household numbered half-a-dozen members plus servants and continual guests; that when she contributed and subscribed and gave, as often and as generously as the need of others prompted—all this wasn't made possible by any idle quarterly coupon-cutting. Harriet earned every penny of it herself, and, beginning at this period, she earned it in the following way:

Through a family friend, Mrs. Otto Matz, came the suggestion that Harry Gordon Selfridge, later internationally known as a merchant, then an associate of Marshall Field and director of the tearoom in the Field department store, was looking for something new and distinctive in the way of gingerbread made in the form of little cakes.

To this woman as she has hitherto revealed herself it scarcely seems as though a more trivial and uninspiring idea could have been proposed. One almost wonders that Harriet heard it— Harriet, of all women, whose interests were predominantly intellectual, whose practical domestic experience was almost nil. She did listen, however, and attentively.

Whether or not Mrs. William Tilden was herself a genius in the field of cookery, her daughter had in some way acquired knowledge that she now put to brilliant use. Without interrupting her school work, she supplied herself with superior materials, withdrew one evening to the kitchen, and there prepared and baked an immense batch of gingerbread, fashioned in the required form.

A reader who may be indifferent to gingerbread as he has known it should not on that account permit himself a condescending thought as to this or any other of Harriet's creations. Any of us who might have eaten of the epochal mixture that launched its maker in a new career would beyond doubt have agreed with the estimate of Mr. Selfridge and his colleagues— an estimate which led to the immediate order of five hundred more cakes.

Five hundred cakes, to be prepared in extreme haste and cooked in an oven which held but twenty-four at a time! And with an inflexible school routine that must be adhered to! A woman with anything short of Harriet's phenomenal energy would not have dreamed of undertaking it. But Harriet did and carried it through. Probably it cost her more than a few nights' sleep, but it yielded an exciting triumph.

This was only the beginning of a new adventure that progressed with amazingly swift momentum.

Since she did not yet know either mental or physical fatigue and since her confidence in herself was practically limitless, she did not shrink when an order came from Selfridge for a large amount (was it six gallons?) of chicken salad. This, she calculated, would require forty-eight chickens, which she boiled, a few at a time, on her mother's stove. The mayonnaise was achieved through the vigorous co-operation of Harriet and the family egg beater.

But a puzzling detail obtruded itself. After the chickens had been cooked, the kitchen was filled with kettles containing a nameless liquid. Tasting this, Harriet perceived that it was nothing more or less than good strong chicken soup. Her immediate decision as to what to do with it was beautifully characteristic. It happened that as a feature of the general decay into which the neighborhood had fallen—for Mr. Tilden had not been the only deflated financier—the opposite house, once the home of a doctor, was now being used as a saloon, toward which long lines of ill-clad men, obviously out of work and stimulated by the idea of the "free lunches" obtainable at that period, hopefully gravitated every day. Harriet, who had been troubled by this spectacle and wanted to do something about it, now sent word to the proprietor of the saloon that each night she would supply soup and bread to any twenty men who might present themselves at her door. And this she did.

In Harriet's own words, "Having provided myself with yellow bowls, and having many crusts of bread left from making bread crumbs, I gave the bowls and the crusts to the tramps as they came in. They sat around my kitchen wall, with their bowls in their laps, and they were well contented with the hot soup on the cold nights. Knowledge of this institution spread among them, until I remember counting twenty-one men seated around my room at one time. It did not occur to me to feel afraid until one night when I was working alone at two o'clock, and a tramp came in for soup. He was perfectly well behaved, but I suddenly realized how unprotected I was in case of need.
. . . ."

With such a start, it wasn't long before the new industry outgrew the Tilden kitchen. Nor could it long continue a one-woman activity, though each process remained under the originator's personal supervision. She approached the whole matter in the spirit of an artist, and her attitude toward the finished products and toward her unseen patrons was, and always remained, that of the gracious hostess offering refreshment to her personal guests—this being happily expressed in the cookbook which she published many years later.

At the same time that new kitchens were rented and new equipment bought, a staff of cooks and other employees had to be secured, which was, of course, the most difficult matter of all. Then, new delicacies had continually to be developed—and here was a suggestion for the name that had to be given to the experiment that in so short a time had become an actual catering business. Keeping her own personality in the background, Harriet called her enterprise the Home Delicacies Association— an accurately descriptive title that was to be famous for many years in Chicago and for a period, and to a lesser degree, in London also. Home delicacies became the fashion. To all large dinners, luncheons, receptions, they were considered indispensable. At the same time, Marshall Field's continued to be a large-scale customer. Even most railroads running out of Chicago regularly supplied their dining cars with Harriet's products. By virtue solely of its own excellence, certainly not because of any commercial tactics on Harriet's part, for she was innocent of any, the business grew prodigiously.

It can now be seen how it happened that when, twenty years later, Harriet Moody's home came to be so extensively frequented by poets and other artists, these guests were daily bidden to partake of miniature banquets. It was merely necessary, in those days, for Bessie O'Neill, who was in charge of the house, to telephone to the factory the number of guests who were to be at dinner, and at the appointed hour containers of ravishing dishes, hot and cold, would be delivered. Harriet's friends well remember these miracles, and they also wistfully recall the fruitcakes and candies that were produced by the workrooms at holiday times and that Harriet would generously send to all quarters of the earth as gifts.

Expressing a natural reaction to one of these bounties, Ridgely Torrence, many years later, wrote her from New York (on March 4, 1919):

"A gilded barge, shaped like a basket, floated up the stairs today and before our shining eyes and wakened palates, quietly. fragrantly disclosed that regal, that imperial, that Olympian CAKE, crowned and anointed with royal orgeat and orbed with gemmy fruits of Elysian orchards. I see it was not addressed to me, but even as an appreciative sparrow that expects at least to dart from crumb to crumb among those that fall from the table of my richer half, I venture to send you this ecstatic chirp.

"As Thoreau said of his birth, it came in the nick of time. Still I could find it in my heart to wish the barge had arrived yesterday, for Frost came here to dinner last night and he is so eminently worthy of the CAKE and the CAKE so deserving of him that I'm sorry they couldn't have met. A King of men and of poets (and he is both) should know the Queen of Cakes."

What distinguished Harriet, at the beginning of her great enterprise, from hundreds and thousands of other women who have turned to cooking because of a need of money was perhaps, first of all, her imaginative approach. Hers was a passion for perfection impossible to a woman not an artist, and joined to this was an immense liberality of view in every direction. To meet the demands that from this time on were made upon her she had to be, as she was, exceptionally intelligent, tirelessly vital, and utterly fearless. Then it was, of course, of cardinal importance that she had a sophisticated palate and could faultlessly discriminate between the good and the not-so-good. So, instead of being the timid purveyor of a few rolls and cookies to a woman's exchange, she became a food magnate, not only producing in vast abundance but actually educating thousands of persons in a knowledge of good food. Yet this industry of hers, in spite of its size, never came to have a commercial flavor and remained indeed so personal an affair that it would be impossible to duplicate or scarcely to imitate it, except on the part of a woman miraculously endowed with Harriet Moody's own attributes.

Could a venture so conducted yield profits? Mrs. Tilden's early instruction had certainly not included the practice of thrift. Moreover, Harriet's whole nature was a protest against cheese-paring, and she tolerated only the highest-grade materials. Also, she paid liberal wages to her increasingly large staff. In spite of all this, and with the heavy attendant expenses, the rewards were, even from Harriet's own point of view, large.

It had been understood from the beginning that these rewards were to be converted, as they promptly were, into ease and luxury for Mrs. Tilden. Servants, doctors, and occasional nurses had to be arranged for. It was an immense delight to Harriet to be able to provide her mother with horses, so that the carriages left over from Mr. Tilden's day—one of them, a "Clarence," remaining always an especial favorite of Harriet's—could be made use of. This entailed a coachman, who had to be provided, too. A detail of particular value to the disabled woman was the installing of an elevator in the Wabash Avenue house. Numberless books were supplied her, for she read constantly. In fact, during the remainder of her life she was to lack nothing that solicitude could devise.

What her attitude was both toward Harriet's filial ardor and toward Harriet's nothing short of sensational achievements can only be surmised. But there is evidence that she accepted these coolly, as she accepted most things coolly. If there was ever a single person in Harriet's devotedly loyal entourage who was able to regard her with detachment, one suspects that it was this mother whom she idolized. Not that Mrs. Tilden was incapable of tenderness. Indeed, she had reservoirs both of love and pride, which, however, she bestowed especially upon her younger son Fred, acknowledged to be her favorite child.

Somehow, one can't help recalling a little anecdote of Harriet's childhood. One day, it must have been in Parkman, her parents went away, leaving the little girl for at least an afternoon alone. What an opportunity, she reflected, to surprise her mother and father by producing a hot dinner for them. Focusing, therefore, her native ability and her good sense, for she can have had no experience, she successfully produced all the essential elements of a dinner which, beaming with pride and affection, she offered her elders on their return.

But instead of being touched and delighted, Mrs. Tilden was sternly disapproving and lectured the child so severely on her naughtiness that the injustice and the hurt of it burned within her for decades.

41

From the moment that Harriet had an income beyond her own small needs, even beyond her mother's needs, she never lacked for human objects of interest and help. No outsider, not even her secretary, can have had more than a general impression of all this. But it was true that, when she considered action necessary (in a given person's behalf), she acted with startling promptness and directness. Writing in 1929 to her friend Miss Ellen Starr, Jane Addams' associate in Hull-House, who had asked her help for a needy person, she said:

"I remember a time when I had asked a service from a banker for a friend who needed to place some stock. The banker said to me, 'Let God take care of him'; and I said .... 'Just for the moment I am God.' This not in a profane sense at all, as you will readily understand, but simply with a recognition of the fact that we are the means divine power has created for itself for intercommunication among human beings. I hope this doesn't strike a wrong note with you; but at any rate it is meant to be reverent."

In fact, Harriet had little interest in money except in using it to develop or patch up other people's lives. For herself she did not desire what money buys and was utterly sincere in scorning "material" things, to use her own adjective. And though she never troubled to formulate any theory of asceticism, her personal life had a strongly ascetic vein.

For instance, though there were five bedrooms in the Groveland Avenue house—where Harriet had come to live, bringing her cooks and her machinery with her, several years after her business had perforce drawn her away from Wabash Avenue[1]— she herself did not occupy any one of them but slept habitually on the swing. She asked little of any abode—indeed, practically nothing, beyond a telephone and, one must add, a coffeepot. When she came to stay in the flat on Waverly Place, she made no reference to the discomfort and even pain that climbing the three long flights of stairs must have caused her bad ankle. In making her frequent business trips to Europe, she chose inex-

---

[1] She had paused on Indiana Avenue in the interval.

42

pensive and far from luxurious liners. Forced repeatedly to live for months at a time in Southern California, her vigorous protest was that the mild climate was too comfortable. And when she was ill one summer in London she wrote, lightly of course, to her cousin Henry Lyman that it was a "vice" to yield, however involuntarily, to a bed as soft as hers.

CHAPTER VI

A FORTRESS CRUMBLES

A DECADE or so later, Harriet looked back almost with unbelief at the serenely successful woman who, in the late nineties, directed a household of her own at 2970 Groveland Avenue, followed two exacting professions and faced the world each day with gay confidence and an untroubled heart. "I thought of myself then," she said, "as an unassailable fortress."

And no wonder. The major problems of her life appeared to be solved. Marriage she felt that she had finished with. Still young and vigorous, with an extraordinary power of drawing people to her, she had filled every moment of her days and arranged for herself, she must have thought, a permanent pattern of living.

Her teaching continued—the lively composite friendship that she carried on with a good share of the most eager and intelligent youth of Chicago. A natural outflowing, this was, of heart and mind, into which it was plain that no element of staleness or slackness could ever enter. As for her cooking industry, that had miraculously flowered. In secret detachment Harriet watched it as she would have watched the progress of an enthralling play. Could it be she, could it be her own energy and initiative, that had brought into being this much-praised affair that turned out food products of acknowledged perfection, at the same time functioning like a complicated engine and yielding money in a volume and with a regularity that she could scarcely have dreamed of? During all those early years she never failed to be entertained, even amused, by her own success, desperately hard though she had worked to earn it.

Meanwhile, her closest human tie, that with her mother, was

always scrupulously tended. Harriet never excused herself for lack of "time" from daily attendance on her cherished invalid. It was her habit to spend almost every night at Mrs. Tilden's house, and the younger women of her household still see her as she gaily whirled home in the morning on an early trolley car (this was the day when trolleys were a novelty and "trolley rides" a popular pastime), lifting from the dust her fashionably long, stiff, silk-lined skirt with a gesture of admirable ease. . . . . Then singing snatches from *The Pirates of Penzance* or *Pinafore* while she made herself ready for school.

In the afternoon, her classes finished, Harriet would begin the day all over again, with her work for the Home Delicacies, experimenting, supervising, and, of course, always humanizing the whole establishment. Later, she would pause long enough to sit beside her mother on the daily drive—that drive which, carriage, horses, coachman, and all, was the especial private symbol of Harriet's success and of the daughterly devotion that had been its source. And yet, mustn't the older woman have seen it as a trifling matter in comparison with the zest and vitality and love with which Harriet enriched her mother's fading existence? . . . .

Lover of life as she was and mistress of the art of living, hospitality was one of the main expressions of Harriet's self. Her home, when she was in it, was always filled with generous interplay of personality, with old friends and new enthusiasms. Those who knew her then delight to speak of her now, to recall the warmth and glow of her personal atmosphere. She seems never to have been tired, never too busy to meet a human demand. Then and later she held a kind of court of youth, for the young people she reached out for sought her with equal eagerness. Also, at this time, for her life thus far had been spent in the conventional world, she held more or less formal "evenings" where she herself functioned in a warmly human fashion. Thoroughly efficient, completely feminine, lovely to look upon, approaching each guest as she did with a special and entirely unforced interest, she was from any possible point of view the most delightful and accomplished of hostesses.

45

In these various ways Harriet Brainard touched a great many lives, and her touch always enkindled. But she went beyond this. Never content with superficial relationships, it used almost to seem as if her instinctive way of expressing an especial interest in a young person was quite simply to invite the object of it to come to live with her. This habit she had, in fact, begun as soon as she had a house of her own to share. The young poet Alice Corbin, who had been her pupil and between whom and Harriet a deep affection always existed, joined the household for the first of several periods. Elizabeth O'Neill, another of her high-school pupils, became a member of the family group and remained in charge of the household as long as Harriet lived. The beginning of Katharine Lyle's long association with Harriet's household occurred a few years later. Mrs. Martha Foote Crow[1] had, since the death of her husband, a professor of Greek, come to Chicago to teach English at the University. She was alone. She adored Harriet. She, too, came to live at 2970.

It was at this time that Harriet had a chance to exercise her maternal instinct by taking into her house and into her affection a four-year-old second cousin, Gladys Plows, who naturally came to be known as Gladys Tilden. So the child's earliest recollections, as it proved, were to be of this delightful grown-up cousin, of Harriet's abundant kindness and affection, and of 2970 Groveland Avenue, the background of it all. The connection lasted but a year or two, until Gladys' mother remarried, but was renewed later on.

In short, Harriet was on the best of terms with the world. She had arrived after the long frustration of her marriage at what seemed an abundant expression of herself. Active in a hundred ways, living her life intensely and joyfully, she scarcely paused to question, to wonder, to look ahead.

---

[1] Martha Foote Crow had an intense, lifelong devotion to poetry. Going to England in the summer of 1894, she must for this reason have equipped herself with a letter to George Meredith, then living alone at Box Hill. On August 15, Meredith wrote to his daughter, Marie (Mrs. Sturgis): "Mrs. Crow of Chicago came to dine yesterday. A really good and pleasant woman."

If this were a romantic novel and Harriet the heroine, you would, of course, at this point sense what was bound to befall her. And befall her it did. . . . .

In the autumn of 1899, Mrs. Crow, thereby following the custom of the household, one day asked Harriet whether she might ask to dinner a young professor who had come from Harvard a few years earlier to teach at the University. He was a poet, and she thought he was lonely. His name was Moody.

Harriet (as Miss Corbin, now Mrs. Henderson, recalls it), well knowing that Mrs. Crow had many enthusiasms, not all of which it may have been her habit to share, assented with rather an absent-minded casualness. So the poet was invited and on a night when, as often happened, there were ten or twelve at dinner. It being understood that he was shy, they placed him next to Alice Corbin who was not only young, charming, and a poet in the bud but who could be relied upon to talk.

Miss Corbin did her best, she remembers, to talk easily with the professor who was an acknowledged poet; and she must have succeeded, for he tried to draw her out, "as a young person writing poetry." They got on beautifully, and, later on, the precociously accomplished Freshman (for she was only that) sent him the poems he had asked to see, and he wrote her warmly about them.

The professor must have felt more than usually at ease with his young dinner partner or linked with her by the gift for writing she had revealed, for shortly after this he invited her to a football game—her first. "I think," she says, "that I occasionally cheered the wrong side. . . . . Anyhow, I know that I was very cold, in spite of much stamping of feet, and the hot beef-tea he fed me; and then he brought me home on the old Cottage Grove cable car, which took about an hour and was little warmer than outdoors.

"At Harriet's it was tea time . . . . and I was glad to be warm again! Among several other people who were there was Mrs. William Gardner Hale, wife of the head professor of Latin at the University. Later, Mrs. Hale undertook to chide Harriet for letting me go to the game unchaperoned with a *dissipated*

47

young poet like that! He had gained this reputation, it seemed, by often being seen crossing the campus early in the morning before classes, with hair dishevelled, and a bedraggled sweater over his arm—*after a night out!* (The "night out" having been spent on the shores of Lake Michigan, in Jackson Park. One of the things Will Moody best liked to do was to spend the night in the open, and to see the dawn and the sunrise. This was true later at Mackinac Island, in Virginia and I think wherever he was.)"

Now it was during this unarranged tea hour that Harriet exchanged her first significant words with the poet to whom at the earlier dinner she had been able to give little heed. No sooner had this happened than she perceived that in a sense he belonged to her—that she would beyond doubt come really to know him.

Externally, what she saw was a blond-bearded young man of medium stature with a ruddy, faunlike face and blue eyes of a peculiar steadiness. Both his smile and his voice were winning. Soberly recalling his friend of many years, Robert Morss Lovett says of Moody in his youth. "It is difficult to think of a human being more perfectly endowed with strength and beauty of body and mind."[2] And in his further description there occurs this delightful sentence: "A guarded joy looked out from his eyes, with gleams of ironical amusement, and now and then his whole being would flame up in laughter."

The room was filled that day with chance callers, none of whom can have regarded the engaging young professor with eyes as cold as those of Mrs. Hale. But in spite of his actual simplicity, he was not easy to approach. Had Harriet made no special effort, she and the poet might have met and parted with nothing beyond the usual formalities. Moody said little to strangers, had no small talk whatever, and did not at first betray the strongly humorous twist of his mind. But his taciturnity was of a friendly sort, and he had a way of watching people closely,

[2] *Selected Poems of William Vaughn Moody.* Introduction by Robert Morss Lovett (Houghton Mifflin Co., 1931); p. lxii.

his dramatic sense enjoining a strong interest in the human scene, however little part he took in it.

Harriet, however, was not dismayed by taciturnity. In fact, a certain resistance piqued and stimulated her. She applied her praticed arts to the young man with the result that within an hour he must have been completely at his ease with her and she in possession of all that for the time being she needed to know of him.

What she may not have realized until somewhat later was the degree to which in the East his gifts were already recognized. So far, he had published no volume. But his "Gloucester Moors," "Ode in Time of Hesitation," and other significant poems had strongly impressed a considerable audience. Sober critics in writing of him had been willing to use the dangerous word "genius." Even as a Harvard Freshman, the shy youth from Indiana had been flatteringly recognized by his fellow-students; and, after his first appearances in the *Monthly*, it was seen that he had no close rival.[3] After graduation at the head of his class in 1893, having completed his course in three years and having spent his Senior year in Europe tutoring a subfreshman, he stayed on at Harvard for two years as graduate instructor, at the same time competently writing and editing textbooks of English literature. He—or a considerable part of him, for there was a duality in his nature—found the Cambridge atmosphere immensely to his taste. It was, in fact, not too willingly and only because his sense of obligation toward certain members of his family made a larger income imperative that in the fall of 1895 he accepted the post at the University of Chicago that Robert Morss Lovett, his close friend, colleague, and coauthor (of two histories of English literature) had procured for him. Here he was, perhaps surprisingly, in view of his shyness, an immediate and brilliant success, even though he never reconciled himself

[3] E. A. Robinson, though he attended Harvard as a special student during a part of Moody's college life, was by no means so promptly accepted; and Moody's close friend and fellow-poet, Trumbull Stickney, belonged to a slightly later period. Philip Henry Savage, who died in 1899, was, however, Moody's contemporary. Percy MacKaye was graduated four years later than Moody.

to teaching. "With every lecture," he wailed a few years later, "I slay a poet."

. . . . The meeting between these two persons, Harriet Brainard and Will Moody, does not need to be overromanticized. It speaks for itself. From the moment of their first talk together each seems to have felt in the other a compelling and inescapable force. In a sense, neither of them was ever the same afterward.

Yet to an outsider, looking on, their association need not necessarily have seemed a romantic one. Certainly, it did not have the usual complexion of a "love affair."

Early in 1900 and not many months, therefore, after their first meeting, Moody's first book, *The Masque of Judgment*, was published. One of the first copies, duly inscribed, was brought by the author himself to Groveland Avenue. Harriet was not at home. But as soon as she came in, she opened the volume, found herself deeply stirred, even startled, by the new power in it, and sat up the greater part of the night reading it absorbedly to the end. . . . . What she had not known before about the man who wrote it she knew now. It is perhaps not too much to say that she based the rest of her life upon this knowledge.

By this time, the dwellers at 2970 saw that among the habitués of the house one was pre-eminently welcome. They knew that Harriet dealt largely in protegés. Moody was far from being in this category. They knew she had countless friends. Yet to no other did she pay such deference. The new poet came with others, more often he came alone. There were long talks and, above all, much reading of poetry. Acquaintance had been catapulted into intimacy. The truth was, and Harriet sensed it from the beginning, that she had formed the supreme friendship of her life—a life filled with substantial and often exciting friendships.

She was now, as we know, a mature woman who had fully developed her bountiful personality and who had had every opportunity to know the world. At her own home and elsewhere she was in the habit of meeting men who interested, often stimulated, her. Nevertheless, of late years not one of them had seriously disturbed her emotional poise.

Now, quite without warning, had appeared a strange somebody who did disturb it. How shall this be accounted for?

It wasn't as if she had found him in any sort of need from which she had conceived a means of rescuing him, as she and almost any other woman would have so delighted in doing. Moody was no Francis Thompson. Neither was he a limp, immature "Morell," helplessly looking about for a "Candida" to cling to. A sound, well-poised young man, quite free of every picturesque vice and vagary, he was equipped with a profession and a livelihood and, above all, concentratedly absorbed in his poetry. Completely masculine, entirely sufficient to himself, he found feminine association agreeable but needed it rather less than the normal young man needs it. Moody was a romanticist, and he had deep emotional capacity. But then and always he stood very squarely on his own feet.

Harriet was a completely genuine human being. And one of the most genuine of her attributes was her feeling for poetry. Moody from first to last typified poetry to her in a deeply satisfying sense. There was something in him, she liked to believe, that transcended ordinary human nature, and to this she precipitately surrendered. All the rest—since she was what she was—naturally followed. In an extremely short space of time Harriet quite forgot that she had been a "fortress"—or even that the fortress had crumbled. In fact, she was never given to thinking about herself at all. She was almost exclusively absorbed in a new and to her a totally different and superior human being, an experience that with all her multiple enthusiasms had never happened to her before.

The attraction was by no means one-sided. Moody was almost naïvely ready to confess that Harriet had overwhelmed him and that she represented something new, dazzling, and wholly admirable. Shortly after their first meeting he promised his University colleague, Ferdinand Schevill, at that time absent from Chicago, that on his return he would be given a "surprise" in the form of an introduction to the remarkable

51

Mrs. Brainard. Reticent by habit in regard to his personal affairs, Moody naturally did not at first link Harriet with himself but thought of her as living in a world other than his own and had, therefore, no reason for withholding from his friends the delightful fact of her existence.

It was true. Their worlds were different. Between two such persons as these there obviously stretched a considerable gulf Each knew it. Yet it did not separate them.

If Moody's feeling for a kind of woman new in his experience had the outward result of making him uncharacteristically expansive—though at first, only; later, he reverted to his usual reticence—Harriet's own recognition of their exciting impact before long altered the ways of her own and others' lives. Having no thought of disguising her rapidly deepening interest in Moody, neither did she try to establish a monopolistic claim in him. To her, it was never an effort to be magnanimous. She was ready to share her poet with her other friends, with her usual circle, so far as these were able to understand him and establish with him relationships of their own. This manner of conducting herself was true of her always.

Since Moody's days as well as Harriet's were filled with teaching and his visits were ordinarily made in the evening, Harriet no longer found it expedient to spend every night at her mother's house but from now on sometimes sent Katharine Lyle in her stead, this, of course, without lessening the number of hours that she was happy to spend with her mother or without violating in the least her rare loyalty. Nevertheless, Mrs. Tilden must have reflected on the change. It may have been as an indirect result of these reflections that later on she betrayed so strong an objection to her daughter's marriage to Moody. It is even said that she extracted a promise from Harriet that the marriage should not take place during her own lifetime. Yet it is not on record that she made a similar effort to dissuade Harriet from her first marriage.

Moody shortly felt very much at home at 2970 Groveland Avenue—"the Grove," as they used to call it. But it is also true that a place, however agreeable, to feel at home in would of itself have meant little to him. He was indeed almost scornfully nondomestic. "I think I am still of the unregenerate in whom sleepy domestic happiness induces *tedium vitae*," he wrote Harriet while visiting some contented household. An explorer by taste and habit, sheer comfort ranked low in his scale of values. But at this time he was still in his early thirties. A middle-aged fondness for sitting by the fire might have overtaken him in due season.

Moody knew well that a poet doesn't encounter every day a woman capable of understanding both his achievement and his unfulfilled ambitions—capable of serving trustworthily as both audience and critic. In Harriet he found these capacities. He adequately valued them and made liberal use of them. Nor were they less acceptable for her being intensely feminine and for her having (though he manfully protested against her "idealization" of him) so flattering a preference for himself. "Sometimes I cannot bear to have you make so much of me," he wrote her a year later, when they had advanced much farther in understanding of each other, "knowing how ordinary are the levels on which most of my life is led, how utterly unheroic I am in all the relations of life."

But their intimacy rested on a deep basis in both their natures. There was no possibility of turning back.

CHAPTER VII

CRISIS

H ARRIET was a Chicagoan who never felt it incumbent on her to defend the Chicago climate. She admitted that at times it was deplorable and in the hot months hardly to be borne, even though she herself had suffered through many a torrid season there. To her mind the spring of 1901, in particular, partook too much of the intensity of a prairie summer. Periodic escape from the city was, therefore, a sound general prescription. And Will Moody, she thought, after a hard winter's work at both teaching and writing would certainly be the better for a few dips into the country.

She, therefore, rented for a season a cottage at Lakeside, Illinois, north of Chicago, and arranged a series of informal week-end house parties. On each occasion she acted as hostess and dynamo, and on each occasion Moody was a guest.

During the evening of Sunday, May 16, 1901, the current house party diminished in number. Up to this point, the usual evening program had been followed: a fire built at the water's edge with an abundant supper cooked and eaten there, the hardships attendant upon too many picnics being avoided by the presence of Harriet's excellent butler. Afterward, it had become the custom to linger quietly at the waterside, listening to Moody's reading of his poems by the flickering fire, watching the starlit water until very late, sometimes even until there were signs of dawn. This was Moody's way, so that every drop of beauty might be pressed from the fresh spring night. There were always a few sleep-defiers, including Harriet herself, who would stay with him.

On this evening certain guests, among them Lorado Taft, the sculptor, and Mrs. Taft, had to return to Chicago. After escorting those who were homeward-bound part way to the railroad station, the remaining guests, Ferdinand Schevill, Alice Corbin, Moody, and others, walked back with Harriet toward the lake shore. This, at the end, was reached by a rather steep decline. It was already night. Harriet, alone for the moment, and ahead of the others, walked along in a rapturous abandonment to the mood of the evening, flinging her arms to the sky. . . . .

Moody, a few yards behind her, was the first to realize that she had fallen. Leaping to help her, he found her sitting on the ground, giving no sign of her suffering but trying, with remarkable composure, to discover by the faint starlight what had happened to her. Even with his help, she could not rise. She had broken her ankle.

Moody managed to cut Harriet's boot from her rapidly swelling foot. They carried her to the house. Expert aid was not available—a serious matter—but the local doctor, with neither antiseptic nor anesthetic and with no light but that of a kerosene lamp, set the bones provisionally. The ankle had been badly smashed, several bones piercing the flesh and one large bone even penetrating the leather of her high-laced boot, a custom-made affair designed for bicycling. Later it was learned that the injury was technically known as a "Pott's compound fracture." Also, the obstacle that had tripped her was the outlet of a drain pipe so that a septic condition was certain to arise.

Tense hours followed. The day of the automobile not having yet come, there was now an enforced wait until the next morning, when the first train that carried baggage and that could therefore accommodate a stretcher would bear Harriet and the others to Chicago.

When, on Monday, the ambulance arrived at St. Luke's Hospital, Dr. Lewis L. MacArthur, an excellent physician and surgeon, had prepared for extreme measures. A description of the case had been telephoned to him by the Lakeside doctor. Also, he had the report of young Martin Fischer,[1] one of the

---

[1] Mr. Fischer had been a high-school pupil of Harriet's and was her deeply devoted friend. He was at this time completing his course at Rush Medical School but was not yet a qualified practitioner. He is now professor of physiology at the University of Cincinnati.

members of the house party, who had come into Chicago early in the morning for this very purpose. Dr. MacArthur, inured to manifestations of hysterical suffering, found, on the contrary, in this new patient a calm, smiling woman who greeted him as though they were both guests in somebody's drawing-room. Harriet had, in fact, amazed everybody by the degree of her self-control, her only concern seeming to be lest her mother, to whom she had telephoned as usual that morning, should learn what had really happened. Meanwhile, she stoically awaited the result of the examination.

Dr. MacArthur's verdict was precisely what he had himself foreseen. Amputation was indicated. But Harriet, still in full command of herself and of the situation, learned that there was an alternative procedure, though this was difficult, dangerous, time-consuming, and to a large extent experimental. She decided, the doctor thoroughly assenting, to submit herself to as much experiment as might be necessary but to retain her foot.

After Dr. MacArthur had operated, doing his best with the shattered and infected ankle, a period of great anxiety followed. So pervasive were the results of the injury that it was not even certain that Harriet would live. For six weeks she was under constant care at the hospital. Then, when they took her home, it was with the understanding that one or more further operations would be necessary and that it would be many months before she could even begin to use the foot.[2]

The accident had involved changes that were drastic and permanent. For one thing, the new handicap meant the end of Harriet's teaching. It meant also that the woman whose outlines and grace of movement had become a legend[3] was never

[2] Harriet always afterward paid full tribute to Dr. MacArthur for his skill in saving her foot, while he, for his part, admired the woman and her courage. At a gathering of surgeons in Chicago a number of years later he described his operations on her foot and their result, and Harriet, by way of demonstrating her gratitude, came herself to the meeting in order to allow her ankle to be seen.

[3] Moody wrote of her in his poem, "A Prairie Ride":

Before me and beside me and on before me swayed
Her body like a water-arum blade,
Like a slanted gull for motion.

afterward to move with any freedom. For Harriet, who, without being vain, could not in all honesty but be aware of these magnificent physical assets of hers, since she had always heard them extolled, and whose lifelong joy in vigorous outdoor life depended on a sound body, this actual alteration of her personality and the enforced revolution in her way of life were particularly cruel.

It would have been impossible, however, to meet disaster with greater courage. The suffering from which she was probably never afterward entirely free she ignored with Olympian detachment, and her own incurable lameness she handled with supreme resolution and skill.

Another change, it may be the most important of all, had been involved in the accident. It seems certain from allusions made by Moody himself that with the happenings of that final night at Lakeside had come a crisis in the relation between himself and Harriet. Brought closely, tenderly together by their common shock, by her suffering and his compassion—perhaps also by a certain chivalrous remorse, however baseless, on his part, for shouldn't he, he may have asked himself, have been able to protect her from the fall?—there emerged the thrilling reality of their interest in each other as man and woman. The irrevocable had happened.[4]

That summer, for the first time, Moody remained in Chicago. During the long hot months after Harriet's return from the hospital he would come every afternoon to Groveland Avenue. It was then that the famous swing was installed so that Harriet, with the dignity that never forsook her and with no suggestion whatever of a sickroom, could remain in a medically approved position on this equivalent of a bed and at the same time, if she chose, receive the world at large. Sometimes the young poet came alone. Often, Ferdinand Schevill, his friend and now more and more Harriet's also, came with him. These

[4] In his poem, "The Three Angels," Moody wrote:
>We had been sweet friends long before,
>.... till this evening's dark mischance, ...
>And yet had not been breathed a sound
>Of love, nor a thought of love been thought.

were the high points of Harriet's days and, one may well believe, of theirs as well.

Such visits were not expressive of sympathy alone. Even Schevill, though lacking Moody's more intimate interest in the stricken figure on the swing, must have been well rewarded for his effort, for the least that you could say of Harriet, even when she was ill and prostrate, was that she was, in the old phrase, "good company." It was a part of her native equipment that she was capable of an easy and unexigent comradeship with men. However shy might be his habit, a man whose very silence chanced to interest her would often to his own astonishment find himself roused to a lively conversational give-and-take. Even when, as now, she lay helpless, one couldn't help sensing her characteristic art of making guests comfortable without seeming oversolicitous. Moody's friend soon realized that a separate and totally unsentimental friendship was forming between himself and Harriet, a friendship that was to yield much solace to them both and that persisted undiminished until her death.

And there were letters, too.

In a note of Moody's, postmarked August 1, he said:

Here is a wild morning-glory which I plucked an hour before sunrise, far south on the lake shore, where I went last night to ask a blessing upon you. It will be withered before it reaches you, but let it be a symbol of that which does not wither but renews itself like the morning.

As I came back the birds were twittering and caroling in all the roadside bushes, and all the ways and moods of passionate kindness on the earth seemed beautiful and right past understanding.

W. V. M.

The middle of August came. On this day, the fifteenth, Harriet was to return to the hospital to undergo a second operation on her foot. As this did not involve danger but would for a time interrupt their daily talks together, Moody fulfilled an agreement with Hamlin Garland to make an excursion into the

West, the West of cattle ranches and horseback riding which was then new to him—the very West, in fact, of *The Great Divide*, although the idea of the play was not suggested to him until several years later. Returning at the end of the first week in September, he joined Harriet and her household in a move to Mackinac Island, a spot chosen because Dr. MacArthur had his summer home there. Harriet had rented a comfortable house and brought with her several young women, including Alice Corbin, Bessie ONeill, "Martie" Butler (one of a group of sisters with whom Harriet had been affectionately intimate since their childhood), and the necessary servants. The three weeks spent there were, in spite of Harriet's invalid condition, memorably happy ones.

With the return to Chicago the near comradeship with Moody, which had given an actual radiance to the months of physical misery, was suspended. In the effort to release himself permanently from teaching, Moody had secured a leave of absence from the University and was scheduled to spend several months in Boston collaborating with Robert Lovett on another textbook. By the time that Harriet came home the University year had begun, but it was for Schevill alone, who had also at intervals joined the Mackinac party, that the academic mill began to grind in more or less the usual way.

For Harriet, now for the first time in her life imprisoned, this was merely the beginning of a period of exquisitely painful readjustment. In the sacrifice of her teaching, which was an intimately personal thing, supplying a valuable and almost necessary balance to her business concerns, a precious part of her life had been lopped off. Now that constant energetic action had had to give way to an enforced passivity, it seemed as if the world she loved and had been a part of floated past her and beyond her reach. Wherefore a sadness more poignant than any physical pain had to be fought and overcome.

A little later she had very slowly and torturingly to learn to walk in an entirely new way, to use and depend upon a permanently disabled ankle. Her success in all this was triumphant, but it was a success for which fresh toll was continually being exacted of her as long as she lived.

It is true that up to this time Harriet's standard of a full life outmeasured considerably that of the average human being, so that now, while she seemed to herself shut off from the rest of the world, interests and responsibilities pressed in upon her far more urgently than upon most well women. The complications of her business, her connection with countless friends, and her absorbing new relation to Moody made up, after all, rather a considerable sum of distractions.

Yet Harriet, the invincible, to compensate for the new and what seemed intolerably rigid limitations of her physical life, reached out in new directions. One of these may be noted. She had not really neglected music, but she now saw that it would be well for her to have a larger grasp of it. So she asked a musician well known in Chicago, Charles Squire, to come to see her. Mr. Squire promptly responded. Of his first meeting with her he writes:

"It was about the last of October, 1901. I knew nothing about her, so was surprised when I was shown into a room where she was sitting up in bed [her swing bed] telephoning. I felt as if I were seeing a great spirit facing life with superb energy, with all the winds of heaven blowing about her, and I could only think of the Winged Victory. . . . .

"She had asked me to come to see if I could give her some insight into the enjoyment of music, something to fill some of the unoccupied moments when she was confined to the house. But it was more the beginning of an education for me than for her."

The association thus formed blossomed abundantly. From now on music and musicians were an abiding element of the life in Harriet's house, while she herself, without neglecting poetry, penetrated into the kindred art much more deeply than before.

CHAPTER VIII

BALANCED INTERVAL

THAT there had been a crisis in the relation between Moody and Harriet was known to no one but themselves. And now that they were a thousand miles apart, only some nimble and extremely perceptive Ariel could have followed the development of their intimacy.

They wrote often to each other, now and later, for there were many and prolonged separations. But the burning of letters seems to have been a habitual activity at 2970 Ellis (earlier, Groveland) Avenue in the later days and, lamentably, Harriet's letters to Moody were destroyed. Yet there can be no doubt that they worthily balanced those that the poet wrote to her. To her correspondents in general her letters were admirable— human in substance and pointed always by her gift of original and telling phrase. The letters to Moody would have borne also the stamp of a woman deeply in love.

There are certain of Moody's letters, such as those quoted a few pages further on, which not only emphasize the depth of their acknowledged emotional interest in each other but establish that from the beginning, though they did not take the world into their confidence, they looked forward to their ultimate marriage. Meanwhile, there were valid reasons for postponement.

For both of them his pursuit of poetry was, properly, the most important fact to be considered. To promote the development of his gift he needed freedom, travel, and, for certain periods, solitude. This was as they both saw it. Indeed, teaching, even intermittently, had now become too great a burden for a man in whom the creative flame was so urgently burning, and the University, in spite of repeated offers and concessions made by its president—who would have been glad to retain Moody by the half-, even by the quarter-, year—was not to hold him in bondage after 1903.

But Harriet was firmly tethered to Chicago, both by her business and by her devotion to her mother, so that for these two an all-the-year life in common must at that time have seemed impossible. Besides, there was Mrs. Tilden's as yet, perhaps, only half-spoken opposition.

Yet at 2970 "Will's room" was always ready, whatever the pressure of unexpected guests might be. Symbolically at least, a light was always kept burning for him. In the winter he would make occasional trips to Chicago, and sometimes in the summer he would join the family group in a rented house on Mackinac Island. During a series of winters that he spent in New York, first in the studio building at 51 West Tenth Street —an especially congenial lodging, because he also in leisure seasons painted creditably in oils—and later in the roomy fourth-floor flat at 107 Waverly Place, he would from time to time cancel engagements on the ground that he was about to devote a number of days to "friends from Chicago." This phrase, ambiguous by intent, was accurate, after all, for Harriet did indeed always travel in the plural, Miss O'Neill, at this time, being her usual companion. She traveled also without losing sight of Chicago or of Mrs. Tilden, seeing to it that each morning a careful report of her mother's welfare was telegraphed to her.

The two close friends, or the lovers, as we may as well call them, shared intimately all the considerable events in each other's lives, though participation, even at a distance—and, usually, it was a distance—in the procession of Moody's experiences, both his triumphs and his disasters, must have made serious inroads upon even Harriet's store of temperamental energy.

The autumn and winter of 1901–2, spent on the task[1] for which he had joined Robert Lovett in Cambridge, were devoted to hard work, at the rate of ten hours a day; but the outcome,

[1] A History of English Literature. By William Vaughn Moody and Robert Morss Lovett. Scribner's, 1902.

according to Mr. Lovett, was particularly fortunate for Moody in a financial sense in that it bought him nearly a year's freedom. As spring approached, the job finished, Moody felt a nomadic urge impelling him toward Europe. First, however, there was to be a reunion with Harriet who, knowing that the poet wished to escape from the chills of New England, brought Alice Corbin and Bessie O'Neill East with her and found a pleasant cottage at Cape Henry, Virginia. Here Moody joined them for a happy interval. On the last evening that he and Harriet were together, he talked eagerly of a subject that was haunting him—the Prometheus legend. The next day he made his start toward Greece, where he was to gather inspiration for his *Fire-Bringer*—and where, also, an accident was to befall him that had nothing short of fatal import.

Climbing Mount Parnassus, in May, he fell, some sharp object wounding his thigh. The hurt did not at the time seem a serious matter. "It is nothing to worry about and will be all right in a week," he reported to Harriet. His immediate plans suffered no change. After drinking deeply of Greece,[2] he spent the summer in Paris with the poet Trumbull Stickney, occupying himself in re-reading the entire body of Greek tragedy, and in the autumn was joined by Robert Lovett in the Tirol, so that it was New Year's before he saw Harriet again.

But three years after the Parnassus incident, again in Europe, Moody hurried home in some distress and shortly afterward, in April, 1905, was operated upon by Dr. Bull of New York for a growth in his thigh. The surgeon could not assure his patient that this was the end of the matter.

In these three years much had happened. From May until October in 1903, Moody spent a fertile period as Harriet's guest on Mackinac Island, she and others joining him at intervals. His immediate preoccupation was the writing of *The Fire-Bringer*, which was to be published the next year. Moody was

---

[2] During months wherein he probably wrote his poem, "The Moon-Moth," with its personal reference to Harriet:

My love, my friend,
My wild one, my soul's need, my song of life!

by no means merely a classicist. He had also a hunger for purely American themes and plenty of imaginative energy to devote to them. So when, at some time during this Mackinac summer, Harriet told him the story of a certain dramatic happening in Arizona, he immediately saw this as the nucleus of a prose play. "He made the first study of the play within the year," Harriet wrote many years later to Ferdinand Schevill; and, before going to the desert with Schevill in the autumn of 1904, an experience he greatly enjoyed, "he had entirely conceived the play and to a great extent executed it." This play was *The Great Divide*.

To Harriet, the insatiable lover of poetry—and of poets—the coming of Yeats to Chicago in this same year, 1904, ranked as a major event. He did not stay with her, as, a decade later, he would infallibly have done. Moreover, socially she found him thorny, for it is remembered that, after one or two unsuccessful encounters, she declined a further opportunity to meet him, protesting that she would not again expose herself to "being bruised by Willie Yeats!" In spite of this, her admiration of him did not lessen, and it is interesting that in forming her opinion of the Irish poet she was not dominated by Moody, her estimate being both higher and juster than his.

"I didn't meet Yeats after all," Moody wrote Harriet. "He must be a good man, to have made so strong an impression on you, and I am sorry now I didn't take more trouble to get at him." . . . .

Publication of *The Fire-Bringer* had enhanced Moody's already very considerable prestige. Even though poetry itself meant so much more to her than any fanfare about it, Harriet can scarcely have helped exulting at the security with which he had "arrived," and she must have had pleasure in the verses that Richard Watson Gilder published in the *Atlantic* in June of 1905, praising a young poet who modestly declined to have even his initials used in connection with Mr. Gilder's lines. Also, Moody's work was now coming to be noted in England.

But the poet who had achieved so much was now for a time forsaking poetry. For many months preceding its production in New York, in the autumn of 1906, the author of *The*

Great Divide—originally called "A Sabine Woman"—had to surrender himself to the trials and uncertainties of the theater. Its immediate success naturally made him known to a public that might never have heard of him as the author of poetry having its roots in Greek mythology. Almost overnight Moody found himself a popular dramatist and the possessor of a comfortable income. These were substantial assets, but neither he nor Harriet would have been disposed to overvalue them.

·Meanwhile, even before the revolution in his fortunes, Moody yielded, as it is evident he had yielded before, to an urge to disregard the still existing obstacles that separated his life from Harriet's. In that summer of 1906 he was spending several months in Cornish, New Hampshire, within fairly easy reach of Henry Miller, who was preparing to produce his play. On July 26 he wrote her:

DEARLY BELOVED,

Let us hesitate no longer about taking the step we have so long contemplated, and upon which, it becomes clearer to me with every minute that I live, our whole life happiness depends. Neither of us can be happy away from the other. We must be together, and we must be so in peace—with freedom from the corrosion of intrusive comment, in the only way in which our mutual life can be gently fostered and molded as we would have it. Let us put all questioning away. I beseech you to do this, knowing in the depths of my heart that it is the way of our salvation.

Meet me somewhere, either in Albany or Quebec; tell Bessie, and bring her with you. Telegraph me long enough in advance so that I may go ahead and make the few necessary arrangements. It will be simpler and better away from Chicago, will it not? Or if you prefer to have me come there first, and to have a few old friends about us, that suits me as well. We will take a house for the fall or winter on the north shore, near enough to the city to enable you to go out or me to come in each day, after the day's work is over.

Is it not clear beyond the possibility of doubt that this is our best and only course? I look to you for a firm and joyous acceptance of this plan, and shall await your word with confidence, dearly beloved, noblest and sweetest of women.

W——

Four days later, not having heard from her, he wrote again:

DEAREST,

I have not written since Thursday, as I expected each day to be off, and to lure you after me somewhere. I suppose you were in Michigan Friday and Saturday, and did not get my letter and telegram until Sunday morning. This is not a letter, but merely the waving of the hand, to let you know that I am well, and eagerly awaiting your reply to the plan I outlined. I had hoped you might be able to act upon it at once, but doubtless it is my fault that you can't. I look for your letter this evening, tomorrow morning at latest. Till then goodbye and God's blessing.

W——

But as he wrote these last words Harriet's delayed reply must have reached him, for he supplemented his letter:

I wish you could make up your mind to adopt the course I suggested last week, immediately upon our meeting. Talking only confuses us, and being together lulls to sleep our sense of the practicalities of the situation. However, I will not argue this further now, since you put it aside with a gentle firmness which leaves me nothing to say. This must not be taken as a reproach.

So, for the moment, that was all. . . . .

A troubling circumstance during these last few years had been the slight but clearly perceptible trickling away of the superb physical vigor that had been Moody's native gift. When, in the spring of 1907, he and Ridgely Torrence planned to take a European trip together, it was sorrowfully acknowledged by his friends that Moody was in rather serious need of this refreshing experience. The two poets wandered through Spain, then Italy. This time it was an Italian hill that was Moody's undoing. On Mount Posilippo, near Naples, he slipped, fell, and told his companion that again his thigh had suffered. It was ominous.

Reaching London, just before sailing, Moody became acutely conscious of his strongest link with home and wrote Harriet (on May 27) that he was "homesick." "If it were possible," he told her, "I would take ship tonight." He goes on, in the same vein in which he had written her less than a year earlier, though now, perhaps, even more urgently:

"In any event, you can expect me very soon, probably by the end of next week. Will you come on to meet me? Perhaps you are too much entangled to get away, but come if you can. And, dearest, you must come prepared to take the step which we have planned to take for so long. You must, you must. It is our only chance of happiness. This absence from you has taught me many things clearly, which I knew before but imperfectly. I will not talk much about this, but I want you to think much about it, as I do, and to the end of having done with doubts. I shall telegraph you the name of the ship I take and the date of sailing; whereupon a little judicious inquiry will give you my date of arrival within a day or two. . . . ."

But this time also, Harriet's judgment seems to have forbidden her to acquiesce.

While Moody was in Europe, Harriet had suddenly found that she also was somewhat depleted. By this time, the valiant creature had herself learned the lessons of overwork and fatigue. Fleeing to Parkman, her country birthplace, for rest and repairs, she wrote to Bessie O'Neill, inclosing some freshly picked violets:

"These grew on the brookside where I found them laying claim to the power that had made me able to walk straight to them with an unlimping foot.

"It is quiet here. God knows what that means, to me; but I see the world with an astral eye, and I am still wondering if I haven't died, and if this isn't the way you feel when you have.

"The 'fireless cooker' increases my doubt. You know the way Marley's ghost went around, with safes and keys trailing after him. Why isn't this my doom? and the whole conception of 'fireless cooking' a coincidence of a state of limbo accorded me as a guarantee that I am not in Hades—not condemned to go."

In spite of the none too buoyant frame of mind that this suggests, Harriet proved no less ready than usual to make warm response to a timid note that she found in her mail one morning. Gladys Tilden, whom she had loved as a child, who had been taken from her and since then brought up in an atmosphere of domestic bickering and fourth-rate theaters, was to come to Chicago with the burlesque troupe she had just joined. Might she, if Harriet wasn't too busy, come to Groveland Avenue for a few moments, to have a little talk, to—well, just to see her again?

By letter, Harriet made an appointment for a certain afternoon. At her first sight of frightened Gladys in purple broadcloth and a green velvet picture hat with plumes, Harriet, half-weeping, took the girl into her arms, and into her life again. Connection with the burlesque company was canceled within a few moments, the girl's luggage sent for, her life arranged.

Harriet could understand anybody's troubles and never hesitated to take a firm hand in remedying other people's blunders. But it happened that she could particularly understand stage hunger, for there is a legend that she herself, like many young girls, had wished to go on the stage. So Gladys was not only established in Harriet's home and sent to a good day school but placed in dramatic classes. From this time on, she stayed for long periods at 2970, attended the succession of schools that Harriet chose for her, went with her to Europe, and, like all Harriet's protegées, acquired for her a deep devotion.

In March, 1908, came the greatest blow that Harriet had ever suffered, in the death of her mother. Mrs. Tilden was old, and it was many years since she had been well. Yet nothing lessened the extremity of the shock. The ordinarily stoical Harriet was completely overcome, and for hours, perhaps days, her terrible desolation found vent in what her cousin, Mrs. Hutchens, described as actual "keening." There could be little direct solace for such grief, but Moody promptly proposed coming to Chicago to offer her what help he could. She hesitated. Could they meet somewhere else, instead? It ended by Bessie O'Neill's accompanying her to New Orleans, where Moody joined them. He himself was not well, she suffering. "It was a distressful time," Miss O'Neill reports.

Hardly had Moody returned to Waverly Place when he himself succumbed to a severe attack of typhoid, so it was then Harriet's turn to join him. When the danger period was past, the summer had to be devoted to convalescence. After lingering, through his weakest time, in Portchester and Cos Cob, he and Ridgely Torrence accomplished a journey to Monhegan Island, off the coast of Maine. By the following winter, still feeling below par, and moved by his habitual urge toward a mild climate, he packed paints and canvases and spent some months in California with the painter William Wendt.

If Harriet's heart, like her house, was illimitably hospitable— and she well knew that it was, for she once said, laughing at herself, that she could love a dozen men at once and that no one man could completely respond to her in kind—she was at the same time the very spirit of constancy. She did not, she could not, waver however slightly in her allegiance to her supreme friendship.

So when, during the early months of 1909, she and Will Moody paused, as they must have done, to take account of the preceding decade, it was apparent that the years had given them much and, except in the grievous matter of Moody's health, withdrawn little and that one by one all severing circumstances had been blotted out.

As we have seen, their patience during the long years of separation had sometimes been near collapse; and once, at least, at a period earlier than the letters from Moody that already have been quoted, they had been, after much talk of marriage, on the point of taking the radical leap. Bessie O'Neill, who was Harriet's companion during a visit to New York, remembers that Harriet would spend each day with Moody in his West Tenth

Street studio (where he lived from 1903 to 1905) and that she herself would usually join them for dinner. There was much talk between them, which seemed only half-serious (though with these two, you could never be sure, they were capable of anything!), of an immediate marriage. Each day they said: Shall it be today? and each day delayed decision. There was a definite arrangement that Bessie should remain in the hotel during certain hours so that Moody, should a decision be reached, could leave his studio, where there was no telephone, and go elsewhere to announce to her: The hour has come!

But the hour did not come . . . . then. In any case, they could not have forgotten that Mrs. Tilden was still exercising her firm taboo—and certainly Harriet could not have borne to oppose her.

Now, years later, practically every element in their situation having changed, marriage, as a serious fact, seemed the logical next step.

Deciding to marry, however, seems easy enough for youngsters who have been in love an intoxicating month or two, who know little, whether of each other or of life, and practically nothing of marriage itself. For maturer lovers, who have long known each other yet who have become habituated to separate lives, such a decision can be enormously difficult and the ways of reaching it often tortuous indeed.

During the latter days of April it was understood in the Home Delicacies Association and by Harriet's intimate circle that, at Mr. Selfridge's urgent suggestion, she was about to go to London to establish a branch of the business. Quiet preparations therefore went on for an absence on her part of several months.

Moody, meanwhile, had returned to New York. At this moment his reputation, both as poet and dramatist, was at its height. *The Great Divide* was still prospering. Another prose play, *The Faith Healer*, over which he had worked and brooded since 1896, had been accepted by Henry Miller and was to be staged within the year. And, almost unbelievable in the case of

70

a thirty-nine-year-old poet who had started penniless, he was now a man of comfortable income.

It is true that for some time doctors had been bothering him with warnings. "Rest," "change of climate," "sea voyage"; by this time their vague prescriptions sounded almost meaningless. So why not forget all about them? There is a new note, sober and determined, in a letter that he wrote to Harriet in April:

"The less we talk and the more promptly we act, the better," he told her, urging that they marry immediately and afterward sail from Canada for England.

One of those April days was irresistibly inviting. Moody asked Ridgely Torrence to join him for luncheon at the Harvard Club and an afternoon out of doors. Starting at One Hundred and Fifty-fifth Street, they walked down Riverside Drive to Seventy-second Street. Moody walked slowly and did not seem overstrong. But he was gay, almost exuberant, and the two talked lightly, jestingly, together. As they reached a high point where they could see both the magnificent stretch of the Hudson and Manhattan's many towers, Moody halted for a silent moment. His eyes clung to the scene. "A citizen of no mean city," he quoted, solemnly. . . . . It was an afternoon of the happiest companionship, vividly remembered and treasured afterward. . . . . The two men never saw each other again.

In fact, when Moody left the city, a few days later, it was with an unspoken permanent farewell to his familiar life there and its network of friends, to none of whom did he confide his immediate intention.

On May 3, Harriet left Chicago, accompanied by Bessie O'Neill, as Moody had proposed, three years earlier. Nobody knew that her destination was Quebec. Here Moody joined her, and on May 7 they were married, sailing immediately for Liverpool. No formal announcements, no personal letters, even to their respective families, were sent out until the two reached London. The effort to avoid publicity was completely successful for the time being, although when the news did reach Chi-

71

cago, nothing but full pages, illustrated in color, would do to set forth the love story of the author of *The Great Divide*.

Such precautions for maintaining secrecy may seem excessive. But his success had placed Moody in a position where he couldn't easily conduct himself as a private person.

The event sadly justified their wisdom. This proved to be no season for a loud and joyous clangor of wedding bells.

CHAPTER IX

GRAY SUMMER

FEW devoted attachments can have been as publicly pursued as that of this uncommon pair. Of late years Harriet had seemed to follow her majestic path through life like the dominant figure in some richly peopled tapestry, alone not in terms of space but by virtue of her superiority and gift of leadership, her various retinues following her at suitably graded distances. Her complicated days seldom yielded any solitude, nor was there often opportunity in the case of herself and Moody for solitude à deux. Their ability to isolate themselves sufficiently for their own purposes, however closely they were surrounded, had a touch of the magnificent, as with royal dinners eaten in full view of the populace or like operatic principals singing an exchange of tender secrets in close hearing of chorus and of audience. . . . .

Now, however, on the friendly, slow-paced English steamer, they were alone and under singularly fortunate conditions. Each greatly loved the sea, so that the crossing was a happy experience in itself, rather than something merely to be endured. England, home and mother of poets, was to furnish their delight during months of precious leisure. All obstacles to their close comradeship had been overcome. A freedom hardly to be believed in lay ahead.

. . . . Or so it must have seemed to them for a scanty stretch of days.

Prompted by some curious prophetic instinct, Harriet had equipped herself with a diary—a diary which, with certain intermissions, she kept during the next year and a half but which was to record not the usual happy stages of a wedding journey but the story of Moody's gradual abandonment of life.

There was to be little of herself in these pages. In one entry, it is true, in June, on the Isle of Wight, the poor woman does describe herself as "exquisitely happy," but even as she wrote the words a cold shudder must have seized her, for she had known very soon or at least profoundly feared that her beloved comrade was ill and of no casual ailment. Moody himself, who kept no diary, doubtless knew this even earlier and with greater certainty.

Less than three weeks after the marriage it had already become necessary to consult a London doctor, who believed Moody's "low health tide an aspect of typhoid convalescence." "So far, he has been in such poor health that I have done little but sigh over him," Harriet wrote to Edith Kellogg, who had been a member of her household in the undergraduate days at the University of Chicago and returned in 1912 to be her secretary.

Nevertheless, the two did a few museums. They saw American friends. Harriet gave what time was necessary to Mr. Selfridge, arranging for the new branch of the Home Delicacies and appointing its staff. Later, they went to Guernsey; they went to Sark; they went to the Isle of Wight and to Jersey. They went to Winchester and Salisbury and, finally, to the Lake District. Meanwhile, Harriet had, of course, to keep darting back to London.

On the surface it wasn't a melancholy pilgrimage, for, besides their devotional attitude toward ancient England and the poets and poetry it had bred, both pilgrims had a warm and humorous delight in untamed human nature. If Moody had been well, they could have had nothing short of a riotously good time together. Even as it was, Harriet could not resist setting down certain incidents that paricularly amused them both.

These records of hers during June and July of that year do reveal her strong native surrender to comedy—but comedy densely overshadowed by a steadily mounting dread.

Leaving London, they went first to Guernsey, where for a few days things went well. They took a drive with a coach and four and the following day repeated it. "Will was in extra good spirits until he got too tired, and I was very happy."

Two days later: "We decided to stay on here another day, but Will was far too tired to take a third drive. Late in the morning we went on the car to an old church and French market—then came home and spent the afternoon reading. Will was very sleepy and frightened me by his lassitude. He thinks he will go back to London and the doctor."

In Guernsey, also, they undertook a visit to the ancient Church of St. Sampson. "We stopped there to speak to an old woman who hung over a gate across the street, and she, recognizing us as her lawful prey, gave the most satisfying account of the age of the church; flanked her statement by saying she had been married in it, and pointed out her 'partner' who was hanging against the house wall like a passion flower, and looked as though he might last forever as there was nothing about him that could decay further. We were so docile to this old lady's histrionics that she suddenly took on a more stately conception of herself and asked us if we shouldn't enjoy being shown through her home and as we went, she pointed out objects of interest with a modest but soaring air. The very heart and core of her residence was a stuffed hen under a glass case. This hen had the expression of self-sufficient knowledge common to her race in life, and was of a dingy yellow color. The woman said she had been a present to her when in life thirty years before, had been a hard layer and a most intelligent bird, and that she hadn't been able to put her away when dead. All this hospitality had been on such a gracious scale that I blushed for Will when I saw him in the familiar side-thrust gymnastics; but the woman didn't. She took the money without a swallow."

It was a week later, at Bonchurch, Isle of Wight, that Harriet sounded her highest note: yet it was here also that she wrote to Bessie O'Neill, who, having made the voyage on a separate steamer, was spending the summer partly in England, partly in Paris, now and then meeting Harriet in London:

"We went from Guernsey to Sark after I wrote you, and Will kept getting sicker and sicker.

75

"We had a doctor every day and some of the time I certainly felt he would never get on the upward trend again. He suffered unbearably. His condition was called 'neuritis' by the island doctor—a good man—and as it seemed to be in his eyes as much as anywhere I of course kept thinking of ———[1] though I didn't tell Will about him. . . . . Most of the time since I left I have thought I might give up the Selfridge matter altogether, but Will seems really anxious to have me go on with it."

On the Isle of Wight they had the adventure, while driving, of coming upon a cottage to rent, which, charming in itself, overlooking the sea, comfortably equipped and even supplied with a housekeeper (it belonged to the writer, Allen Upward), seemed without any possible drawback. "Here," Harriet writes, "was everything we had been seeking." Yet, "as we drove away from it, we realized how *little* we wanted it. My heart ached at the thought of Will's being stranded alone in it; and he turned from it as if it stood for desolation."

Ordinarily no two persons could have known more clearly than these travelers precisely where they wished to go and why. But Moody's illness had upset their values and confused their judgments, leaving them in a bewildered blur.

By the first of July they were both back in London.

"Will seems inclined," Harriet writes, "to settle down and take the rest cure. I feel restless and anxious over his condition and at a loss what to do."

After all, they continued their wanderings, the next point being Jersey. "There is no resisting the charm of island beauty," Harriet wrote. But for Moody this beauty had no recuperative power. "Will did not seem so well this morning," is Harriet's sad refrain.

On July 9 she says:

"I feel most afraid of the effect of continued novelty on Will's nerves and constantly pray him to let us *settle* somewhere in the country, either here or at home, and get away from

[1] The reference is to a close friend of the Tilden family, whose severe nervous breakdown had been followed by suicide.

76

exertion and from hotels. I think he will do it in the end. I pray he may not wait too long."

Here, as in other passages, one is struck by the role that Harriet is playing in this new marriage. Both because of her husband's impaired health and her own unquestioned habit of arranging the lives of everybody about her, one would expect to see her taking a rather authoritative lead in these summer adventures. On the contrary, she seems to subordinate herself with extraordinary and touching completeness, and even when, as in this case, she questions the wisdom of her husband's decisions, she nevertheless accepts them as final.

Among the distractions that they found in Jersey was a visit to the lighthouse at Corbière. On returning, Harriet made a comment in her diary which, however curious and baffling, is a contribution to the study of this remarkable woman's complexities. "This lighthouse trip," she says, "marks a unique experience in my mind, and its human aspect seems to furnish food enough for one's whole impression of this world's life. I often feel that my being is pitted against one of those remorseless manifestations of natural power, and, since it avails nothing, I feel myself snuffing out like the moth in the candle."

On certain days the two were able to enjoy themselves almost in traditional tourist fashion, as when they climbed to the castle at the top of Mount Orgueil.

"I can give no idea of the pleasure we had in wandering through the old castle. The approach from the sea side is magnificent, the ruin overwhelming in its beauty and its grim fitness for the life that was carried on within it—the external elevation magnificent from the land side, where we took our departure. We climbed to the top of the ruin, up devious winding stone staircases, and in imagination 'flung all the banners on the outer walls' as we were beset by the hordes of the enemy. On the highest tower the wind rushes like an advancing army. Will gathered flowers for me, going up and down, poppies first, and last the lovely rose-colored wall climber for which we know no name."

And later, in a cheerfully exploratory mood:

77

"Will went to St. Hélier and brought back a dog cart and a substantial, strongly individualized black horse which he had already accustomed to the name of 'John.' With these we set out on the pleasantest day of our journey. We drove over the gently undulating country, constantly ascending, however, until we reached the bluff coast which hangs over Bouley Bay, Will often addressing humorous remarks to 'John,' and often breaking out in admiration of a beautiful tree-shaded lane, a handsome old pile of buildings, or an effect of light and cloud-shadow on the landscape. By the help of a map of the island, for which I had great respect and Will but little, we found our way without much questioning of the passers-by; and particularly because, as it turned out, ours was a straight road with no turnings. We passed the market women going and coming on this drive, most quaintly dressed, young and old, in transparent muslin caps. Will of course succumbed to the charm of each one who had any claim to beauty. At Bouley Bay we found a small hotel where we had luncheon. . . . . The view of the bay and the surrounding country was fine though, to me, not so good as I had been led to expect by the gentleman in Guernsey who had vociferated that 'Bouley Bay wanted a lot of beating.' . . . . We drove back over a longer route than we had come. . . . . As we knew neither the name nor the place of the stable where 'John' belonged, we confided our difficulty to him, and he threaded his way through a maze of narrow streets and brought us home."

But it was only a few hours later, on the evening of this same day, July 10, that there was a collapse of all this fragile gaiety.

"Will takes such a despondent view of his present state, mental and physical, and of his prospects for future health, that it makes my heart break. I don't know what to do, and sit holding my helpless hands and praying. The out-of-door days seem to have been salutary. I think it would be good to spend weeks this way, and better still in America, with a *home* to return to."

Here as elsewhere during the summer, during the many hours when Moody was too tired or too ill to move about, Harriet soothed his melancholy and her own by reading aloud. Her assiduity in this practice may be measured by considering only a partial list of the books they read. Wells's *Food of the Gods*, and Maeterlinck's *The Blue Bird* belonged to the period. After visiting Jersey, they attacked Hugo's monumental *Toilers of the Sea*; and after flirting with the idea of renting Allen Upward's cottage, they read this writer's *Yellow Hand*. Volumes of Jules Verne, Eden Philpotts, and Gilbert Parker also occupied them.

After returning to London alone, Harriet records:

"At Guernsey I went ashore with Will for the half hour the boat was to lie there, and was sadly tempted to stay over one day and take the ride to La Gouffe. In resisting this temptation I shed some outward and many inward tears; especially as I have never in my life sacrificed such a noble pleasure to such a squalid duty without its inserting itself in my memory as an irreparable error. Will, my dear, beautiful friend, stood on the dock, when my boat pulled out, so that I saw him as long as the dock was visible." Having arrived in London, "I passed a wretched night. First not sleeping, then pursued by direful dreams."

On July 21 they left London together for the Lakes. At Windemere, the next day, there is the entry:

"Rain pouring down too much for any excursions. Will walked about a bit and reported the place as the thing he had always been looking for."

Soaked with English rain, shaken by her companion's misery and her own fear of what might lie ahead. Harriet's resilience was by this time nearly spent. Though as valorous as ever, she could react no further to whatever of comedy their encounters may have yielded.

By the end of the month the reappearance of the sun, which powerfully and beneficently affected Moody all through his illness, must have proved cheering to Harriet, too, for she was able to write from Prince Town, England, to Bessie O'Neill:

"We drove yesterday from Oakhampton over here, stopping at Tavistock for luncheon—a glorious drive. Will is no better. I don't know whether he will go to London or not, but I really think he had best, to see the oculist and to try the osteopath. .... The sun shone out yesterday afternoon and it is bright this morning. We are driving with one horse and a four-wheeled cart. This is of all things in the world the ideal thing to do, and I wish we had three months to spend in this way. The country seems more finished than Philpotts shows it, or rather the towns, but otherwise he is proved a great portrayer. Our drive over the moors, between the tors, was too wonderful to grasp and made me ache with my own inelasticity."

The summer's struggle against the inevitable was almost over.

CHAPTER X

BLACK WINTER

AFTER a brief entry in the diary on July 29, 1909, there is a silence. The reason is clear enough.

Harriet could no longer bear to set down what seemed to be the plain truth. Her husband's condition had become more and more alarming. London doctors, themselves puzzled, were not helpful. By September there was no longer any choice as to what course the Moodys should follow. They took a steamer bound for home.

In Chicago, Dr. Hugh Patrick, neurological alienist, after examination and consultation with Harriet's friend and surgeon, Dr. MacArthur, and with a third physician, made a diagnosis of suspected brain tumor. Dr. Patrick was excessively urgent in speeding the patient to Baltimore and into the hands of Dr. Harvey Cushing, cranial surgeon at Johns Hopkins. So on October 6 the sick man entered the Baltimore hospital under the care of two special nurses, Harriet being given a room near him.

Dr. Cushing was admittedly first in his field. It was well known that in February of this same year he had operated successfully for brain tumor on General Leonard Wood, who had made a sensationally quick recovery. Cushing's provisional diagnosis of Moody's case confirmed that made by Dr. Patrick. On October 25 he operated, with "exploratory" intent, and in November there was a second operation. A third, which confessedly would endanger the patient's life, was commonsensibly rejected.

Removal of brain tumor, which, as everybody knows, is now classed among the everyday feats of surgery, was then extremely hazardous affair, even when performed by the most eminent of practitioners. Partly because of the uncertainty of the case, a good deal of secrecy was observed. At the same time that certain newspapers stated that an operation had been performed, without mentioning its nature, Dr. Cushing (out of consideration for his distinguished patient) publicly denied having performed any operation at all and instructed Harriet to say that her husband was suffering from "nervous prostration as a sequence of typhoid." Harriet, in great perturbation, wrote her Chicago household, urgently repeating the doctor's very words, which, since the anxious women had followed the case from the beginning, they must have found oddly confusing. The idea was, of course, that if Moody were to recover, it was better that the facts should not be known; and Harriet, in the extremity of her concern, seems to have persuaded herself that the facts did not even exist.

After undergoing, at Johns Hopkins, all that medical science and warm personal interest could do for him, Moody, with Harriet, spent a short recuperative period in Catonsville, near Baltimore, where plans for the next move were discussed with profound anxiety. It can scarcely have seemed to anyone that the patient's condition had at all improved. He was weak, suffering, and almost totally blind. In fact, Harriet, hopeful as she strove to be, was obliged to note in the diary, which from now on assumes a different character, that he seemed actually worse in six important respects, namely, sight, speech, memory, pain, nervousness, and slowness of response. This discouraging statement was framed two weeks after leaving the hospital.

Moody's own leaning being toward a warm, dry climate, Southern California was at last decided on, Dr. Cushing assenting. The two were to be accompanied by Moody's only unmarried sister, Charlotte, who had had a nurse's training and between whom and her brother there existed an especial sympathy,[1] by Klemet Torp, a capable Norwegian manservant, and by Sunday, a young Irish setter. Through sheer natural gaiety

[1] Moody had always felt a brotherly responsibility for Charlotte, and from now on Harriet also adopted her as a sister. After Moody's death Charlotte was to take her place as a member of the Chicago household.

and doggishness, Sunday was to make an important contribution to the morale of the harassed group.

Harriet's exigent responsibilities in Chicago could, of course, no longer count with her. Life now had one meaning only and one object—to accomplish that cure of her husband's condition for which Dr. Cushing held out a possible hope. Upon this her concentration was complete.

In spite of her youthful dallying in the field of medicine, one would suspect that, of all women, Harriet had perhaps the least natural affinity with the sickroom. Supremely healthy herself, previous to her accident, and with small interest in detail, her real attitude, which she repeatedly had to overcome, must have been one of sincere distaste for illness and its messy trail. She was always a complete stoic in regard to her own suffering. Toward suffering in others, it is true, she was warmly compassionate. But she abhorred discussion of symptoms by laymen and was far from being of the tribe that pursues you with concrete remedies on the ground that somebody else has profited by swallowing this pellet or that nostrum.

Yet it happened that during the latter half of her life she had considerably more than a normal share of illness to deal with. Moreover, in each case she rose magnificently to the immediate need, as in the final year of her father's life, her mother's long invalidism, her brother Will's illness—which she was shortly to have to face—and the present cruel ordeal, the nature of which had pretty well defined itself.

In dealing with this desperate malady of her husband's, it was important that she concern herself particularly with his frame of mind. It was her job to bolster his hope, reinforce his courage, strengthen his desire and determination to live. If she had no special gift—though it may be unfair to her to suggest it—for replacing bandages, she could at least set at the disposal of her greatly loved patient the abounding treasuries of her mind and heart.

Through November and thereafter she resumed the entries in her diary. From now on the pages were to become largely clinical, with few intervals of lightheartedness, as during the

83

English summer before the cloud had irreparably darkened. Of Moody's own depressed state she says (on November 21): "He is by nature a great humorist, but for the past year has been grave of speech"—a reflection suggesting one way in which his departure from normal health had been apparent before their marriage. But "I now notice," she continues, "a recurrence to the humorous outlook that seems to strengthen a little from day to day."

It was only a day later, however, that she wrote, pitifully enough, to Bessie O'Neill: "Every day's anxieties are more than I can bear, and my daily chance to write varies from ten minutes to an hour, or more, according as Will sleeps or wakes. You must understand his condition is very critical and that we are watching him for signs of improvement, sometimes with a little hope, sometimes with almost none."

On December 6 they left for California. "Will is traveling wonderfully well and is not suffering," she wrote en route. Arriving, they spent a week in Riverside, then went on to Santa Barbara, stopping first at the Hotel Potter, later taking a cottage that Moody thought "one of our lucky finds," and also renting by the month "a lazy horse." By way of diversion for the invalid, reading aloud was again resorted to, in what seems prodigious measure. During the first weeks, among other books, a complete reading of *Robinson Crusoe* is noted, also Victor Hugo's *Ninety-Three*, *The Tale of Two Cities* (the first work of Dickens that Moody had ever cared for), and Maeterlinck's *Life of the Bee.*

By Christmas Day, Moody's sight had improved considerably. There was an attempt at celebration, and holiday packages were sent and opened.

During all this California winter, Harriet noted with extreme care and fulness both the invalid's variations in mood and also his complete physical history from day to day as though she were looking far beyond the moment and thought such a chart, for that is what it amounted to, might be medically serviceable, if not in Moody's own case, then in others.

January brought a special and inevitable disturbance to the

carefully protected invalid. On the nineteenth of the month his play *The Faith Healer* was to be put on in New York by Henry Miller, who was himself to play the leading part. For years Moody had lived with the idea of this play, his first drafts of it having considerably antedated his writing of *The Great Divide*. Both the play itself—which was shortly to be published, the proofs having to be read during February—and the production were matters of the deepest concern to him. It would have been almost equally agitating, therefore, whether his drama had fared well or ill.

As a matter of fact, the play was to some degree discounted before its opening. "He had the advance New York clippings concerning the *Faith Healer*, and .... bore all this with his usual uncomplaining acquiescence, and without allowing himself to be downcast," Harriet wrote at the end of January, 1910.

Though enthusiastic telegrams from his close friends naturally followed the *première* and though Miller himself wired: "I believe the play will live," the production was not a success, and *The Faith Healer* was shortly withdrawn.

After this, there followed a downcast period. Discouragements of various kinds piled up. "I find myself dreadfully tired," Harriet wrote to Chicago, "but I hope and keep hoping; and if Will gets safely better, I know I shall be well."

In a lighter mood she writes: ".... We had a week or more of terribly bright hot weather here and our little cottage felt like a pill-box on a gridiron..... Just at this moment a magician's mantle fell on us in the shape of a soft gray fog which has lasted now three days and gives Will more freedom for staying outdoors than he has had since he has been sick. This the grocers and all people who want us to stay say will never lift till the first of July; while the casual Santa Barbaran says it doesn't exist now and that no fog is ever seen here."

With the coming of March, there was a breath of hope. On the sixth, "Will feels assured of his complete recovery." Yet he became restless, inclined toward a new scene. He considered Colorado Springs, then decided to cling to California. On

March 16 a move was made to Los Angeles, thence to Hollywood.

Dr. Cushing had, of course, been kept informed, and shortly after the arrival in Hollywood there came a letter from him, cautiously worded, on the whole, but saying, nevertheless: "I am pleased beyond words at the present status of things." The month passed fairly cheerfully. On Easter, the twenty-seventh, Harriet records: "Today the assurance comes that he will get well." But she was speaking of some inner and, alas, impermanent conviction, for not many days had passed before again she was forced to face the naked facts and to face them in stark loneliness.

She wrote to Bessie O'Neill on April 8: "I can hardly tell you the truth about myself now, because the arc of my vibrations is so terribly long and these alternations so unbearable. . . . . Yet I keep this all hid even from myself when I can for I am trying with every power God gives me—or to speak with a deeper sense of reverence and mystification, with all I can reach or find of God's good gifts within myself—to bring to Will through gentleness, hope, love, and the 'sense of healing that the whole world needs.' . . . . Into this metaphysical state penetrate these awful business revolutions. I must not entertain them if I want to save Will's precious life. I dare not disregard them for if the business were to go to pieces I don't know how we should all manage. I have to keep them to myself as far as possible for every reason; and sometimes I feel like a package of dynamite that will explode under the pressure of a baby's finger."

Although this is the first reference, in Harriet's own words, to her business worries, it may be taken for granted that she was already familiar with the troubles that were intermittently to beset her for the rest of her life. That she had been obliged to be away from Chicago for so long is a natural explanation of the fact that things weren't going as they had gone at the beginning; but it is not the only explanation. As her business had become larger, it had inevitably become less personal in its actual character. But Harriet's own conception of her creation continued to be a personal one, her methods even dangerously personal. It wasn't only that the word "labor" had come to have a very different significance from what it had had when Harriet placed in the family oven her first pan of gingerbread. What counted more was that, through the exercise of too personal a choice, she would place in a responsible financial post a man who, too greatly tempted, would betray her. Wounded, but not hardened, by such a defection—magnificently and, alas, fatally trustful in the human race—she would repeat this course. Her rich creativeness, her extravagant liberality, accounted for her success, but they were not the qualities to protect her against happenings such as these. Cold business methods, even ordinarily prudent supervision and "checkups" where her employees were concerned, she never practiced and would have scorned to introduce into her system.

During this agonizing month of April, Harriet felt hope itself deserting her. Her husband's life was ebbing before her very eyes. Medical science had done its best and failed her. On April 27 there is a heart-breaking cry from her, in a letter to Chicago: "I am bound here hand and foot, only praying and looking to see Will better. . . . . I cannot write of it. I try to hold myself steady. Sometimes I succeed. . . . . You can never know what all this has been for it could not be put in words. If I could die of it, it would be a rest."

It is significant that the last California entry in her diary had been made four days previous. The courage with which she had recorded the tragic story was, for the time being, spent. She did not open the little book again.

Meanwhile, California temperatures were mounting. The coming summer had to be arranged for. It seemed reasonable to take for a few months a small house outside Chicago, and there was much correspondence with this in view. In the end, however, the Groveland Avenue house itself was chosen as most comfortable for the invalid, and there they both, Charlotte of course continuing to be with them, remained from May

87

until September when they went West again, this time to Colorado Springs.

In July, Percy MacKaye, on his way to California, stopped off between trains in Chicago, visiting Harriet's house, where he "felt encouraged by an apparent rally in Will's health. . . . . We caught our last glimpse of Will walking south on Groveland Avenue with his happy setter dog, Sunday, leaping about him."

Moody's comfort and pleasure that summer were greatly increased by Harriet's acquiring an automobile, her first one. Anton Schedl, the German who had been Mrs. Tilden's coachman, now fitted perfectly into place as chauffeur of the new car, a post that he was to occupy for the next twenty years. Harriet always placed great reliance on Anton and maintained a warm personal interest in him.

But nothing could really help the dying man. It was with the most tenuous of last hopes that the journey to Colorado Springs was undertaken. Here, on October 11, Harriet sent word to Chicago: "Will is better than when we left and having said even that I have said more than I am permitted." . . . . On October 17, 1910, the cruelly stricken poet died. . . . .

Harriet's valor and endurance had been tested on the rack; and she emerged from the ordeal unbroken. Not now, more than at any other time, did she need to rely upon the strength of others, her own strength, as always, even supporting those about her. Also, in the midst of this shattering of her personal life, she embraced a mystical palliative.

Twenty years later, writing with her usual sincerity and absence of trite phrases to her friend Esther Dale, the singer, whose brother had just died, she said: "It can scarcely be explained what it is all about, this life and death. Under certain circumstances where the intimacy has been great enough to justify it, one is immediately uplifted by the consciousness that the intercourse that has existed can never be broken. *I had that experience completely when Will died.* But under other circumstances that consciousness of perpetuity does not protect one and then the crash of death on life is almost insupportable."

And at about the same time she wrote to a stranger: "When

my husband died, in thinking it over, I realized that he had given me all that he had to give to any human being, and I realized too that such a gift would not be measured in the least by time. This gift had been enough to fill my life with joy and confidence and so it should remain and so it has."

The story of Moody's life has a brief epilogue. Ten days or so after his death, Harriet went to New York, Charlotte Moody with her. Ferdinand Schevill went also, custodian of an urn containing the dead poet's ashes. In New York this group was joined by Ridgely Torrence, who, a few days earlier, had been with Harriet in Chicago.

It was a windy day of flickering brightness. Boarding a train at the Pennsylvania Station, the group left it at Far Rockaway and walked the short distance between the station and the stretch of sandy shore.

Here the two men set to work assembling sticks of driftwood from the beach and, contending vigorously with the wind, contrived to build the ceremonial fire that Harriet had planned.

Then, wrapping themselves in rugs, for it was near November, they clustered about the flames; and the little audience devoutly listened while Moody's *Fire Bringer* was read aloud by Schevill and Torrence alternately. Afterward, Harriet read the Ninety-first Psalm. Then Schevill, walking to the edge of the waves, committed to the ocean, which all this time had stormily foamed and tossed and waited, the almost substanceless handful that the urn had held.

. . . . The final parting accomplished, Harriet was now alone in a sense and to a degree that she had never known before.

PART II

CHAPTER XI

RABINDRANATH TAGORE

IN FEBRUARY, 1913, the Bengali poet and mystic, Rabindranath Tagore, then practically unknown in the United States, was staying at the University of Illinois, in Urbana, where his son was a student. Harriet Monroe, having arranged for the poet to come to Chicago, turned to a quarter that had never failed her and asked Mrs. William Vaughn Moody to receive him as her guest.

There could be no more astonishing sign of a new weariness in this prodigiously vital woman than the fact that she begged off.

Harriet had just returned to Chicago after having spent the greater part of three heartbreaking, energy-consuming years away from home. Not even the briefest interval for seclusion or for healing had been possible after her husband's death. Instead, the failing health of her brother Will had so engaged her concern (his wife then being held to the bedside of her dying mother) that on the day following the afternoon at Far Rockaway she took him to Europe; later guided both him and his wife to California, where she stayed with them for a time; afterward brought them back to her home in Chicago; and, finally, suffered the shock of his death. There had also been illnesses of her own, and in the year past urgent business cares had taken her three times to England. She was desperately tired—and dulled.

But, after all, what had now been offered her was a genuine human experience of no common order. Persistent refusal of Miss Monroe's suggestion would challenge the whole tenor of her life. Deliberating overnight, she realized this and hurried to the telephone in the morning. It was then arranged that Mr. Tagore and his family were to come to her almost immediately.

Once more the house where poetry had so often been eagerly celebrated was made ready for a poet's entrance—while its hostess foresightedly withdrew to accomplish a careful reading of Tagore's *Gitanjali*. Miss Monroe had just sent her the recently published volume, with its warmly appreciative Preface by W. B. Yeats.

Tagore came—a leader in the throng of poets who were to frequent the house during the next fifteen years. With him were his son Rathi and the latter's lovely young wife, Protima, as well as the poet's English secretary, W. W. Pearson.

Many a lionizing American woman would have eagerly welcomed such a group as this yet would have been unable to resist exploiting them a little—or much. And, the visit over, guests and hostess would still have been strangers.

Intrusting one's self to the hospitable care of Harriet Moody was a different matter. Tagore himself, by his voluntary renewals of the association, again and again, by the many warm letters that he addressed to Harriet, and by the dedication to her of his *Chitra*, acknowledged the genuine friendship that was now to come into being.

As for Harriet, she was regalvanized by this new meeting and by what it promised. Exhausted as she was, it was never a "rest," in the usual and for her intolerable sense, that she needed. Indeed, her whole being rejected passivity. Tagore's visit set the machinery of her life, her true life, in motion again—though this machinery could not in any case have remained stilled for long.

For a brief period, then, it may have been for an hour or two, after the Indian family arrived in Groveland Avenue, their hostess was probably content to admire their beauty, picturesqueness, exquisite courtesy, and profound reserve. The younger Tagores, in fact, in filial deference to Rabindranath, scarcely spoke at all in his presence. Harriet, too, could easily manifest all that the occasion demanded in the way of courtesy and grace. She could even be reserved—for a time. But since the Tagores strongly attracted her, it wasn't to be expected that she could maintain a neutral exterior very long. Spending the first

94

evening together lent form and reality to the new relationship. Harriet was an eager seeker for wisdom; Tagore, the seer, was accustomed to dispense it. Figuratively kneeling at the feet of the Oriental, the middle westerner did not find herself repulsed.

This first meeting she described afterward, dwelling on the inner kinship that she had felt with the new poet from the first. "There was not a moment," she said, "when he was strange to me."

During the weeks that followed, for this visit was no overnight affair, East and West accomplished a happy fusion. It is possible, of course, that the adjusting was largely on the part of the Occidentals, for Mr. Tagore may have been a little exigent in an unintentional and charming way. Light is thrown on this by a note of Harriet's written, during a later visit of the Tagores, to an acquaintance with whom she had been unable to arrange a meeting: "I am more than sorry to have missed seeing you when you were in Chicago. I am sure it would be difficult for you to imagine just the kind of restraint that fell over my household because of the presence in it of Mr. Tagore. Not that he would wish to restrain us in any way; but his preoccupations of mind are such as to leave him quite oblivious of the current life about him and the result is that we have to adapt ourselves when he is here, to possible changes in his plans."

Harriet's usual form of hospitality toward an especially valued guest, which was to enfold him in a metaphorical embrace while leaving him all the actual freedom he might wish, was mingled in this case with her extreme fervor of discipleship. She strove earnestly to learn from the prophet dwelling under her roof while devoting her exceptional competence to assuring his welfare. In addition to providing every possible comfort for Mr. Tagore as well as for his family and friends, she also helped liberally, as he found, to create his American audience. Knowing her was in a sense his introduction to the United States.

With her guest's sensitiveness always in mind, Harriet carefully selected poets and appreciators to meet him but never too many and never, it seemed, the wrong ones. The social atmosphere that she supplied even yielded a few permanent associations, as in the case of Alice Corbin and her husband, William Penhallow Henderson, the painter, who made a portrait of the poet.

Evenings at 2970 were now devoted to listening to Mr. Tagore—either to his talk, which did not mean conversation, or to his reading of his own poetry. Harriet Monroe has recorded: "[Tagore] was then unknown except for *Poetry's* first English printing of some of his Gitanjali in December, and Mrs. Moody could have had no idea whether her three guests from Bengal would fit into the daily scheme of an American household. That she found them most adaptable and companionable, and formed a lasting friendship with the distinguished poet of the East, was her well deserved reward. And the editors of *Poetry* shared in it when they gathered many evenings that winter around her hearthfire to hear him chant his songs in their Bengali rhythms, and to be stimulated by his wisdom and rich spiritual experience."[1]

When, in February, Mr. Tagore was invited by Professor James Haughton Woods of the department of philosophy at Harvard to speak at Cambridge, Harriet's sense of responsibility for the poet's well-being was so great that she decided to go East with him, taking a member of the household as usual. Passing through New York, they were joined by Ridgely Torrence, who remembers that the Harvard lecture, given in the professor's own large classroom, was meagerly attended, in striking contrast to the tumultuous crowds that greeted Mr. Tagore in this country three years later, after he had won the Nobel prize and after American bookshops began to call attention to mountainous masses of his books.

Back in Urbana, in March, Mr. Tagore wrote Harriet, acknowledging her kindness and indicating something of the degree of dependence on her that he seems already to have felt.

I haven't sat down to my writing yet, putting it off on some idle pretext or other. The first pull is always unpleasant and I am coaxing my mind to put its yoke on with good grace. I hope I shall be disposed to make a beginning tomorrow morning.

[1] *Poetry: A Magazine of Verse*, XL (April, 1932), 53.

My bridemother[2] is bravely trying to evolve some kind of order and decency out of the topsyturvydom of the domestic anarchy that prevailed during her absence. She had to exercise an amazing amount of ingenuity in getting up our meals the first day after our arrival. But you must admit that want of ingredients is much too formidable an obstacle to overcome by a mere tour de force, and cream toast, I venture to say, is almost an impossibility if you have no cream. But our prospect is getting brighter every day and we are feeling hopeful. So you may banish all anxiety from your kind heart about the proper supply of our nourishment.

I have got a very nice letter from Dr. Woods asking me to prepare three more lectures to be read in Boston. I have also a request from the Editor of the Atlantic Monthly to write for his paper an account of our school at Bolpur, specially the philosophy of education underlying it—which I shall do.

Rathi has begun typing my poems—I won't call them translations. . . . . I will be sending to you the original copies as they are being typed, and if it is possible for you to have three more sets of copies made, it will be of help to me.

I send you the letter I got from Mr. Okakura. As he will be passing through Chicago, perhaps you will be glad to ask him to your house.

I cannot tell you how I miss your loving care which has been one of the rarest good fortunes I have met with in the West.

Yours,
RABINDRANATH TAGORE

A few days later he wrote again, also from Urbana, in reply to Harriet's invitation to return to her house:

DEAR FRIEND,

Indeed it will give me great pleasure to spend the few days we have in hand in your company before we leave for Europe. I think I shall be able to come to Chicago by the time you come back from New York. But, why talk about California, dear friend? Surely, you are not thinking of deserting us, taking our

[2] Mr. Tagore's daughter-in-law, Protima, wife of Rathi Tagore.

bridemother away, leaving two hapless male members of our family unprotected and uncared for. I don't see any use of my going to Chicago just to catch a glimpse of your vanishing form and live in memory of it the remaining days in that noisy town. No, I am not going to put up with such utter neglect. I have a better game to suggest. Make Chicago our California, and fruits and flowers and sunshine will not be lacking if we all set our minds to it. So that is settled. Vive la Chicago.

I do not think I shall be able to make a longer stay in this country than till the middle of the next month. In the meanwhile I should be glad to get some opportunities to replenish my exhausted coffer by lecturing if that is possible. But I am afraid it is not. The time is short and my temperament is unfavourable.

I have begun writing and the windows are being opened in my mind, the light streaming in, and a sense of freedom filling my heart.

I am sending you some more of my manuscripts. To whom shall I address them when you are absent?

It is a grey evening—everything is so quiet, no traffic in the street—only the bell ringing from the Catholic church in our neighborhood.

Your

RABINDRANATH TAGORE

Some weeks afterward the Tagores sailed for Europe, having again visited Chicago in the interval.

From the "Olympic," in mid-April, the poet wrote Harriet a farewell letter, which, however it may impress anyone who did not know the writer, certainly to Harriet herself had no excessive flavor of piety. At this date neither knew that they were shortly to meet again.

DEAR FRIEND,

We shall reach our destination tomorrow night, and before I leave this steamer I must tell you how truly your friendship has become a part of our life, and I feel since now your sympathy will be a source of strength for me in all my works and aspirations.

Last Monday was the first day of our Bengali New Year—and we three had our prayer that morning at a corner of the saloon. We could thank God that our life had been richer by union of hearts in His name and in His service and that love had been waiting for us in places we had never known. This year the New Year's day has come to us while crossing the sea and I feel that my life has been launched on a great voyage, laden with love and hope and good wishes from dear friends.

I hope we shall meet again; but if we do not, let us feel assured that our meeting has been fruitful of God's blessing, that it was not mere social intercourse, pleasant and passing, and that it will help us in some measure in the fulfilment of our life. Let us march onward in God's broad path to the emancipation from the narrowness of self, to the dedication of our lives to His love and service, and feel that we are walking side by side. Mourn not for the past, be not overcome by the present, break yourself away from the daily trivialities of life, from the interminable web of nothingness, turn your face to Him in joy who is infinite love and life everlasting.

Your affectionate friend,

RABINDRANATH TAGORE

It happened that almost immediately Harriet's business again called her to London. Or is it possible that the urgency of the summons was colored by her unselfish wish to smooth still further the philosopher's pathway? She delayed somewhat, being unwilling to leave the country until the child expected by her brother Fred and his wife—their first and only one—should be safely born. The baby girl arrived on June 5; Harriet sailed immediately afterward, Edith Kellogg accompanying her. Happily, she arrived in London just in time to see a presentation of Tagore's play, *The Post Office*. "It made a great impression on me," she wrote to Charlotte Moody, "but I must say I don't think the Irish Players the best ones to have produced it."

By June 22 she was living in the flat at 16 More's Garden,

Cheyne Walk, S.W., Chelsea, where she and Charlotte Moody had stayed during two earlier London visits. Knowing that Henry James, whose work she greatly admired, then occupied an apartment in the same building, Harriet one day recognized the novelist in the lift and and made him a profound obeisance. Since Henry James once declared to his English friend Arthur Benson, "I am singularly accessible to all demonstrations of regard," it seems a pity that he was not impelled to throw formality overboard and to prove his susceptibility on this occasion also—even though, after all, neither Harriet nor Mr. James really belonged in the other's universe.

This year she had left a part of herself behind in Chicago. The birth of the Tildens' little girl meant almost as much to Harriet as to the parents, and the child's existence remained always one of the most important elements in her life. When speaking of this newly born infant to whose actual self she had had no opportunity to become attached, she could write, as she did, to the child's mother: "I try to get the little baby out of my mind because I seem to be inclined to think too much about her, but I keep on dreaming about her when I am asleep and I find my mind reverts to her over and over again in the daytime. . . . . It is hard for me to understand why it is that these claims of relationship are so strong"—it was clear that she had been moved to her very depths and by no transitory emotion.

The link with the tiny creature in Chicago was strengthened by the fact that little Alice Harriet had been named in part for Harriet herself. With this start, and with her strong family feeling, Harriet would, no doubt, have cared much for the child, in whatever fashion she might have developed. But as the little niece proved to be lovely, intelligent, and winning, Harriet's pride in her as the years went on was almost equal to her immense love.

No sooner was Harriet established in More's Garden than Mr. Tagore with his family accepted her invitation to join her and remain her guests during the summer. To this spot literary London pursued him.

"Mr. Tagore is being lionized extensively," Harriet wrote to

Ferdinand Schevill. "I think he is doing his best to get away from it .... but he is not very successful."

In order to undergo a slight operation Mr. Tagore shortly entered a London hospital. While he was detained there, Harriet slipped over to France, joining her cousin Henry Lyman who had also had a Parkman childhood and with whom she was always on the happiest comradely terms. These two, with Edith Kellogg, spent a ten days' interval in motoring in the French Alps, near Grenoble, an excursion greatly to Harriet's taste. Reporting on this to the Chicago household, she wrote: "The motor ran into perpetual snows and around curved precipices where you knew you could dash off thousands of feet to the bottom in•another moment; and all so swift that the obvious instant between you and an unconscious death was too short to worry about. It was joyous."

Such words, from Harriet, implied no morbid leaning toward death, which was far from being a part of her temperament, but rather an intense love of life. Only life, as she understood it, mustn't be too humdrum.

Escaping disaster on the edge of mountain precipices, Harriet encountered it, after she had hurried back to London, in the form of the superlative English strawberry. Its excellence, she believed, was her undoing. After eating as many as she wanted, she fell painfully and prostratingly ill with what she described as a "rheumatoid infection," which kept her in bed, suffering acutely, for weeks.

This circumstance, inconvenient though it was, proved not the slighest barrier to hospitality—and hospitality on a scale resembling that at home. Bedridden, Harriet had both to give time and attention to the affairs of The Home Delicacies, which was her reason for being in London at all, and, also, being responsible to her guests, to direct the labors of incompetent servants. With the exception of her sickroom, the entire flat was made over to the Tagores and their stream of visitors, the hostess herself being perforce invisible. "Mr. Yeats came to call upon Mr. Tagore but of course I did not see him," an unfamiliar and thwarted Harriet records. But she does not remotely suggest in her dictated letters nor, one may be sure, did her mind harbor the thought that her cherished guests made life more difficult than it would have been in any case.

Brooding always upon little Alice Harriet, the enraptured aunt wrote to her brother: "Couldn't you afford to insert Converse . . . . in the baby's name? Then part of her name would represent mother." This was, accordingly, done.

On July 31, 1913, she was engaged in characteristic plans. Writing to the sculptor Jo Davidson in France, she says: "Mr. Tagore is at present comparatively free and will be glad to pose for a few days, more or less, if it suits your convenience to come over here now. I don't think you would ever regret making a study of him. I must suggest to you that he is very sudden in his movements [that is, likely to leave London] and that it is really necessary to take him at once in order to be sure to get him.

". . . . In coming to London . . . . you may not see me but you will find the Tagores in the flat with me here, the drawing-room of which is an alleged studio."

At the same time she reported to Ridgely Torrence: ". . . . Mr. Tagore's influence is growing rapidly all the time. His children' poems are to come out in the fall, exquisitely illustrated from India. A volume of his essays is being published by Macmillan. *The Nation* is publishing a series of his stories and a series of poems on death—very beautiful. In the midst of all this, he is really standing aware, I think, of the fire by which he is being chastened, but also, ... ready for the chastening and willing to withdraw from all . . . . adulation into the best beloved work of his school. His heart is fiery, but it is also broken and contrite. . . . . I have greatly enjoyed meeting William Rothenstein, his friend. I am sure you know of his paintings from the Museum in N.Y."

A few days later, having heard from Jo Davidson that he would come to make the bust of Tagore, she writes regretting that she cannot ask him and his wife, Yvonne, to stay with her in the flat but proposes that they lodge as her guests elsewhere in the building and come to her for their meals.

This portrait and all other immediate matters having shortly

102

been accomplished, the Tagores, toward the end of August, were ready to sail from Liverpool for Calcutta. Harriet would have been glad to leave London at the same time, particularly as the More's Garden flat was no longer available. But as she was not yet able to travel, it was arranged that she and Edith Kellogg should occupy for a few weeks the house of the painter William Rothenstein[3] at 11 Oak Hill Park, Frognole, Hampstead, which happened to be for rent. This proved to be an agreeable experience, resulting in a friendly connection. "Mr. Rothenstein," Harriet wrote to Alice Corbin, "is a man of wonderful nature, ... intellectual, far advanced in the spiritual understanding of life. I like him well." By the middle of September she was so far improved as to be ready to sail for home.

At about the same time, on board the "City of Lahore," Mr. Tagore wrote her:

Beloved friend,

The weather is all that could be desired. There is just enough agitation in the sea to remind us it could be much worse. The sun is godlike and most extravagantly exuberant. He has snapped his pursestring and is scattering gold upon every beggar of a wave which is clamouring and raising its arm to him. The sky is drowsing, drunk with an excess of light—and the air is full of dreams—dreams of a heaven from whence they have strayed and cannot find their way back. My days are silent and full. I occupy a solitary corner in the unfrequented lower deck and spread out my heart over the blue and smooth out all its creases. How I wish you could come with us and share our gladness. It breaks my heart to think of you spending your days in the dismal gloom of London, lying in your sick bed. I devoutly hope you are out of it by this time and are restored to your unbounded cheerfulness and well being, filling your surroundings with your overflowing life and goodness. . . . .

Accept my grateful love.

Yours
Rabindranath Tagore

[3] Later, Sir William Rothenstein.

No sooner, almost, had Tagore forsaken European shores than one result of the impression he had personally made that summer in England, following upon the admiration that his writings had excited in Yeats and others, began to shape itself. The belief in him as a man, as an artist, and as a power for peace became transmitted to the high councils functioning in Sweden, and, some months later—quite unexpectedly, it would seem, to the recipient—the Nobel prize for literature for that year was awarded to the distinguished Indian. So shortly after he reached India what he describes as his "ordeal" began. Few of the notable persons to whom this prize has been awarded, particularly when awarded in absentia, can have found the experience so upsetting. Mr. Tagore wrote to Harriet:

SANTINIKETAN, BOLPUR, BENGAL
December 23, 1913

MY DEAR FRIEND,

It is such a great delight for me to have your letter and to know you have got back your usual abundance of health and activity. I am passing through an ordeal. My time is uselessly wasted in trivial formalities. I am assailed by the curiosity of the multitude. This burden of the wasted days which brings me neither work nor rest is an enormous strain on me. The honour is for my country, the prize is for my school, and for me is left this great disturbance which I am trying to bear with as good a grace as is possible.

Yesterday was the anniversary day of festival of our ashram. We had our divine service and the boys sang beautifully. Our sunny winter days are lovely and everything here breathes of peace and the intimacy of a spiritual presence. My heart is full of gladness and love. This exuberance of space and sunshine seems to have turned the blood in my veins into wine, spreading a golden inebriation far into my being. I wish I could show you the little ones in my school, their whole body and mind astir with the joyous impulse of young life. Yet even in their restlessness our Indian children have the expression of a wistful tenderness in their large black eyes which is perfectly pathetic. I wish I had no other distractions but looking after these boys, helping them to grow in grace and strength.

Please remember me kindly to all our friends in your household.

Your affectionate friend,
RABINDRANATH TAGORE

A month later Harriet found herself again appealed to in so urgent a strain that it must have chagrined her to acknowledge that in this case no solacing action was really within her power.

SANTINIKETAN, BOLPUR, BENGAL
January 22, 1914

MY DEAR FRIEND,

I am still suffering from Nobel Prize notoriety and I do not know what nursing home there is where I can go and get rid of this my latest and my greatest trouble. To deprive me of my seclusion is like shelling an oyster—the rude touch of the curious world is all over me. I am pining for the shade of obscurity. I hope you have not already tired of my name being discussed in every newspaper and you do not despise him who has been dragged from his nest of dreams into the most crowded market of public applause. Why do I not have a word of sympathy from you in my time of distress?

I hope you have completely recovered from your illness.

Your affectionate friend,
RABINDRANATH TAGORE

And again (on February 4) he wrote her:

MY DEAR FRIEND,

I have just come back to Bolpur after a tedious course of dissipation in Calcutta life and I am beginning to feel that life is a noble gift to use and the world round us is precious. The spring is in its full flush of youth, the mango trees are in bloom, and some of our summer birds have become absurd in the repetition of the refrains of their music. I am trying to forget the strains of my Nobel prize. I hope I shall gradually regain my mental *health which thinks nothing of leaving letters unanswered and of being vigorously rude.*

I am sure you have got my "Chitra" by this time and have forgiven me for the liberty I have taken in dedicating it to you without waiting for your permission.

Yours,
RABINDRANATH TAGORE

Indeed Harriet must have known of the *Chitra* dedication considerably before this date. Thoroughly as she deserved it, this was a handsome gesture on the poet's part, and it is pleasant to think of the happiness it must have given her. Apropos of this matter, Sir William Rothenstein wrote to her with great enthusiasm, praising the large heartedness, the "unbounded and spontaneous" hospitality that had called forth the *Chitra* dedication

And from Santiniketan, in March, Mr. Tagore wrote:

After a long wild career in their motor car Rathi and Protima have at last joined me in my school which is nearing its summer vacation. It wasn't a day too soon—for I needed very badly to be taken in hand by my little "bridemother." I have just that touch of illness brought about by fatigue which is sufficient to ward off unnecessary intrusions but slight enough to cause no anxiety to friends. The warm fragrance of spring is around us and it would have been all wasted upon me had it not been for this beneficent indisposition which has provided me with a reasonable excuse to be idle. Please remember me to all my friends.

Your affectionate friend,
RABINDRANATH TAGORE

CHAPTER XII

E. A. ROBINSON—VACHEL LINDSAY

HER "master," Tagore, was now at the other end of the world, possibly never to be seen again. So Harriet, freed from the absorbing preoccupations of the past year, began in the early part of 1914 to look about her a little. Though the Indian seer had aroused in her an almost idolatrous reverence, she had many sides and multiple capacities. Poetry was more than ever her dominant interest, and as always it was an interest that manifested itself in extremely active ways. Just now, however, there was lack of a human focus that should be both significant and near at hand.

After Moody's death she had turned naturally and confidently to his close friends. A lasting comradeship with Ridgely Torrence had developed at that time. The link with Percy MacKaye had been formed even earlier, when Will Moody had brought his friend to her house. With E. A. Robinson she had exchanged a few letters in her husband's lifetime, and in 1911 she had consulted him while preparing for the publication, in 1912, of Moody's *Poems and Poetic Dramas.*

A conscientious critic, Robinson then sent her detailed comments and recommendations, at the same time registering his warm admiration for the work of the man who had been considered his rival.

After this, the relationship between Harriet and Robinson progressed—but gradually, as was Robinson's instinctive way, rather than at the impetuous pace that Harriet herself usually contrived, believing that in such matters no time should be lost.

When, the following October, she sent him a copy of *Poetry*[1]

[1] *Poetry: A Magazine of Verse,* I, No. 1, 1.

containing "I Am the Woman," a poem he had already praised, he wrote her from Cornwall-on-Hudson: "I was glad to see Will's poem in print. . . . . Barring possibly a chorus in Murray's version of the Medea I know of nothing with which to compare it."

Yet Harriet must have been more than a little distressed when he continued: "What you say of my own poetry is very complimentary and encouraging. But I am sorry to have to state that I haven't written a verse in two years and that there seems to be nothing in sight. There is some in the distance but I cannot attempt to say when it will come near enough for me to capture it. It looks now as if I should have to waste a few more years over more or less experimental prose to pay for my venturing into that apparently forbidden country to which I was called and hauled. I should like to contribute something to *Poetry* and I would if I could. Sometime in the future, if its pages are still open to me, I may be able to send something.

"I shall not see much of New York until October when I hope to see you again—and Mr. Schevill, if he is still there."

A month later, however, he had better news to send and wrote her in a tone of confidence:

DEAR MRS. MOODY,

Your note came just as I was on the point of sending this poem [Eros Turannos] to Miss Harriet Monroe for her magazine—that is, of course if she should want it. But it occurs to me that you might like to see it yourself, and that you might not consider it an imposition if I were to ask you to read it and forward it to her.

As for the Porcupine, I shall be glad to send it to you as soon as I have restored the original and only sensible ending—the same that you know. But the play has been entirely rewritten and so far as the language goes is almost another thing from the play that you read.

In the meantime, I have to thank you, as always, for all your friendly interest in what I do and in much that I don't do. I'm

108

back with my original trade now in earnest and have about the fourth part of a new book due.

I wonder how much more the Lord is going to stand from me, sometimes, but he is lenient just at present and I won't invite his impatience by calling his attention to the fact.

Yours always sincerely,

E. A. ROBINSON

Will's letters[2] are mighty pleasant reading. . . . . It is a great pity there are not more of them.

So they had really become friends, and by neither of them was friendship held to be a casual or ephemeral affair.

But Robinson, MacKaye, and Torrence all lived in the East. At that time she saw little of them. In any case, however, she would have kept a watchful eye upon the field of poetry itself, and she could not have failed to note that a new poet was now vigorously blossoming at her very door, that is to say, in the pages of *Poetry*. This was a middle westerner—an inveterate middle westerner, as it proved, in spite of his many wanderings —from Springfield, Illinois, named Nicholas Vachel Lindsay. Lindsay was far from being a beginner. He had, in fact, been writing for a decade. Also, he had already invented his vocation of twentieth-century troubadour and tramp, gathering experiences from which he was shortly to formulate his "Rules of Beggary for Poets." For the first time with this new poem, "General William Booth Enters into Heaven," had he made a definite and permanent splash. As usual, Harriet made no mistake in reaching out toward this original young man.

To a letter that she sent him, he responds from Springfield with a pleasant naïveté:

MRS. WILLIAM VAUGHN MOODY:

My dear Friend: I am indeed honored that you should seek me out, and coming to Chicago again, I hope to visit you. I shall come sometime next fall or winter.

[2] *Some Letters by William Vaughn Moody.* Edited with an introduction by Daniel Gregory Mason (Houghton Mifflin Co., 1913).

Mr. William Vaughn Moody is closely tied up with the memories of my beginning days in Chicago. About 1902 or 1903 . . . . Prof. John Kenyon . . . . presented me with Mr. Moody's poems and the memorizing them and all, are bound up in my . . . . life at that time. . . . . .

I hope you keep Mr. Ficke[3] in the notion of bringing me. I am sending you just about my latest copy of Rhymes to be Traded for Bread. . . . . .

As for "The Congo," it should appear in the Metropolitan for May, or at least some time soon.

Yours sincerely,
NICHOLAS VACHEL LINDSAY

For the impulsive creature that Lindsay then was, postponing his acquaintance with Harriet until fall would scarcely have been in character. As a matter of fact, he came to see her in June, two months after the preceding letter; and he came without escort. She detained him for dinner and in the early evening took him, with others, for a drive through the parks. On this drive Lindsay recited "The Congo," then unpublished, with tremendous vehemence, while, on returning to Groveland Avenue, his rendition of "The Firemen's Ball" (Miss Kellogg reports) "actually made people congregate in front of the house, thinking there was a fire inside."

Harriet was delighted with her visitor's abounding talent and overflowing personality. And they got on so well together that, after returning to Springfield, he wrote to her again. As he himself once said, in speaking of his lonely midnight hours, writing was really easier than not writing, when letters were addressed to a comprehending mind. In Harriet, though he did not look to her for a sentimental response, he nevertheless divined the sympathy or, at any rate, the willingness to give him close attention, that his temperament required; and from now on for many years he wrote her often, voluminously and apparently quite without reserve, so that the mass of his letters amounts almost to an autobiography.

[3] Arthur Davison Ficke, the poet.

Thus there were no delays, hesitations, withdrawals, in the progress of this friendship. Two month later Lindsay had accepted an invitation to spend a month in the New York flat, while Harriet was at work in her characteristic way asking her New York friends to meet him and successfully introducing him at Cornell University as a man with "an inexhaustible fund of poetic imagination."

Learning that Lindsay's meeting with at least one New York poet had come off happily, Harriet wrote in July to Percy MacKaye: "It gives me much pleasure that you have been in New York with Mr. Lindsay and enjoyed him. He certainly is a fresh and real experience. I find myself deeply interested in his various utterances, for example, 'The Santa Fé Trail,' 'The Firemen's Ball,' etc. I know you too are delighted with them. How thrilling he makes them with his prodigious rolling voice!"

But this being midsummer, E. A. Robinson was safely tucked away as usual in the MacDowell Colony at Peterborough, New Hampshire, and may have been well content that this was the case. Though as sincere and, indeed, as kind a person as Harriet herself, in his utterly ungregarious way, he shrank from new encounters. Several weeks after Harriet had told him about Lindsay, he wrote her:

DEAR MRS. MOODY,

. . . . I should be glad to meet Mr. Lindsay if I were in New York, and still hope to meet him sometime. His chants in "Poetry" are, I fear, a bit too radical for my antiquated taste (I used to think I was modern) but I like his "General Booth" and I believe in the man. It seems to me that he has not yet found himself. I'll be glad if you will send my Porcupine to the above address. . . . . I am going to rewrite the first act and sometime I may publish the thing—that is, if Van Zorn is not too much for the Macmillans. I don't know why I have never mentioned it to you. Perhaps because I felt intuitively that you wouldn't like it very much. Anyhow, I'll send you a copy when it comes out.

111

What is this that I see in Poetry about Will—or rather a book[4] about him. If it is something that you recommend I wish you would ask the Literary Club[5] to send me a copy with bill.

My brain has been a vacuum for the past three or four months and as a consequence I'm not on good terms with nature. But I see signs of recovery and I feel symptoms of another attack of work.

I hope to see you again when I get back to town.

Later on, it was arranged that Lindsay should give a characteristic recital at Carnegie Hall in October in order to make himself better known in the East. No entrance fee was to be charged. Endeavoring to insure the quality of his audience, Harriet wrote to a number of friends of her own. Appealing again to Percy MacKaye, she said that Lindsay "cherishes the remembrance of your kindness and friendship."

In a letter to Robinson written for the same purpose and at the same time, which was just after he had sent her a copy of his prose play *Van Zorn*, she charmingly if rather ambiguously signs herself, "Your faithful student," a phrase she uses in no other letter, implying, perhaps, that if she hadn't so far been wholly captivated by *Van Zorn*, she was doing her best to accomplish that surrender.

Before the Carnegie Hall affair took place, Harriet wrote to Lindsay himself:

CHICAGO, Oct. 21, 1914

DEAR VACHEL,

. . . . *I have written Mr. Robinson and Mr. MacKaye and to several other friends telling them to bring any literary New Yorkers to your reading. I believe they will all do something toward your audience. I should like to be there, if possible, myself. As to patronage, I am a sorry patroness. I never know the rich or the influential. I have known several real poets, and I have a few loving friends in New York, who could, do and will,*

---

[4] A booklet on William Vaughn Moody by Edwin H. Lewis, teacher of English literature at Lewis Institute, Chicago.

[5] Publisher of Mr. Lewis' book.

112

care for your work. In any case, anything that friendship and gratitude for your abundant gifts can help me to do for you, I shall be only too glad to offer.

A month later, Robinson writes to tell Harriet of his regret that he had returned to New York too late to see her, during a visit she had recently made. The play he refers to is *Van Zorn*. The news that he was writing poetry again must have especially pleased her. He says: ".... To return to my own play for a moment, I have been led to believe that most of the seventeen who have read it have skimmed the long scene between the two men at the end of act first. As this scene is in one sense the whole play, a failure to get it is rather disastrous—particularly if one gets sleepy over pp. 60, 61. I don't see how any language could be clearer than that which is printed on those two pages, and therefore I'm at a loss to understand why about everybody who reads the play fails to find out what it is about. You don't tell me whether you had difficulties or not.

"But I'm not playwriting this winter. I'm getting together a new book of poems and one that will, I hope, not be the cause of so much mental indigestion on the part of my friends as this play of mine seems to have produced. Perhaps it is a warning for me not to follow after false gods, but to take what the friendly gods have given and to be glad that they have given it. I don't pretend to know how much it is worth. That's for time to decide. There seems to be nothing for me but to work and to make my letters short. I was glad to be told that you are to be here in January."

Even though Robinson's prose work may have interested her less than his verse, this fact had not prevented her from trying to help him stage his play; and, with this in view, she had urged Margaret Anglin to read *Van Zorn* and had attempted to bring about a meeting of the poet and the actress. All this Robinson acknowledges in the following letter: "I should be very glad indeed for a letter to Miss Anglin, and I thank you sincerely for calling her attention to *Van Zorn*—which, by the way, seems to be giving certain people a good deal of trouble. I wrote

113

it to please myself, and I seem to have succeeeded admirably. There seems to be an inclination on many sides to let me be King Ludwig—without Wagner. The difficulty seems to be that I did not make V Z's attachment to the girl sufficiently evident. Of course this could have been done easily enough, but I am pig-headed in not seeing the necessity of it. In fact, it seems to me that such a proceeding would make his position rather banal. I know that Time will settle the matter; and if the book— I don't insist on saying the play—is what I think it is, it will eventually be found out. If it isn't what I think it is, it will go the way of dead dogs, and be properly forgotten.

"I am working on a new version of my *Porcupine*, bringing Rachel more to the front, and making her give a more satisfactory account of herself. The rest of it will remain substantially as it is, with many minor changes.

"So now you have another long letter, and all about myself. . . . ."

In December of this year, six months after the beginning of their acquaintance, Lindsay felt sufficiently at ease with Harriet to write her three letters of intimate self-portrayal, the first dealing with himself as an artist, the second as a (disappointed) lover, the third as a son. He was still in Springfield. On December 2 he wrote her:

My dear Harriet Moody:
Thank you for your prompt letter.

I am living my real life here again in Springfield, calling on my oldest friends, talking to the local politicians I liked best— late at night—and being N. V. L. again. Helping rather lazily with the chores, and seeing all things going on their ancient round.

The room where I write to you I have inhabited since my thirteenth year. It holds an awkward bookcase I myself made in that year, and in it are some books that date from before then. Every picture on the wall is a souvenir of an old friend, and has a story to it as long as the Mississippi River, one might say.

114

My room is always rather grubby and mussy, for I take care of it myself mainly. The view out the window is pleasant. I can look out over the Governor's yard. Governor Dunne can be seen in the evening in good days in the summer, walking among the bushes with Mrs. Dunne.

Piled all around me in odd places are poetry-books folks have sent me to read, and some prose. What memories I have had tonight! I only wish I could open the door to you. These very old memories have a certain cosiness I wish I could divide.

You have no idea how much of me this room shuts in—you who have only seen me on the stage as it were—acting (sincerely enough), speaking lines I myself have written here—yet even the writing self seems extraneous sometimes, as tonight in the midst of the past.

Why do I talk so much about this? Because the thing above all that occupies my conscience, is the matter of doing what is the next inevitable duty or pleasure of N. V. Lindsay, maker of this bookcase and friend of these pictures. Here my sins, my weak spots, my failures, my self-challenges are all about the same that they were in 1899, we will say, my second year of college. I must stay in the same old game to beat the devil and conquer destiny, and not let any outside noises deflect me. Anywhere but in this room and on the road I am in deadly danger of believing in that new dramatic caricature of myself the Reviewers depict. I am in danger of believing my own exaggerated advertisements, and living in them, rather than my ancient soul.

Sometimes I think I should issue another war-bulletin full of bitter truth about this town, to set them all against me once more, for it seems to me my soul was more in harness then, when it walked alone, than now when those that like me the least speak with sweet tongues.

My work requires the ascetic and the celibate. I should renounce money even more strongly than I do, love poverty more. I should hate what I used to hate, for that big social hate was better than the petty spites of wounded vanity I cherish today. I am glad you want me to go on the road. It will be worth doing, even if it breaks my neck. You have no idea how when I am out of this room I reach back to my former ascetic self through today's roses, with the fear that I am losing it. Beauty and sweetness move me far more than they ever did before. I almost forget to mistrust them sometimes.

I have the spiritual hungers of a Franciscan ninety years old, yet I am suddenly loaded with a flowering outer self, and a blood-beat more like twenty than thirty-five. I am just beginning to understand the passionate ways of my girl and boy-friends that I remember at College, that were a subject of amazement to me then.

Yet my work—which has my heart of hearts—goes on like the illumination of a manuscript in a monastery. Today flatteries and publicity and the intoxication of the crowd threaten to drag me away from the missal. My literary self, or the monk that takes care of him, and sits inside of him by this bookcase, would know just what to do every day, and enjoy it with unalloyed pleasure, if this other Siamese twin with the hot-blood was not always hanging round, and buzzing more and more.

But unless I am mistaken, the monk will win in the end. He thinks quite clearly, and the other fellow never has his wits. The monk gets around his bacchanalian brother, by telling him, at a desperate crisis, when all other arguments fail, that it is his business to be a gentleman, at least, and by other spiritual diplomacies the monk wins.

Well, this is a lot of nonsense. I have no doubt I will write on these matters much more clearly, from the road, if I ever get there.

I remember how in Chicago I wrote a long and ardent letter to Herbert L. Willett—from my very soul—asking for his friendship and help—and was treated in a grand and scholarly manner for my pains. I wanted to know someone—no matter who—whose brains and position I could respect, with whom I could thresh out the questions that were shaking me to pieces. As it was I trod the winepress alone.

It is Monday morning. The hired girl stayed at the house of a

116

friend this morning—sick, so I have been washing and wiping the dishes. This is one chore I really enjoy doing. Now I am at my desk for all morning, and I plunge in a moment into my movie-book.

With love,
VACHEL

The second letter may be particularly revelatory in that it has the sound more of one close friend lamenting the loss of another than that of a passionate lover bemoaning the desertion of his beloved. "Ascetic"—"celibate"—Lindsay had described himself four days earlier, with perhaps a sensitive perception of the true course his destiny should have followed, freed from the uncertain swervings of what he calls his "heart angle." This time, he writes:

MY DEAR HARRIET,

I must confess to a certain lost feeling when I take my pen in hand tonight. For about nine months the good and beautiful Sara Teasdale and I wrote to each other all our minds and hearts, and she is going to marry another man, the 19th of December. She was in many ways the most intimate friend I had had for years and the best understander, the most natural. We were just alike in much that it would take Henry James to show. She was hard to give up, and now I have an empty rattly hollow-pumpkin sort of a place where she belonged. I will tell you confidentially that practically all the complimentary poems in The Congo were written to her. And The Spice-Tree. She walks through all the latter part of my book. The wicked daughter of Babylon in the earlier part was the cruel lady who preceded her—and I shall never cease to be grateful to Sara for helping me to forget her, and giving me a new faith in and respect for woman in matters of Romance. I can always say "Thank God she stands between me and the insults of the past."

She did me good and not evil every hour of our knowing each other, and I have one more poem to write her, I hope. But I have a sort of baffled feeling tonight. I have told so many things

117

to the dear lady about myself. I sort of lived in the palms of her hands, so many things I have told her that she and I must forget or will forget. I feel rather empty and puzzled and say—"Is the only way to make myself clear to myself, and steady my life and thought, to write out all these things again, and rewrite all my resolves once more, and all my aspirations and puzzlements and the silly routine of my little struggles? Why must I go spinning my web over again like a spider to catch the fly of my own thoughts? All these webs torn down so often—why must I go round and round?"

I wish I had an angel for a friend who would always show me myself infallibly, listen to me interminably, remember everything I said encyclopaedically and never weary of the job. And in the intervals of silence tell me interesting things that had been happening to him from the beginning of time.

The Epilogue of the Congo book was written to Sara after we had parted, I knew or almost knew, for good. And forever, it proved to be. There are times when I think of her just like that Pysche-poem, or as though she were Beatrice. And then other times I get that rattly feeling, as though my heart were a gourd— so far as Human Passion is concerned. And then I think of my North Star, and reflect rather wanderingly, how thoroughly consistent my artist-author life has been, and what a wavering scrappy fragmentary destiny I have from the heart angle. From the beginning to the end—just like fate.

And, finally, here is his account of his origin—of his "folks."

I haven't given you the right notion of my Mama. She is unquestionably the most powerful personality I have ever known, and one of the literary intellectuals of the first rank. She has taught me most all I know and I am still acquiring information from her.

In character though not in outlook Papa and Mama are much alike. I think within his own province he is more of an original—he is an absolutely unconquered Ishmaelite, in his determination to do everything his own way to the last ditch. A man with a most restless energy, great self denial—absolutely preoccupied with his family and his work, and believing in hard work. . . . . I get the credit of all I ever do from my mother. The Lindsays class me as a Frazee through and through. But they are wrong. My father has a nicer sense of the particular word than my mother, who is more lavish and eloquent. In his middle age he used to be a much more musical reader of prose or orations than Mama. When he was young and full of fire, he just loved to read the Speech to the Jury—at the Cronin Trial, for instance. . . . . And in every practical task to this day, he goes at everything with a certain pioneer ingenuity, which I think I inherit when I approach the problems of versification. Everything cold or mystic or Buddhistic or non-human in me I get from my mother (though she has many other qualities), while I get from him everything romantic, individual, lonely and rebellious.

Papa and Mama practically met in Europe. Children of Kentucky and Indiana pioneers, Papa had practiced medicine about nine years—near Springfield, and Mama had taught several years in a Girls' School in Kentucky. She and Miss Eudora Lindsay were chums and fellow-teachers and they saved up till they had enough for a year in Europe. So about 1874–75 they started, after all the study and preparation that two young school teachers would give.

Papa insisted on going along. He reported first for inspection at Grandpa's house. He had planned to spend the next year in special study in the Vienna hospitals, and he just made it a year earlier. So the three went together, presumably with auntie for chaperone. They became engaged in Dresden, and Papa nursed Mama through fever in Paris. All sorts of things happened. Papa and Mama were married at Grandpa's on their return. Then they came straight here. The house was filled of course with European photographs, especially the standard European art stuff of the day, and all my childish years were filled with their reminiscences of Europe. Going to Europe then was a bit like going to China now. They did not go back till my youngest sister was half grown. She has been there with them three times, and I went once.

119

In between they have camped of summers out West. I have gone with them three times to camp, no, four, but I generally spent my summers in this empty house, concocting Village Magazines,[6] etc.

Now, I hope you have some notion of my folks. I think the very fact they did their courting in the European Art Galleries has something to do with a lot of things I unconsciously take for granted. They are still unabashed restless haunters of Art Galleries, Chinese Palaces, and Colorado Camps as well.

And there wasn't anything in China to be readily got at, that escaped them in this six months, you bet. They approached it with the wisdom of years, and the directness of seasoned travellers, and being grey-headed, they were overwhelmed with Chinese reverential ceremoniouness for old age, which quite set them up, I assure you.

Well, now, Good morning.

With love,
VACHEL

By this time, well equipped as he already was with parents, Lindsay had also become to Harriet almost a son.

[6] The name given by Lindsay to a series of pamphlets written by himself and circulated by him in Springfield.

CHAPTER XIII

JOHN MASEFIELD AND OTHERS

WHEN Harriet wrote in a personal letter, midway during these crowded years, "one's life goes on from high point to high point of human intercourse," she described accurately what her own existence meant to her. It was precisely these peaks of experience that she was forever scaling; 'it was their tonic air she always longed to breathe. Valleys of labor and struggle lay between, for Harriet was neither sentimentalist nor idler, and her life was not an easy one. But for her exalted satisfactions this staunch pilgrim was willing to pay the necessary price.

In her friendship with Tagore she felt that she had achieved nothing short of a Himalayan summit. With the drift of English and Irish poets toward this country in the years immediately following, new and unexpected heights, in the human sense, were successively to reveal themselves.

In January, 1915, in the course of a visit to New York, Percy and Marion MacKaye introduced to her two strangers whom she instantly adopted as friends. Padraic Colum, the young Irish poet, friend of Yeats, had just come to this country for the first time, straight from the Abbey Theatre and the turmoil of Irish politics. With him came Mary Colum, his wife, later to make a distinguished reputation in the field of criticism. Harriet, who never wavered and fidgeted while waiting to see what other people might think of an artist or his work, made her own prompt estimate of Padraic Colum and acted accordingly.

Writing to him a few days later from Chicago, she refers to the efforts she is already making in his behalf and modestly remarks: "One of the privileges consequent upon my long association with a poet is that I am sometimes able to serve the cause of poetry in some simple way."

What she actually did was to write cogent letters not only to Cornell, her own university, but also to friends holding key positions at the universities of Chicago, Illinois, and Wisconsin. Besides approaching Chicago clubs, being herself an influential member of several, she reached out toward connections of her own in cities outside the state. The energy and conviction with which she repeatedly supported her belief in a new poet were successful in this case as in scores of others.

In March, Padraic Colum came west to fill the engagements that had been secured for him, and "Mollie and Padraic," as they were to be henceforth, paid Harriet a visit that resulted in warm personal friendship and in an invitation to go to the Cummington farm in the summer.

Meantime, there was at least one figure in Harriet's personal group of poets who kept her fully and frequently informed of all the events of his individual world. Vachel Lindsay wrote her from Springfield about himself, about his writing, and about what he planned to write. He was now seriously affected by thoughts of the war.

In an undated letter written about this time, he confides to her:

Well, I have spent most of my day in this room, but have not written a line of my book. Here is the outline before me. I have sat gazing at it with serene inertia, and rank cheerful stupidity, Quaker-meeting style.

That's the first stage, the hen on the nest. . . . .

My Papa and Mama are grand folks, and the trip to China has done them lots of good. Their tone has completely altered. They are really quite buoyant for them. Always I really enjoy them in a sober way, more than any other humans I know, and now they are great fun.

I feel slowly shaping itself within me the dream of my next poetry-book, coming in two years, perhaps, but the critical and strategic volume, as you know. I want it to be as democratic as Bryan and Mark Twain, but that gives but the dimmest idea of

122

what I have been thinking about. Certainly the chants should not lead in the next book. I do not want to be known for any one mannerism. I want to be as rousing as a Chautauqua oration, and at the same time carry a sort of smoking censer with me. I keep thinking of the Catholic mass, the Gregorian music, and the work of the Ancient wizards. I think the war has made the American temperament more pliable, and much more tender and deeper than it has ever been—but war poetry is the last way to go at it.

Perhaps, to put the picture in two words, I want to write rhymed quatrains that are at the same time incantations. And then I have a certain decorative, pictorial type of verse in mind, like marble inlay of various colors around the niche that holds the colored inlaid state of the Spirit of Illinois, we will say. . . . .

Your letter has just come. . . . .

Thank you for the invitation [to come to Chicago]. But here I stand—this rock shall fly from its firm base as soon as I, until this book is written.

"If I should," said Mrs. Dorking, "Then my eggs would all get chilled."

"No they won't," replied the chicken, "And no matter if they do," etc. . . . .

Mrs. Dorking stays here on the nest.

Very sincerely forever,

VACHEL

This retreat to his "nest" was the sequence of a lecture trip to the East in the course of which, for the first time, he had seen and talked with E. A. Robinson.

"I have met . . . . your friend Robinson," he had written from Washington on February 2, 1915, coming home from New York, "and admired him, though he was too shy and abashed by me loud fresh ways or something. Maybe the next time the manners of N. V. L. will be more moderate. . . . . I see Mr. Robinson has to be taken quietly, alone. That's hard to do when everyone wants me to exhibit my good health and physical culture and recite all over the place."

123

Harriet herself seems rather to overstate the purport of this letter when, writing shortly afterward to Robinson, partly to thank him for the gift of a new edition of *Captain Craig*, she says: "I hear from Mr. Lindsay that you and he have met and grown very friendly together. I am glad of this for your sake as well as his, for I make sure that this unquenchable and noisy boy will seem as rich in his offering to you as he does to me."

And, she adds, referring to her own effort to bring about a meeting between Margaret Anglin (who had starred in the original production of *The Great Divide*) and Robinson (with his play, *Van Zorn*, in mind): "I am enclosing a letter from Margaret Anglin received today. It will speak to you for itself. . . . I am sure you will get her something that will give her a chance to grow again."

To another confidence of Lindsay's, at about the same time, she was less responsive.

"I am much rejoiced," he wrote, "that Macmillan's are going to bring out Webster Ford's *Spoon River Anthology*. It is great stuff. I send you the last installment. Don't you dare to refuse to admire. Also mark my words. It will be one of the literary sensations and the literary landmarks. In one year the literary world will be at his door, eating from his hand, we might say. He has said hundreds of things in the anthology I wanted to say in the *Village Magazine* and wasn't man enough or artist enough."

"Webster Ford," was, of course, the pen name used by Edgar Lee Masters in this connection only. Masters, then practicing law in Chicago, had published a number of books of verse cast in traditional form and was one of a small group of local writers frequenting Harriet's house at this time. During this year of 1915 he was to publish the *Spoon River Anthology* under his own name. The poems had already appeared, a few at a time, in *Reedy's Mirror*, published in St. Louis. William Marion Reedy, editor of this journal, was the discoverer of the new Masters who, while himself feeling somewhat timid as to the radical character of this departure of his, was for the first time to become widely known. But in spite of her friendly feeling for its author, Harriet failed to join in the wide and deserved acclaim that *Spoon River* promptly received. The content of the poems fell just outside the boundaries of her large liberality. To her, their tone was "negative," and the destructiveness of this epithet, as she used it, can hardly be conveyed.

Coincidentally, Carl Sandburg became, if not a daily habitué of Harriet's house, at least a more or less frequent visitor. After this period she often made warm references to him. An especial bond between them was a canine one, as Harriet continued to breed Irish setters, descendants of Sunday and of Beau Brocade. Sandburg wrote to her, some time in 1915:

DEAR MRS. MOODY:

A referendum in our house yesterday was unanimously for acceptance from you of One (1) Irish Setter, and I was placed under special instructions to compose a Song of Thanks for a Dog. In any event I shall get for you the Chippewa Songs among which is Song of Thanks for a Pony. The choice is for a dog of January, 1915, since you are so good as to offer such a wide range of choices. I shall try to reach you by phone re where the dog is to be seized for transportation to Maywood and a subsequent career as watchguard and playmate for the wife and daughter of a Scrivener.

Yours faithfully,
CARL SANDBURG

Transcending, at all times, all other news in interest was news—any news—from India. So the announcement, doubtless reaching Harriet in March, of Mr. Tagore's actual proposed return to America must easily have reduced all other coming events to a blur of insignificance. His plea to Harriet, in this letter, that she subordinate "profits" to poetry is probably the most unnecessary piece of advice ever offered—though she knew it was intended waggishly. From this time on, though he did not arrive until the following year, his coming loomed ahead, an event of primary importance.

From Calcutta, February 18, 1915, he wrote:

MY DEAR FRIEND,

We are arranging to visit Japan about September next. Have you any idea where you will be then? Why not meet your poet in the land of the rising sun? We can follow his fiery track till the East and West become one somewhere in the neighborhood of Groveland Avenue. Did you not plan this meeting at your fireside! Of course, plans are enough as plans—they have their beauty—but there should be occasional realizations, just enough to give them a flavour of probability. Do come, my dear friend, and let us have some of your delightful ice creams in Japan. Don't you plead business. Business should never be one-sided, it must not fix your mind to its profits only. There must come times when you should recklessly rush to losses and be glad. The element of loss is the element of poetry in business. Business would be deadly to the spirit of man if it were wholly successful. There should be at least one poet among your business advisers to represent this side—the freedom from the tyranny of desire for success. I hope I have convinced you.

I shall let you know the dates and other necessary details when I know them myself. But if you have communications with Rathi, you will have more accurate and satisfactory information. The children are happy and they are looking forward to this trip with eagerness. You know how glad Rathi and Protima will be to see you, especially the latter who so heartily enjoyed being spoilt by you.

With love,

Yours affectionately,

RABINDRANATH TAGORE

Friendship with the Colums progressed to everybody's keen satisfaction. From the Cummington farm Padraic Colum wrote in late August:

(THE MOODY FARM, WEST CUMMINGTON, MASS.)

THE LOG-CABIN, 29th August, 1915

DEAR FRIEND,

We are sitting in the log-cabin in the utmost contentment, listening to the rain beating on the roof and pitying "Sultan

126

Mohammed on his throne." It is grand here. Mollie is becoming a person of rude health. She has been out twice on horseback and she takes to it naturally.

I wonder what your plans are! Have you fixed up anything about going to England. If you haven't, you ought to come down here. The world is a very distracted place, and it has few places as peaceful as this.

I am writing a fantastic comedy, big drafts of which I wrote in another epoch of existence. I have hopes it will go here. I am sending you the first instalment of "The King of the Cats."

Take all good wishes from two who are very devoted to you—Mollie and myself. . . . .

A blessing with you.

Yours always,

PADRAIC COLUM

It was by now apparent that Padraic Colum was the precursor of a series of European poets who became Harriet's guests and, almost overnight, her friends. A major figure among them was John Masefield, who in January, 1916, made the first of several visits to Groveland Avenue. Both the poet and his poetry excited her fervent admiration. Here were no "negatives"—as in Masters' case—to shrink from! Also, Masefield proved to be a teller of enthralling tales, adventure stories of the heroic order, which seemed to come from him without thought or preparation and to which Harriet and her circle listened delightedly, evening after evening.

But this, after all, may have been no more than Harriet had looked for, for from Masefield she had expected much. Though her guests usually came through introductions from friends held in common, this poet she had directly invited, for she "had to know the man who wrote The Everlasting Mercy." Long before she knew him, she would quote him familiarly and speak of herself as a "widow in a bye street."

Shortly after the first visit, she wrote to the University of Illinois in the effort to secure an engagement for "our beloved John Masefield" who had been "a wonderful inspiration to all

of us in Chicago." Masefield's own letters to Harriet show a
warm response to her friendliness, even though the phrasing
tends to be formal. A Briton in every sinew, his earlier experience in this country would not seem in the least to have Amer-
icanized the future laureate. From Indianapolis, on January 27,
he wrote her:

DEAR MRS. MOODY,

Thank you so much for all your friendly welcome to me. I
have many grateful thoughts of your beautiful kindness.

If you can really bear with me, I shall be very glad to see you
again, on Tuesday next, when I come from Nashville, but I do
want you to look on me simply as a friend, if you can, not at all
as a guest.

Warm greetings and thanks to you.

Yours very sincerely,

JOHN MASEFIELD

And not long afterward, the following very human and sincere letter came to her from St. Louis (February 15):

This is to say that I reached Urbana safely and made the
Clinton train in style, and was in good time here.

Indeed I don't know how to thank you or any of your household for so much generous kindness given or trouble taken. It
will all be a beautiful memory while I live, and for your own
share in it all I don't know how to begin to thank you.

One little thing I would like so much to do. I was very much
interested in what you told me about ———. I've lived that kind
of life myself, and as a much older man I would like, if I might
be allowed, to give a hand. Are there any books that he would
find useful in his studies? I would love to make him a free list
in a bookstore up to ——— dollars or so. I felt shy in proposing
this in person, thinking that—perhaps, as a B——, he might not
like such an offer from me, during the war.

It was charmingly kind of you to have me with you.

I miss Miss O'Neill's sad Irish face so much.

Thank you very very much for all the happiness of my stay

with you. All greetings and good wishes to you and all of your house.

Yours most warmly,
JOHN MASEFIELD

Established favorite though he promptly became, even Masefield's prestige was somewhat obscured as the time drew nearer for Mr. Tagore's return to America. As a sequence of the Nobel prize, Tagore had recently been knighted. And he was widely read all over the world. These circumstances did not, however, increase his stature in Harriet's eyes. Nothing of the sort was necessary.

Also through the Colums there was introduced to Harriet's friendship the accomplished French writer, H. A. Jules-Bois, who thenceforward lived almost uninterruptedly in this country until his death. For several winters in succession M. Jules-Bois lived in Chicago, doing much of his work at Harriet's house and dining there almost nightly. Being especially interested in Moody's *Faith Healer*, he translated this play into French.

Meanwhile another Hindu, Dr. Ananda Coomaraswamy, had come to America with a letter of introduction to Harriet from Mr. Tagore. So in March, Harriet invited him and his English wife, Ratan Devi, to stay with her while they were filling some lecture-recital engagements in Chicago. This visit having been accomplished, Harriet gave an account of it in a letter to Alice Corbin Henderson.

"Now the Coomaraswamys have been and gone. She sang her Indian songs—four recitals in the Little Theatre—every time filling the house fuller, until it might be fair to say as many were turned away as got in. Her singing is very beautiful and new, a wonderful revelation about music, the understanding of which would reveal to me a secret I have long guessed at, but never been able to draw near to. She also sang at home for us innumerable English folk songs. She had an unbelievable versatility in these songs, was very dramatic, and altogether

129

charming. I did not know there were so many delightful ballads and songs of this kind in the world.

"Dr. Coomaraswamy introduced her singing in the Little Theatre each time, with a brief talk about the difference between western and eastern music, and the difference between what he called the art songs of India and the Indian folk songs. .... I make sure Will would have been deeply interested in his books, which he brought with him and showed to us. He also talked a great deal about Indian painting past and present. .... Dr. Coomaraswamy's continual statement about India is that it is now finished, and that the only soil upon which ancient Indian artistic ideals can flourish and develop is the soil of the west. It has been announced here that the Coomaraswamys will return for another week, beginning June 5th, and if Pond doesn't upset this arrangement with the bookings he has made for them, we expect to see them back.

"We have all been very much interested in the Kennedy-Frasers and their folk songs of the Hebridean Islands. These two, a mother and daughter, preceded the Coomaraswamys in the town and in our household, and the general result is that we are all humming different folk songs at the same time, and that a kind of new pandemonium has been created in the ever fertile atmosphere of 2970."

Mrs. Marjorie Kennedy-Fraser and her daughter Patuffa, introduced by the MacKayes, had been Harriet's guests in the course of a series of recitals from the songs of the Hebrides, given throughout the country. Mrs. Kennedy-Fraser was not only a musician for whom an admirer could claim that she was "the greatest figure Scotland has yet produced in music" but a woman of exceptional intelligence and charm and a writer as well. Harriet found both mother and daughter unusually sympathetic, and all three shortly formed a close friendship that lasted many years.

Two months later Sir Rabindranath's arrival seemed imminent. Harriet wrote again to Alice Corbin: "Now as regards the news of the hour. I have had a note from the great Rabindranath, which I enclose to you, hoping that your conscience will prompt you sometime to send it back again, because I am fond of every little scratch of his pen. . . . . He will be coming into Seattle sometime about the 8th or 10th of August. I should like to rush out to the coast to meet him, but I . . . . shall be waiting for him here."

A little later she learned that the poet had been delayed. From Yokohama, on July 16, 1916, he wrote her: "My departure for America has been postponed till the 21st of August. We shall reach Seattle about the 16th of September. The name of our steamer is Canada Maru. I wish you could meet me in Japan. It is a beautiful country—and there are lots of things we can learn from these Japanese."

Restraining herself, with who knows how much difficulty, not only from spanning the Pacific, but even from leaping to California, Harriet stayed on patiently in Chicago, writing to Mrs. Seymour, at the University of Illinois (Professor and Mrs. Seymour were close friends of the Tagores) on August 15, "Isn't it wonderful that we are to see our beloved Robi Babu[1] again?"

In October, at last, the eminent guest was due.

"Mr. Tagore is arriving tonight," Harriet wrote on the twentieth. "It is one of the few real human communications to meet him."

This time, the Poet, who was always capitalized by his admiring hostess, was limited by his lecture engagements to a two weeks' stay. After he had gone, Harriet wrote to a younger friend, the sculptor Lucile Swan Blum, that she had been "happily busy" with her guest. "Certainly," this letter said, "those meetings after death can be no stranger than the return from a different continent of a friend whom you had never expected to see again. If you get a chance to hear Mr. Tagore's lecture of 'The Cult of Nationalism' don't fail to do so. It is on the whole the most significant utterance of this hour."

Later, on his way back to the Pacific coast, Mr. Tagore made a farewell stop with Harriet, after which she wrote to a woman friend: "I should have written you long ago except for the unusual distractions of having Mr. Tagore and his retinue in my

[1] Term of affection by which close personal friends addressed Mr. Tagore.

house and being for the most part subject to their wishes. Mr. Tagore has now gone on to California. He is speaking tomorrow in Los Angeles and is to sail from San Francisco on Wednesday the 17th. He had quite a little attack of cold brought on by exposure, but he made a good recovery. He is happy in the thought of getting back to India with its congenial climate and to his beloved school. . . . . We think him more interesting than ever."

Meanwhile, she wrote with greater expansiveness to Alice Corbin Henderson, who, since Mr. Tagore's first visit in 1913, had moved with her husband to Santa Fé.

DEAREST ALICE:

. . . . To take up first the subject of Mr. Tagore. He spoke of you often when he was here, and he missed you, spoke of the possibility of starting home on the Santa Fé and so stopping off to see you. He looks unusually well, a little stronger in every way, and younger than when he was here a few years ago. He has had the most astounding success, as you will learn from the papers, wherever he has been, although of course he has also received adverse criticism. You will have read his lecture which has been printed over and over again and will know that his great message to the west is one opposed to nationalism. He sees in the war the natural outcome of the selfishness of western organized life. His manner of delivery and the fervor with which he presents his ideas give him a kind of domination over his hearers that you would imagine Joan of Arc would have. I have been feeling that only a prophet walking through the various involved countries of Europe and speaking a divine word could avail to break up the war. I never had thought of Mr. Tagore in this connection, but when I saw what he was able to do I thought that he might be able to do even this great thing. He is never-the-less in some way dissatisfied or tired of the work that he has undertaken, and I hear from his secretary that he has cancelled all his dates after Christmas and is going to sail from San Francisco on the 7th of January.

He will be in Chicago for a day or two on his way west, and

132

when he comes I will get him to write his name in the new books and send them on to you. If he does go to Santa Fé perhaps I could go too and together we could visit for a few hours or a day or two. His going will not in the least depend upon my ability to go, and I almost venture to hope he might stop over to see you.

Nothing that I can say of Mr. Tagore is altogether adequate. He is himself inexpressible and in many ways more uplifting in his influence than ever, though perhaps a trifle less simple in his outer bearing. He has translated a few of his earlier plays, poetic dramas, which in their advocacy of peace and love might well have been written for the present hour. They will, I suppose, be published too. They may even now be going through the press. Since he went on to New York I have not heard very much from him. . . . .

Padraic Colum is visiting me and giving a few talks on the revolutionary poets whose posthumous poems he edited a short time ago. . . . . Lindsay was here for a couple of weeks the last of November. He was arranging for some dance interpretations[2] of a few of his poems, and gave a program in the Little Theatre and one in Mandel Hall. These programs were speculatively received with a strange mixture of challenge and affection. I can hardly say whether they were successful or not, but they interested me. . . . . Alice Harriet is growing to be a big girl and is saying the only clever things ever said by a little girl of three and a half. Just as your little Alice did, and all other little boys and girls have done since the world began. She is wearing a fur suit and looks quite grown up.

Earlier, she began a letter to Mrs. Kennedy-Fraser by asking: "What knight was it who was so fit for his favorite cause in every way except that he could not raise his sword hand? I seem to be under the same kind of enchantment as regards my pen. It is the last thing I am able to 'take in hand.' "

This (1916) had been a year filled with happenings. But Harriet was not so absorbed by them that she could not find

[2] By Harriet's young friend Eleanor Dougherty, sister of Walter Hampden.

time to devote to the encouragement of a young American boy who wished to write poetry. This was Harold Hart Crane, of Cleveland, then only sixteen years old, who so impressed Harriet with his native capacity that she was largely responsible for his insisting, in spite of family discouragements, on adopting poetry as a career.

In March she had written to Marion MacKaye: "On my way home from New York I stopped in Cleveland and there discovered a young boy (this time a rich one) who interested me exceedingly. He is about the age of Robin,[3] deeply absorbed in poetry, writing some himself, and getting ready for Harvard. He is, I believe, in his last year in the high school. . . . .

"This lad is Harold Crane, the son of Clarence A. Crane, manufacturer of . . . . chocolates."

And at the same time she wrote to the young poet himself: "Both the mood and the pictures of your *Nocturne* seem to be very true. The realization in phrase is not quite equal in quality, it seems to me, to . . . . the verse melody and the mood. I have a deep conviction that you are following the real right lead for you in giving all to poetry.

". . . . I shall be glad to have you write me whenever you feel like it, and whenever anything comes to me that I think would interest you, I will send it to you."

The friendly association with young Crane, and critical help in regard to his writing, continued through his earlier years, and when he went to New York to seek his poetic fortune, he was still more or less under Harriet's aegis and came equipped with letters to her friends.

[3] The MacKayes' son, Robert.

134

CHAPTER XIV

ROBERT FROST—W. W. GIBSON

ROBERT FROST had now become a compelling figure. Harriet had been more and more clearly sensing his quality from the time he returned from England and published *North of Boston*, so that she was fully ready to respond when, in January of 1917, Eunice Tietjens, poet and coeditor of *Poetry*, asked her help in arranging for Frost to come to Chicago. Springing to the opportunity, Harriet wrote Mrs. Tietjens that the Woman's Club would be glad to hear Mr. Frost in February. "I shall be working diligently," she said, "to find something else for him at that time." Her diligence was, as usual, effective. Later she wrote the poet of the engagements she had obtained for him and invited him to be her guest.

Though Harriet was, naturally enough, a somewhat different woman to each poet who became her friend—a disciple to Tagore, a Cordelia to Lindsay, and so on—she was most completely herself with those who had the gifts of humor and gaiety. It was their sharing of these live elements of companionship that had strengthened the bond between herself and Moody before illness had sobered him—and her, likewise. When he would come to Groveland Avenue in the years before their marriage, they would often spend entire evenings sitting together on the swing, absorbed in lively, laughing talk and seeming not to know that other persons often passed through the room. A quiet member of the household, who had often noted this, was asked outright what sort of thing these two talked about.

"Oh, it was all fantasy," she said. "They would follow one whimsey to its end, then seize upon another. And they were universes away from the rest of us." . . . .

Both Padraic Colum and Ridgely Torrence had made strong appeal to Harriet's affection because of their natural buoyancy, thus helping to restore a quality in her that had been partly dormant for several years before she knew them. Now Robert Frost proved to be another poet after her own heart. They understood each other at a glance, and Frost's playful extravagances in familiar talk delighted her. The friendship then promptly sealed remained firm through Harriet's lifetime.

Frost's Chicago visit was, after all, not made until March. A letter that he sent her from Franconia, New Hampshire, in August, shows at what an excellent understanding they had arrived. The step that he lightly pretends he had hoped to be dissuaded from taking was, of course, his affiliation with Amherst College—Harriet having naturally suggested, with Moody's experience in mind, that college work limited a poet's necessary freedom. He wrote, on August 12, 1917:

DEAR MRS. MOODY:

Unless I put off writing a while longer I can no longer conceal from you that when you are in West Cummington and we are in Franconia the distance that separates us is almost hopeless. It is not for a practical-poetical like me to teach geography to a poetical-practical like you, but by the map I should say that one of us would have to set at naught some two hundred miles to reach the other. (Let it be said in contradiction that they are beautiful miles.) It seems to me you ought to be the one to do the setting at naught—you with your automobile and your superannuated horses.[1] . . . .

I require of you that you shall come [to Franconia] as an act penitential for not having come to West Cummington before we left Amherst and for probably not intending to stay in West Cummington till we get back to Amherst. I am past the help I particularly wanted of you in June, namely, advice against a step I was about to take, because I have taken the step. There is nothing left but to help me not to think too hardly of myself. Come and give me that.

[1] Those that Mrs. Tilden had used.

No, but you will come, won't you?

And I will tell you when I see you how much I care for Will Moody's poetry. Just rough enough with beauty to show a man's assurance that beauty can't get along without him.

Always sincerely yours,
ROBERT FROST

And, two weeks later, on September 2, he wrote again:

DEAR MRS. MOODY:

All hearts are set on Thanksgiving with you at West Cummington. Here's looking forward!

And if you think you could stand me twice in the same winter, get me the readings in Chicago. They would have to be crowded into short space. I mustn't be away from my college long. I should be grateful for the break in the college winter, however, and I can't say I should object to the extra money to pay my wartime expenses.

A few more favors like these and you will have earned the right to come right out and scold me for having tied up with Amherst. I wonder if I have made a very great mistake. It can't be a great mistake when I can so easily undo it. Don't think too discouragingly of me or I shall feel the depression even at this distance and even though you don't speak.

Do you make out just what the name of the place in West Malvern is where Wilfrid abides? Print it on a postcard for me, if you do, and end my perplexity. I didn't pay attention when Wilfrid said it and he writes it as badly as some people write poetry.

Always sincerely yours,
ROBERT FROST

The "Wilfrid" mentioned in this letter is the English poet Wilfrid Wilson Gibson, whom Frost had known well during his two years' stay in England and who had recently come to this country to give readings, bringing with him a letter of introduction to Harriet from Mrs. Kennedy-Fraser. His first visit at Harriet's house, in February, 1917, where he renewed his acquaintance with Frost, proved a permanently gratifying success.

Shortly after he left, Harriet wrote Alice Corbin Henderson: "We have just had a very happy visit with Wilfrid Gibson, who seems to me one of the most real people..... I suppose you have had Mr. Gibson's books and maybe you like them and maybe you don't. To me .... the quality of his thought and the general impartment of his being are in many ways very suggestive of Will. He is coming back here to spend a few weeks."

And she adds: "When I was in New York in January I saw the first production of the revival of *The Great Divide*..... After the play began there was no doubt about its success..... All the comments of the newspapers were as long and as sympathetic as if the play had never been seen in New York before, and I understand it is still running on there, with great success."

Frequent letters came from Lindsay in the next few months. One written from Springfield on April 8 shows him troubled by the war, by his own possible part in it, and by the bogy of matrimony.

MY DEAR CORDELIA[2]

No doubt this is the resurrection hour, for it is one minute after midnight—Easter morning. Yet I am thinking of death, not of life. I am thinking if I died tomorrow by any sudden accident, I would say with my last breath I had had far more than I deserved or expected or could hold of the joys and privileges of living, and I would say it if I died by burning alive, and I would say

> Who has given to me this sweet
> And given my brother dust to eat,
> And when does his wage come in?[3]

It is as strange an Easter as the world has ever faced, and it is shameful not to realize its irony, and it will be a pity if any one makes of it a sanctified nominal Easter. It is an Easter in which

[2] Lindsay's usual form of address to Harriet; from then on.

[3] From William Vaughn Moody's poem "Gloucester Moors."

138

to hold one's breath. I cannot think of the resurrection but of the cannon fodder—that is and that may be. I wonder how many that die today can look back happily—and say they have not been cheated? It may seem strange—but I feel tonight that my life has been full even without the satisfied fire of which Mrs. Browning writes in her sonnets. I have always been haunted by the notion of a sibylline princess of her sort—somewhere at the end of the road. Yet I doubt if I will ever be more than a brother with such a one. My very few bonfires have been built by women of another sort. Way back in my soul I have felt that my north star did not guarantee me much in the world of passion. My writing destiny seems so absurdly clear and simple and steadily developing—in a slow year by year way. I have always felt I would pay for it finally by a smash-up in no way connected with my ink-bottle—probably some unusually bad luck in love, and my luck has not been especially good. It has been a sort of intermittent farce; a joke that was all on me, if I forget the mere agonies, when the mortal self was racked.

Why should I trade my most secure star for my most insecure one? I cannot bear the idea of selling my pen for one day—no, not for Juliet herself. And I know of no Juliet but would want me to trade it for a hat or a Ford, sooner or later—which is quite proper—but I could not endure it. I would feel much more justified in enlisting—with all my doubts about war. I still love Tolstoy more than any dream of Juliet, and even American war more than any such fancy.

Why should I write this to you? Because my Mama is at me to get married to most anybody that is decent and proper, as it is proper a Mama should, with a youth of thirty-seven on her hands. While not intense about it—she is perfectly frank—and argues the economics with me—offers me the house, etc. But really it is not the house. I really haven't met Mrs. Browning and if I did, I have so much more faith in my ink-bottle than my heart's luck that I would not give Mrs. Browning a very good chance to write her sonnets. They all want to be wooed so. They want you to swear by high heaven you will have them or die. Then perhaps they will look you over. I would infinitely prefer they would do the swearing. A lady bold enough to take the risk might grab me, if she would state her case in plain terms, like Queen Victoria. But such a suggestion seems so outlandish to them, I do not dare offer it in sober terms.

Well—in one year, you may see me doing my duty in the trenches of Mexico or somewhere and I will be paying dearly for my independence! Ought I to go to Belgium with Roosevelt? I have lived long enough—and had more than my share. Tell me what? Ought I to enlist?

With love,
VACHEL

Before he wrote the next letter (on May 11, 1917) Lindsay had seen Harriet and now gratefully reveals the extent to which she had been able to soothe his nervous dread.

My DEAR CORDELIA:

Yesterday I typewrote the Booker Washington Trilogy (for book publication in some far day), and incorporated all the changes worked out in your parlor, and the whole thing came back and I enjoyed it again, and the crown Eleanor[4] made me, that I keep hung in sight, looked gay again.

When I realize what chunks of your time I took, and how boundless and sympathetic was your hospitality, I must thank you all over again. I have taken you too much for granted, like the sun and the stars. I have let you do me endless good, hardly realizing you were doing it.

And I appreciate your advice on the war. I cannot come to your farm this summer, since I must be in or quite near Springfield for several family reasons. I will try to help some of my Sangamon County friends to harvest.

. . . . The plans for my writing this year begin to fall into more attractive form. The Golden Book of Springfield progresses. It will be nearly all prose, and I wish to make it a book better prepared and with more driving power than anything heretofore done. And by the simple method of taking more time, and pouring into the hopper a tableful of notes I have accumulated for four years, I may get the cumulative quality I covet—more

[4] Eleanor Dougherty.

140

than in other writing of mine, perhaps. But this involves fastidious and prolonged selective revision.

Anyhow I have just discovered a method of using endless accumulated material that has put me in good humor with myself. It will be the longest hardest drive I have ever made on a book, and this summer I want to harvest for my country's sake. But aside from harvesting, this is my work, and I will be able to fight "these times" behind this barricade—I hope—this barricade of notes! This barricade of serener years!

This evening I saw a lovely annual dancing exhibition by the Y.W.C.A. It was as good as the daisy fields. It is really the rallying point for all the serious dancers of the amateur sort among the patrons, and as pretty and well costumed and unconscious a home-talent affair as one would wish to see. Exceedingly wholesome. They serve Jesus better than they used to. It is a part of my pride that my missionary sister was the original projector of this Y.W.C.A. Now they fill an arsenal with lovely dancers, innocently taught.

Your letter is in my mind—but it is too late at night to shake up the room hunting it. Thank you indeed for it. The substance of it is in the back of my head.

My love to you all. If little Miss Lovett[5] ever dances for you, give her my most respectful good wishes. I thought of her tonight—seeing so many children her age doing their prettiest. "Spring came on forever," said the Chinese Nightingale. . . . . .

The world does not seem like such a desert or a hell-hole tonight. Here I am behind a fragile barricade of dusty papers— and feel as well defended as if they were endless entrenchments. They read like a novel, it has been so long since I looked them over.

I am discovering on my table endless notes and projects that I had clean forgotten. My table is as exciting as Grandmother's proverbial attic.

God bless you, Cordelia.

From
VACHEL

[5] Ruth, the younger daughter of Robert Morss Lovett.

141

In a third letter, written June 7, Lindsay shows himself brooding, as he so often did, on the horrors of lynching and brooding also on the personal protest he might ultimately feel compelled to make. Also, the passage in which he expresses his personal devotion to Harriet is striking in its sincerity.

. . . . Let me tell you of a virtuous act of mine. When that black was burned to death in Memphis on hearsay without trial, I printed my protest in the local paper—and sent fifty copies of the protest out to what might be called my literary dragnet. That is, I sent out twenty-five copies to my dragnet among the editors and the other twenty-five to editors of Southern papers. As a result I know I prompted at least five editorials along the line of my clipping and there are more coming.

Put it down in your memory, my dear Cordelia, that some day I may die for the nigger. Sometime when they want to burn one without trial, I intend to climb on the pyre in his place, or with him. If I go to the trouble to make such a protest, I hope you will see to it that the point of the protest is not lost. As a matter of fact, I value my carcass and hope if I have to give it up in any cause—every bit of the sacrifice will be strategic. I know this is egotism. But I made up my mind long ago to protest against burnings alive for all there was in me. I haven't the least doubt that some day I will have the complete chance to protest. These things represent the margins of our savagery—and the battle must always be fought on the margin, if it is to be won for democracy.

Dear Cordelia—I want you to know you are a real person to me, fighting your great life through. I know you have many friends of life-long faithfulness and that others pass by you in a slow procession and you find in two or three years they are somewhere else. I hope you will never find me somewhere else. I hope you will think of me here at my desk as one who wants to please you. If other people turn up oftener, I think you will find as years pass, I at least come around in due season.

I have just typewritten seventy-five more pages to go into the back of a new edition of the Congo—everything I have recited

142

for the last three years. Eleanor shall have her paragraph in the poem-game section. Also I have two boxes of papers on the Golden Book of Springfield, that I hope this time next year will be a book. If the war goes on, I fancy that this time next year I will be drafted. The present draft of ten million will give four armies of five hundred thousand, I would guess. Then there would have to be another registration of men 30–40. And I would be 38. So I give myself one more year of writing, harvesting, reciting, etc. and assume I will be drafted next June. If I get the Golden Book done, I will be pretty well satisfied, I assure you. But I would rather make my choice of deaths—and die for the nigger. I am quite sure they need it.

Well—well I didn't know what I was going to say, when I took my pen in hand, except to send my good will. I hope I have done that.

My love to everyone,
VACHEL

By this time the friendship with Wilfrid Gibson had progressed to the point of close understanding. On leaving the country, he wrote Harriet on June 18, 1917:

DEAR HARRIET:

We parted very hastily after all at the last moment, and I am afraid I took a very unceremonious leave of you! (and I didn't say "Good bye" at all to Miss Moody, to whom my apologies!) But though I said nothing then and can say nothing now, I know you will understand just what my stay in Chicago meant to me. And it looks as if that really was to be a leavetaking. Everyone here advises me that it is just as safe to sail now as it will be for many months, or even years, to come. It appears that only about one per cent of the boats that sail from America are sunk and that the liners are sailing backward and forward regularly. An English naval officer who was here yesterday said that if I sailed at a time when there was no moon, there was really little risk. So it really looks as if I might as well chance it. Russell Loines is to get particulars on boats, and I expect I shall be sailing in a fortnight or three weeks.

*Well, you know just how much your sympathy and under-
standing has meant to me at this time—and how often and how
affectionately I shall think of my Chicago home.....And the
way you took my wife and baby to your heart means more to
me than I can say. You know I am always inarticulate, excepting
now and again in a poem, but you also must know that my
meeting with you has meant to me.....*

*It is very lovely here on a hill looking over woodlands to the
sea and the weather hot and bright. I suppose we shall next
meet in England, at Malvern, I hope—and the war over.....*

Good luck to you always!

> Yours, gratefully and affectionately,
>
> WILFRID

His journey accomplished, Gibson wrote her again:

> JOURNEY'S END, WEST MALVERN
> 27th July, 1917

DEAR HARRIET:

*Well, I am home, and it is real Journey's End! It took the
boat just twelve days to zig-zag its way across the Atlantic.
Though we escaped attack, we had an anxious time, as we
should have been a wonderful prize for the Germans. We carried one of the most valuable cargoes that has ever crossed the
Atlantic, and the passengers we carried made the voyage an
event in the history of America and England. I wish I could
give you the exciting details, but I don't want this letter to be
delayed by the censor.*

*I have been home just a week and America is already a dream
—but O! such a wonderful dream—a dream that must influence
all the rest of my life.....*

*The hills of home are even more wonderful than I remem-
bered them. I am writing this in my little attic workroom, and
gazing out between the sentences over fifty miles of rolling up-
land towards the Welsh mountains. I am writing it very badly
because I have been clipping the garden hedge all morning and
my hand is tired.*

144

We seem to be getting plenty of food. It is hideously dear—but the country is certainly not starving. I have let the military authorities know I am back, and I am now awaiting a summons for medical re-examination.

Well, when are you coming over to see us? I am afraid you will find our English hospitality very meagre and frigid in comparison with American—but you know it is our way—and you shall have as warm a welcome as we are capable of giving.....

Yours affectionately,

WILFRID

Harriet, for her part, had written (July 17) to Mrs. Kennedy-Fraser: "Wilfrid Gibson stayed with us quite a long time. I cannot tell you how deeply indebted I feel to you for having added this truly important episode to my life..... He became the friend of all of us, and we all loved him and parted with him with great regret."

A little earlier had come a letter from John Masefield:

OXFORD, ENGLAND, July 7, 1917

DEAR MRS. MOODY,

.... The time in France was very exciting and only occasionally very dangerous. I saw "the breaking up of the ice," when the enemy began really to fall back on the western front, and that was a most wonderful and unforgettable time, like nothing else in the world. Now I am rather out of things, in England again, doing my official work, and though it is interesting and pleasant work, it hasn't the color and romance of the army in France, nor the gaiety.

You will see that this is from a new address, which will be my permanent one now. It is up on a hill, close to the single elm tree mentioned in Matthew Arnold's poem of Thyrsis. There is a school of scoffers who say that the elm was an oak and has since been cut down, but I will not let anyone depreciate house values in this way.

There is just a chance that we may be coming to America again at the end of this year, though of course very much de-

pends on events. It will be splendid to see you again and to see how much the little girl has grown. I expect she is a big creature now. Please give her my love, if any dim trace of a memory of me remains with her.

If any of your friends are coming to England with American contingents, will you please let me know, so that I may look them up. I shall be here, and in London, with occasional visits to France, for the next few months, as far as I can see, and I would love to see your friends and welcome them after so much welcome from you.

All greetings and good wishes and blessings to you and all of your household.

Yours very sincerely,
JOHN MASEFIELD

And, at about the same time, the following note arrived from Omaha:

DEAR HARRIET MOODY,

> *From strong hills round about Omaha*
> *and singing bushes of prairie roses*
> *I send you a Sunday afternoon greeting.*
> *Luck and health to you.*

CARL SANDBURG

It had been a grief to Harriet to learn that Mr. Tagore had had "another serious attack" of illness on his way back to India, but later news had been reassuring. On July 17 she wrote Mr. Pearson, the poet's secretary, that she had heard Tagore was in the mountains. "I love to think of him . . . . in a place where his spiritual outlook will not be disturbed by . . . . rasping details . . . . which are so uncongenial to him and so unsuited to the serene majesty of his noble personality."

And to Mukul Dey, one of the young Hindus whom she had known through Mr. Tagore, she wrote: " . . . . Also I was glad that you stayed with the poet, prophet, our master. It is such a wonderful privilege, and you, naughty boy that you are, are dear to him. He needs that everyone who enters his life even in the slightest degree must always remain a part of it, and live as far as may be in accordance with his own inner harmony. I always try to be worthy of the great privilege of having joined his inner circle, and I am sure you are doing the same, and that this will prove one of the greatest inspirations of your whole life."

A department of Harriet's life which meant much to her during the years 1912–22 and to which she gave faithful and devoted attention was her trusteeship at Cornell. This summer, at the close of her first five-year term, she made her official report of what had been accomplished. It would seem beyond question that her work as trustee had been of significant value to the university and particularly to its women students, whom she considered that she represented and whose welfare she did much to advance.

In August, Harriet made her annual visit to Cummington, and Lindsay wrote her there.

MY DEAR CORDELIA:

.... The ten chapters of the Golden Book of Springfield— and that is all the chapters—are pretty well blocked out—the heavy work of arranging the book is over—and the main work now is the actual writing, which will consist of going over, rewriting Chapter one fifteen times—then Chapter two—and so on through ten. Then the whole book five times. Out April, 1918.

Next—I will be reading proof in a week or two on The Chinese Nightingale and other poems—out about Oct. 15, 1917, by the usual rate of speed. My publishers preferred a new book to my proposition of an enlarged Congo.

Finally—I have signed a contract with the Macmillan Company for a book of pen and ink drawings, to come out a year from September. How I will get them done, I do not know. Somebody will have to make me an artist again. I have not

147

drawn a line for seven years. The backbone of the book will be the drawings you have already seen. Yet Marsh asks me for one hundred drawings—a wonderful order, but I have me doubts!

You-all wait till the Golden Book of Springfield is done! The one object of that book is to make you sorry you were not born in Springfield, Illinois. With the most Jesuitical art, I accomplish the feat—see if I don't.

As soon as I finish this book I will be more reconciled to the possibility of being a soldier. The book represents six years of planning, and I just can't throw six years of that sort away. I may deceive myself, but I feel by next April I will be much more reconciled to stopping bullets, having uttered the main things suppressed. Then I will look around—and see if the war is over —and consult you—what to do.

I send my very best wishes to the Luther Shaws.[6] I make my deepest bow to Miss Moody and kiss her hand, acknowledging again her charming hospitality, which shines in my memory yet—and so helps to make this August a holiday. I can hear you all chattering—and send you as much of my heart as you choose to eat. View it as pound cake.

Very much yours,

Nicholas Vachel Lindsay

John Masefield wrote on September 11, reporting on his removal to Oxford:

Dear Mrs. Moody,

I've not been anywhere since I came here, and do not even know Oxford yet, nor any of the colleges; and I haven't been at Iffley. All these things must wait for the peace, which will, I should think, come suddenly, like the passing of typhus or yellow fever; one hour the patient is at the brink of death, in a very violent condition; and the next he is out of danger and the doctor is thinking himself rather a smarthead. It is the unexpected that happens in life. "The end men look for cometh not."

Always your sincerely,

John Masefield

[6] Caretakers of the West Cummington farm.

At the close of the year came a characteristic message from Robert Frost:

DEAR MRS. MOODY:

We get a sense from your pranks of your being all around us but at the same time invisible like a deus ex machina. (Do you know that I never noticed before that "the deuce" by which we swear is no more than the deus with the "eu" pronounced as in Zeus?) We meet someone who has met someone who has but just now seen you and heard you speak right here in Amherst. We hear you speak ourselves out of the empty air. We are fed by you with candy in a tin box like a bolt from the blue. We get your promise in writing that if we are good and have faith, our eyes shall some day (some day this winter) see a better land than this, namely Chicago—

"Where never wind blows loudly, but it lies" etc.

You know the rest—all that boastful Sandburgian, or should I say Burgundian, "with beaded bubbles winking at the brim." I suspect he was paid to do it by the Consolidated Real Estate Agencies to boom Chicago farms. And that was why he was winking. And you can tell him I said so.

But it is hard to have faith in these days when you can actually hear it preached from the pulpit that if those who have only one talent don't know enough to bury it themselves a committee of eugenists should bury it for them, and I own to a growing doubt whether you exist as a person at all, whether you may never have been anything more than a principle of good or evil whose promises aren't worth the paper they are written on.

Nevertheless, I am, I Profess,

> *Yours as faith-full as circumstances permit,*

> > PROFESSOR F.

CHAPTER XV

A SALON?—ROBERT NICHOLS

IF HARRIET ever had what many people like to call a *salon*, it was now (1918–19) at its height.

She herself would certainly have disliked to be known as a *salonière* and must at some time or other have said so. Indeed, her hospitality was so individual, so unimitative, that it would be a pity to apply a shopworn label to it, and, for the rare thing that it actually was, our language has not so far mustered an adequately descriptive term. What should be understood is that this hospitality was not a matter of mass arrangement. In every case, Harriet invited a person to her house because he had captured her interest or liking, because she saw in him significance or promise of significance—but never, of course, as contributor to any social design of her own. Nor did anyone recommend himself to her because of being a member of any group or because of having repute as an "intellectual," for Harriet distrusted such. Fusion among the persons she did invite she gave little thought to. That took care of itself and to such an extent that men and women who might not otherwise have dreamed of seeking each other out were afterward conscious of an inescapable bond in the mere fact of having shared in Harriet's friendship.

It is not important whether one name or another be applied to Harriet's nightly gatherings. But there is the question whether a *salon*, by definition, is obliged to occupy a given point in space; for the striking fact must be met that Harriet's *salon*, or whatever it may be called, was not limited, after all, by the walls of that unpretentious Chicago house that was thought of by so many as the very symbol of hospitality. The house had an unforgettable character of its own that Harriet

150

had given it, a character inseparable from hospitality of a sort both generous and distinguished. But she herself really occupied a personal territory of wide area. Its center shifted with her movements; that was all. A day after leaving Groveland Avenue cosharers of her territory would group themselves about her in New York. A week later the same thing would happen in London. The background seemed in her case to be almost negligible.

Anyone who has followed her story to this point will have realized that an almost inordinate capacity for warm, sustained interest in other human beings was this vital woman's supreme gift, accounting for all the directions that her life followed. Multiplying distractions, as the years went on, never lessened this urge. Nor was there any capriciousness in her friendships. She gave always with an understanding—on her own side—of permanence. Conscious within herself of more love in the large sense than she had outlets for, she had little understanding and sometimes little patience with emotional aridity or emotional parsimony in others.

A poet whom Harriet knew familiarly came to see her one day, complaining bitterly of his lot. He had no one to love, he told her; nor was he loved by anybody. His loneliness was intolerable.

"You poor fish and frog!" she burst out. "If you really had love in your heart, the first person you might meet as you went out in the street would suffice for you to pour your love upon. You do not know what love is!"

If Harriet herself had been a normally self-regarding person, who loved with prudence and gave with discretion, she would never have played the significant human role that must be attributed to her.

At the same time, a captious critic might take the view that this was a life wastefully lived. That is to say, Harriet squandered her gifts of mind and heart upon whoever might need them with the same magnificent recklessness with which she benevolently squandered her income when she had one. As she did not "budget" her material resources, except perhaps in

151

theory, neither did she thriftily apportion her affection or her deep human interest.

Indeed, it is rare enough that a person so equipped by nature pays so little heed to his own gifts. Not that she was in the least self-distrustful. But in some ways her ego asked unnaturally little. And self-interest can almost never have been the motive for any action of hers, which is certainly an extraordinary fact. Yet she remained as unaware as a child of the trend of her actions and would no more than a child have dreamed of analyzing her own motives or experiencing a complacent afterglow as the sequence to a feat of magnanimity. Her almost irrational unselfishness was the outcome of no contortions of conscience.

It goes without saying that at all seasons poets ranked highest in Harriet's hospitable concern and that among the poets themselves a natural hierarchy existed. As John Masefield stood high in the scale, it was a keen pleasure to Harriet that another visit to America brought him to her door again at the beginning of 1918. Their relationship was never close, and he always observed that barrier of formal address which was so lightly leaped, at her desire, not only by easy-going Americans, but—and one wonders how!—by many a Briton likewise. But his letters to her were always warm, sensitive and sincere, as, for instance, the following, sent from Des Moines on February 6, 1918, after he had left her house:

Dear Mrs. Moody,

It was a great pleasure to me to see you again after these two years, but I don't know how to thank you for all your kindness and thought for me during my stay with you. You gave me a very pleasant happy time, though Lord, when I think of it, it makes my heart ache to think of the flood of world which I brought into your quiet home. Thank you for your kindness, and for the great care with which you fenced me round.

I am afraid you are having a very sad and anxious year, with many personal anxieties as well as the troubles of the war. I hope so much that these personal troubles will soon pass, and the war, too, and that we may then meet again, here or in England, in a happier world. I hate to think that I came to give you so much added bother.

All greetings to you, and thanks, and to all the members of your household, all so kind to me.

Ever yours sincerely,

JOHN MASEFIELD

Another cherished experience, during the winter, was a brief visit from Robert Frost. So Harriet tried, when she went to her Cummington farm with Ridgely Torrence in May, to see Frost, who was then at Amherst, and to take up some of the threads which they had left suspended. Failing to meet him, she wrote him from Chicago about the misadventure and concluded her letter: "Having a desire to make you a present of the very best thing I can think of among all possible gifts, I hereby bestow upon you my three volumes of your books, which you carried off with you in such a conscienceless way. I have decided to give them to you in order to save you from the stigma of grand larceny."

In June he wrote her from Franconia, New Hampshire, as follows:

Don't you begin to see why I haven't written to you? I have been holding off for better terms. I wanted you to discover for yourself without being told what more was expected of you if we were to become old friends. Don't think I haven't appreciated your many kindnesses. The chance to visit you in Chicago, your wild attempts to visit us in Amherst, your promise to visit us in Franconia, the gift of the beautiful shirt, the gift of my own beautiful poems (complete in three volumes) which I may or may not accept—the gift of the Oxford Book of Verse, the acknowledgement that in looks at least I surpass ——— —all these are much but they are not enough. Add to them the acknowledgment that I can write a letter when I try and they are still not enough. They amount to no more than poor consolation for what you withhold. I am not a person

153

to be put off with consolation prizes. You must see that. Nothing short of two or three major concessions will satisfy me and I may as well name them here and now, though to be worth anything to my pride you should be first to name them. I half suspect your having shut your eyes to them on purpose. But you haven't, have you? You require to be shown what my demands are (at this very moment you are trying to guess what they are likely to be) but once you are shown I think you will not be backward in meeting them. Well, they are these two:

You must acknowledge that I am really and truly democratic as no Englishman is or can be.

You must acknowledge that I am a better poet than ———. He will do for the present. We can consider other poets I am better than, later. . . . . .

I shan't insist in your putting all this in writing where it might be used against you; you may come to Franconia and deliver it by word of mouth. But deliver it you must before I write you even a formal letter to say that I got safely home from Chicago and am now a sunburnt farmer with half my farm under my finger nails.

Remember me to any who haven't forgotten me.

Always sincerely yours,
Robert Frost

A trying summer followed. It can scarcely have been easy for Harriet to realize the climatic marvels in her own near-by Ohio of which Ridgely Torrence wrote her (from Xenia) at the close of June: "If Chicago has such skies as these today, the Lake must shine enchanted like a vast horizontal rainbow. This year's green seems to be uncommonly intense, a rain-intoxicated emerald like that of England, and scattered among these golden counties of ripe wheat, the effect is fair dazzling to the brain. As I stood with an old farmer at the top of a hill overlooking a valley of these paradisal summer splendors, he expressed our common emotion in these words: 'It looks almost like a kind of scenery.'"

Her brother Fred having suffered a slump in business because of the war, Harriet arranged that he, his wife, and the five-year-old Alice Harriet should spend the summer at the Cummington farm, she herself driving them there and fetching them home at the end of their visit. It is characteristic of Harriet that she, hard at work in the Chicago heat, which she heartily disliked, worried continually about the family that she had stowed away in the cool Berkshires, writing daily letters and so on by way of assuaging what she assumed to be the tedium of their exile. As the young niece continued to be the object of her immense devotion and the source of an almost maternal pride, reports that the child was "homesick" were a shock and disappointment. Later, she was correspondingly delighted to hear that Alice Harriet was learning to ride a horse. "I am glad for everything she dares," she wrote to the little girl's parents, "and confident that her daring will be to a good purpose sometime." Harriet herself had been a good horsewoman and was a supreme exemplar of fearlessness.

Meanwhile there had come from Mr. Tagore a letter that both disturbed and tantalized her. He wrote from Calcutta, on May 13, 1918:

My dear Friend,

I thought I would startle you one fine morning in June by presenting myself at your door and quite naturally taking my seat at your breakfast table. I had engaged my passage, packing was done, Rathi and Protima were ready to accompany me, when some newspaper cuttings from Japan informed me that there was a prosecution of some Hindus in San Francisco in which the prosecution counsel implicated me, saying that my last tour to America was undertaken at the instigation of the German Conspiration and my real motive was to join the revolutionist party. Such a sublime piece of invention took my breath away, the more so as the counsel said he had documentary evidence to support the charge. Evidently documents can be manufactured in the devil's own factory to support any charge whatever, and therefore for honest truth documents are naturally rare. What I can say against such incrimination can

155

only be oral, which can have effect upon people who already trust me. Unfortunately this is a time when people's minds are unsettled and their moods are unreliable. So after due deliberation I came to the conclusion that it was best for me to give up my visit to your country. For it is sure to be very unpleasant for me if there is the least possibility of misunderstanding and mistrust pursuing me while I am on your soil. There is something which is so undignified in this affair that it fills me with disgust. However, this unnatural state of things, prolific of monstrosities in all forms of untruth and injustice, cannot last forever. Therefore I still entertain hope of one day finding my way to your table, and enjoying a generous portion of your ice cream and your warmhearted friendliness.

With kindest regards to you,

Your affectionate friend,
RABINDRANATH TAGORE

There was never a year or perhaps even a month of her life when Harriet wasn't having some fruitful connection with one or with a score of the idealistic young creatures who persistently sought her out. It was in this year, 1918, that a group of students from the University used to come to her house to discuss poetry and to read aloud what they themselves had written. This was entirely on their own initiative, and Harriet merely played the part of auditor. As one of them afterward put it, "Harriet just let us come!" However, she had a definite personal interest in certain members of the group. One of them was Glenway Wescott, who had not yet written any fiction but in whose early verse Harriet saw something original and promising. Another was young Kathleen Foster, at that time Wescott's fiancée[1] and herself an experimenter in verse.

After his return to England, John Masefield, finding that a younger friend, the poet Robert Nichols, was about to go to

[1] The engagement was subsequently broken. The young girl later married Donald Campbell and continued to be a close friend of Harriet, as well as her staunch ally and support during the final disconsolate years. Her third daughter, happily born within Harriet's lifetime—and properly proud of her name—is Harriet Moody Campbell.

156

America, did a double service, as he rightly thought, by supplying the young man with a letter of introduction to Harriet. Having immediately written to invite Mr. Nichols to visit her, Harriet made a point of informing herself about his capacity as speaker. While in the East, she contrived to see and hear him and found his "an enthusiastic, graceful young fellow, with very good delivery." So she wrote to Cornell, recommending him and saying: "I am now keeping track of his dates."

After his Chicago visit, which came off in due course, Nichols wrote:

PITTSBURGH, PA., March 31, 1919

DEAR MRS. MOODY,

Forgive if this letter contains no sense but it is written under trying circumstances. I am in a pseudo-marble saloon, on all sides is a desert of leather and oak armchairs and acres of spittoons: using these are countless numbers of that god the Average Man—a coat, a bowler, a bag (at his feet), a cigar stump in his mouth, a vacuity in his eyes. The future of the world, we are informed, is in the hands of that individual—My God!

Thank you very much for an entrancing time; my behavior I admit was chequered—but so are my feelings at present. I have to forget my troubles at intervals by a solemn—or unsolemn—travesty of myself on another plane—i.e. feel like Hamlet—act like Pierrot-Pantaloon: Hamlet and P. P. arc cousins.

I had a bully time and like Chicago best of American cities so far.—Love to all.

Thank you so much, most long-suffering of hostesses.

Yours very sincerely,
ROBERT NICHOLS

Earlier, she had heard from Robert Frost, making the welcome promise of a visit.

AMHERST, MASS., March 19, 1919

DEAR MRS. MOODY,

(Still to keep to a mode of address that no one else of equal pretension to your friendship seems to use):

Though I'm not as well as I ought to be and there are other

157

obstacles in the way of our getting to Chicago to see you this spring, I am resolved to try to make it if only for a very short visit. You'll have to squeeze both the lectures into the one week, April 14–19 and leave me Tuesday the 15th free for a little talk I may do for some of the free verse gentry.

We'll talk over the summer school plans when I get there. It may be I had rather put off the summer school till a year from now. I could keep it (if it would keep) for something ahead to prolong life a moment if I should burst my bonds here as teacher and run wild again. I strain at these bonds all the time and of course they only cut deeper the more I strain. It might be a good thing if you mustered against our coming your religion, such as it is, to help me endure what I ought to endure for my sins and my family. You can tell me your idea of duty and I'll counter you with why I think nobody that talks round poetry all the time or likes to hear talk round poetry can ever write poetry or even properly read it for that matter. I suppose simply that it is the nature of God to have it so. It is not that generalizations from poetry are so wholly bad if they make themselves as it were spontaneously and after the fact. God has only made them fatal when they are used school fashion as the approach to poetry. The general notion having been laid down by the professor, it then becomes possible to enjoy the particular poem as an illustration of it or as a case under it and as nothing else.

But don't mistake my getting mad about it in your presence for getting mad at you. You may be as much to blame as you please for this or anything else, it will make no difference to me: I shall remain

Always your devoted friend,
ROBERT FROST

And Padraic Colum heralded his own and his wife's immediate coming:

NEW YORK CITY, 22nd May, 1919

DEAR HARRIET,

There are coming to Chicago two very good friends of mine, Mr. Clement Shorter, editor of the London Sphere, and Mr.

W. H. Massingham, editor of the London Nation. I told them you would see them and they are anxious to know you. Mr. Shorter particularly is very delightful (his wife by the way was an Irish poetess, Dora Sigerson Shorter, who died recently). Ask Sandburg and Lee Masters to meet them. Mr. Shorter has an introduction to Harriet Monroe.

And we—Mollie and I—shall be in Chicago the first week in June. I am going on to Colorado Springs to lecture there. If there are any lectures in Chicago, hold on to them for me.

PADRAIC

It cannot be said in the case of any of Harriet's English friends that they took her gracious reception of them for granted. Their letters themselves are sufficient evidence of that. On an unrecorded date in July, she notes, in another letter to Mrs. Kennedy-Fraser, a further pleasant happening: ". . . . Too bad you didn't see more of Wilfrid [Gibson]. I am very fond of him. I don't know whether he told you he had given me the great happiness of making their next child my godson. Through this kindness I am now made for the second time a god mother. My other godson is the child of Alfeo and Beatrice Faggi."[2]

Not long afterward came an interesting bulletin from the Hebrides:

LEWS CASTLE, STORNAWAY
3rd August, 1919

DEAR HARRIET,

Here we are in the extreme north of the Hebrides and we have been motoring, Patuffa and I, over great expanses of moorland, of deep blue hills and hills of Harris.

The folks are busy fetching home the peat for fuel, peat cut early in the year and now dry enough for stacking. And the young girls look so lovely in their dark petticoats, blue aprons reaching to the hem of their skirts, blue shortgowns (i.e. blouses) and blue kerchiefs bound about their heads and they carrying round-shaped creels on their backs held by a rope

---

[2] Italian-born Chicago sculptor and his American wife, who were Harriet's close friends.

coming round the shoulders across the chest. There is not another outstanding feature on the landscape—only the long white road curving its way to the hills between interminable downs of peat-moss and stacks of drying peat of a lovely dark brown, awaiting the harvest.

Then at times we see them moving homeward again from the temporary turf sheilings where they have been spending the last few weeks. And amongst their goods and chattels always an old-fashioned churn.

This is the last spot in Europe, I believe, where these summer migrations still persist. They not only fetch in the peat but they take the cattle with them to feed on the uplands. . . . .

MARJORY AND PATUFFA

For her own country refreshment Harriet motored as usual to the Cummington farm, taking her brother's family with her. From the farm she reported (on September 18) to her home in Chicago: ". . . . I had a graceful, incorrigible note from Robert Nichols, every sentence—as one might say—marked 'confidential' and 'strictly between ourselves,' though the Lord knows why.

". . . . The baby [six-year-old Alice Harriet] has pink in her cheeks and is as amusing a little rowdy as you could wish to see."

Her ear being always inclined toward India, Harriet at about this time heard news that did not seem greatly to surprise her. Mr. Tagore had renounced his title, a decoration of his personality to which Harriet, at least, had never attached great value. But she was concerned lest his action have an unfavorable effect in England. Indeed, her mind was never at ease where the Poet was concerned.

CHAPTER XVI

HOLLYWOOD

L IKE the traveler of sound equilibrium who is classed as a "good sailor" even on a heaving ship, Harriet adapted herself with astonishing poise and, in fact, with enjoyment to the violent changes that often replaced the routine of her Chicago life. Indeed, change was itself a part of this routine. During a good part of 1920, for instance, she was obliged to forsake personal and business interests in order to fill, theoretically at least, the post of consultant and supervisor while her husband's play, *The Faith Healer*, was being filmed at the Lasky studios in Hollywood. The situation was that Lasky, of the Famous Players–Lasky Corporation, had invited her to be present at the filming as the company's guest, with expenses paid. Harriet's desire was to work and contribute as much as she would be allowed to, but she did not yet know how circumscribed her role would be.

This play had been a beloved project of its author. It had failed on the stage. Harriet could hardly have helped feeling tenderly toward it. She could hardly have helped welcoming its reintroduction to the public, even through the medium of the motion picture. After dashing several times to New York for preliminary consultations and after the signing of the contract, she set out for the West in March, believing that the filming was to begin immediately. By a happy chance, Padraic Colum, whose wife was then in California, had the same goal; so Harriet was assured of one of the traveling companions whom she would most eagerly have chosen. On the train she worked on the scenario which she had been asked to write for *The Faith Healer*, and Mr. Colum helped her with her letters. The sense of haste, of pressure, was exhilarating. She was braced for immediate action.

161

It is true that *The Great Divide* had already been shown upon the screen, by the Lubin people, but this had been in the days of silent motion pictures, in 1917. Harriet had been fearful in regard to that early project. It had been the first step into an unknown territory. She had felt keenly her responsibility in turning over Moody's work to commercial agencies. In that case, however, she had by no means been invited to supervise the filming. The whole affair had been of a remoter character and its success only mediocre.

But she believed that she was now in a position to protect the play and its author and, also, that the whole matter could be speedily accomplished..

Once established in Hollywood, she was soon forced to shed her innocent misconceptions. Nothing happened, it seemed to her. Nobody did anything. She of course became usefully familiar with the milieu. But three weeks after her arrival she wrote that "nothing tangible has been accomplished." When, after two weeks more of what seemed almost complete inaction, the Home Delicacies urgently demanded her return, she was allowed to go home with the understanding that she would be back in the summer. Meanwhile, one important step had been achieved—the choosing of a cast. One of Harriet's former pupils (many of whom reappeared all through her life, always under happy circumstances) was scheduled to fill the leading role, that of Ulrich Michaelis, the Faith Healer. This was Milton Sills.

Hollywood left behind, one of her most urgent concerns, not only at that moment but during a large share of that year, had to do with Cornell. Holding the honorable post of membership in a committee appointed to choose a new president for the university, Harriet did not take this responsibility lightly. From the first she had a candidate of her own for whom she worked with energy and deep conviction. This was Vilhjalmur Stefansson, whom she saw as a man of originality, power, and distinction and whom she seems to have believed available. Discussing "the Stefansson situation," Ridgely Torrence wrote her at this

162

time: "The chance for Cornell to avail herself of him is such as comes most rarely to any institution and it seems to me that everything should be done to bring it about. If students are ever to be stimulated to think for themselves, then Stefansson is the man to do it. To think for oneself is to be a discoverer and Stefansson is a Discoverer par excellence."

But the situation resolved itself differently, and Mr. Stefansson did not become president of Cornell.

It wasn't surprising that Harriet made the return journey to Chicago in rather a dismal frame of mind. Her personal associations with Hollywood and Los Angeles, which she had known first during Moody's fatal illness, had been painfully revived. The climate was at all times unsympathetic to her. And she was now able to realize all the difficulties that lay ahead—the unwelcome concessions that at the very best she would have to make in regard to the screen version of the play.

In a letter written after her return, to Richard Offner, who had just given up his post as professor of art at the University of Chicago, she says: "It was a glance into a perfectly new world, a world in which time and space are obliterated and details emphasized and ignored in one and the same breath. I stayed there five weeks. In the middle of July I am going back again. It is a wonderful country. . . . . Enchanting, and to me quite rejectable. I don't know when I have felt more completely isolated or more lonely."

This loneliness she evidently did her best to avoid during the second Hollywood sojourn, beginning the middle of July, for she now took with her not only Edith Kellogg but also Charlotte Moody and Mrs. Frazee of Louisville, Charlotte's niece and a close associate of the Moody family.

Surrounded and fortified as she now was and with the domestic background of her own that was always important to her, for she and her companions were informally keeping house in a rented bungalow, Harriet made her usual prompt adjustment, reconciled herself to the vagaries of the studio personnel, and learned studio terminology.

Moreover, life under any conditions would have taken on a

163

radiance from Rathi Tagore's letter, which shortly reached her, confirming the fact that he, his father, and Protima were definitely to arrive in the autumn. Replying to this, she assured him: "I shall be back in the East before your approach and shall meet you in New York. Do let me know as long in advance as possible about your bookings."

The motion-picture studio was so near the bungalow that Harriet could walk back and forth. "She went faithfully to the studio every morning at nine," Edith Kellogg remembers, "conferred with the director and with the man who had the lead— Milton Sills. . . . . Adolph Menjou had the part of Mr. Littlefield, and a blond named Ann Forest that of Rhoda. . . . . I think she saw the entire play 'shot,' even to the parts made 'on location.' She also saw the 'rushes.' It was all very friendly and agreeable."

In August, Harriet wrote cheerfully to Ferdinand Schevill that "Will's beautiful Faith Healer" was being filmed. "We have a porch on which we sleep, Edith and I, undeterred by the fact that we lie almost precisely on the road[1] over which an incessant procession of motor-cars rushes. It is good to sleep out of doors. I wonder we don't all insist upon it the year round. . . . . I don't know whether you remember Milton Sills. He may even have been a pupil of yours. He is going to play Michaelis, and will do it well, I believe. The atmosphere is so replete with bank surplus . . . . and everybody so assumes that you have all the money in the world, I find it hard to keep from shrieking out that I am living on my last dollar from day to day. . . . .

"The inner shrine here is conducted by a round table of . . . . plutocrats. I can see them there, wagging their heads, while the activities of the studio are going on without, and betting on the probable intake of proposed stories. Some of the people longest in the studio have never seen Mr. Lasky to speak to him. . . . . I have myself reached a kind of aristocratic position by reason of the fact that I saw him and spoke with him first of all."

[1] Sunset Boulevard.

To Mrs. Henderson (Alice Corbin) she wrote in an earnest mood, the following:

DEAREST ALICE:

.... If you only could come out here for a few weeks I know you would be deeply interested. .... I have felt from the first that there is something far more important in the photo-play than is recognized by the "wise and prudent," but I do not think in the least they have struck their pace yet. I don't believe, for example, in the idea of making over another man's play or story, although we are doing it with the Faith Healer, I see in the screen plastic material or fabric on which a great dramatist could portray his vision much more immediately than by first putting it into phrase, and then striving to get it into voice and action, or onto the printed page. Now, the photo-play starts with what might be called a dead idea, because it has originated in one mind and another mind is trying, not any too piously, to express it. But if the creative artists should conceive his story in terms of the screen, it would be a different matter. It would be, as it were, plunging his hands in the very stream of life. You know how stupid a copy of a picture or a translation of a poem is.

The photo-play of today is such a thing; but it won't always be so. One of the things that excites my artistic passion is that the drama has always been hampered by delimiting considerations of "time" and "space" whereas the red blood of life running through it is the vital conception of "progress." The photo-play can shake off these old snake-skins of time and space and revel without artistic sacrilege in the primordial passion for progress. You know how the highest word of praise in France for a work of art is that "il marche." Well, the photo-play can, must and will march, like an untrammeled Pegasus.

I am convinced that the writer and director of a play must be one and the same person. And if one wants precedent for this, why consider how Shakespeare wrote his plays, fairly sitting on the stage. You see how absorbed I am in all this.

For your part, it is just the place for you; and you and Willy

165

would make an incomparable team for writing and producing living things, with living models. A great artist must see the screen as his medium, I repeat, and produce his composite work with living models. The camera is a marvellous coadjutor, catching the nuance of inspiration as it springs into being in the mind of the actor who is portraying a part. "Something too much of this!" . . . .

Hollywood's Community Theatre, which was, of course, quite distinct from the motion-picture industry, was a refreshing resort for Harriet during these long weeks, and she was delighted when it successfully presented Ridgely Torrence's Negro play, *The Rider of Dreams*, in one of the frequent revivals following its Broadway run in 1917. Her strongly sympathetic interest in the Negro race, manifested so often in her life, would have drawn her to this play even if she hadn't valued it as drama—or even if she hadn't had close friendship with the playwright.

Among Harriet's guests during this summer was an old friend, Mrs. Ella Ayres, who made a stay of several weeks. In October, some time after Mrs. Ayres' departure, Harriet wrote her, noting that she had moved to another bungalow and reporting on a remarkable instance of mob psychology, many ailing onlookers at the filming of *The Faith Healer* seeming to believe that they themselves might be healed.

"Behind us," Harriet writes, "lives a lady afflicted with various kinds of mild mania. She has 22 Angora cats, professes to some form of spiritualism, and is a painter of poor pictures. The twenty-two cats having some charm for me, I suggested on our first interview the possible exchange of a young and inconspicuous cat for a reasonable sum of money. But it turned out that she had not a single cat too many, and only feared her cat increase might not keep pace with her desires. She is, however, a good poor thing, and rather diverting to talk to.

"All last week we were on the ranch doing out-of-door crowd scenes. I wish I had it in my power to describe the varied excitement this has afforded me. Four hundred people gathered around the exterior of the Beeler house on the Lasky ranch. The exterior is as independent of the interior as the interior you saw was of the exterior. A ten foot porch on about four foot elevation from the ground runs along the entire fifty or sixty feet of the outside front of this house, and gathered around the front of this or drilling around the sides of it or off into the dusky oak forest by the side of it, these people come to be photographed in long-shots and close-ups. They represent every nationality and every possible kind of experience. Among them are the soldiers that we saw at the ball. There are many really sick and many not at all sick who seem sicker than the sick ones. They are operated on by a kind of religious fervor, and many of the sick ones are believing they will be healed in the course of the play. It is a very fatiguing experience, but one of the most incredible interest. I only wish you could have seen it."

From England, whither he had gone that summer, Vachel Lindsay had written her a good deal less confidently than when on American soil, so Harriet replied to him, as often, maternally: "And you have been in London and have not quite liked it, apparently. How terribly too bad! You have only to go out to Oxford and present yourself at Boar's Hill to find our wonderful friend and your true admirer, John Masefield, and begin to love yourself again. Or, take a train and go to Malvern to find Wilfrid Gibson and another loving friend of your own as well as mine. Or a single night would bring you to Edinburgh and the Kennedy-Frasers.

"What has become of Robert Nichols and his enthusiasm and determination to present you to your British public? . . . . I only wish I were to be there in London and knock about the old town a bit with you."

As always, whatever her other preoccupations, she was deeply concerned with the welfare of young Alice Harriet, now seven years old. Writing her brother, who had spoken of choosing a school for the child, she said: "I hereby enter my protest, which I fear will not have much weight. Why not let her have modern language work this winter and go on with her music? Those are

167

things she can't get later. School is like hoeing corn—you can always hoe corn when you want to, though I don't see why anyone particularly should."

This view, although her colleagues on the Board of Trustees of a great university might not all have shared it, was the considered opinion of a wise woman and a distinguished teacher. To her surprise, perhaps, her advice did prevail in the Tilden family. Alice Harriet was not submitted to the traditional school routine until several years later.

Mindful, too, of what she considered her own obligations, Harriet, although half a continent away from home, accomplished a good deal of long-distance hospitality. She had asked Miss O'Neill to arrange a farewell party for Charles Squire, who was coming to California, and wrote from 6319 Sunset Boulevard: "It makes me happy that so loving a party is to be held at our house. . . . . If you get this before the party, diffuse my love as well as your own into the general atmosphere. . . . .

If Mme. Oda Nielsen presents herself at the house, either personally or by letter of introduction, offer her anything we have—the suite, if she cares to stay with us, the car, when she needs it, etc. And give her my most cordial greetings. Paul Leyssac[2] introduced her to me. She is said to be the greatest living actress of Denmark."

The months spent in Hollywood might have been considerably prolonged if, at the beginning of November, Harriet had not been called home by what seemed, and in fact was, her brother's grave illness. The telegrams received en route were increasingly encouraging, however; and when Harriet arrived in Chicago, he met her at the train. The attack he had suffered was a precursor of others, increasingly serious.

So, to Harriet's great disappointment, the picture was finished without her, as the management did not accept her offer to return at her own expense.

No sooner was she back in Chicago than she had the pleasure of receiving another book dedicated to her, together with an explanatory letter from its author, Padraic Colum. Mr. Colum wrote (from New York, on November 7): "Every day for the

[2] Famous Danish actor and Hans Christian Andersen interpreter.

last two weeks I have been expecting that your book would be out—the Eddas with the dedication to you—and I wanted to send it on as I wrote. But there has been delay after delay. At last it is out, and I am sending it on. It looks nice, and I hope you'll like it. And I'm glad to have a book out with your name to it. I have another book coming out in about two weeks—*The Boy Apprenticed to an Enchanter*, and I'm going to send on a first copy to Alice Harriet. I hope I'll be with you to read some of it to you. You'll find in this envelope some poems of mine.

"Well, and how has everything been with you since? How about California? Have they come down to business with you? And did you have a good holiday out there? I hope that you have had the best. I haven't been able to find Ridgely since I came to New York, and I wish he was back here. I am sending you a poem of his that was in *The Dial*.

"'Well, you'll be asking what's the news with us? We've had great trouble in getting settled down in New York, but the trouble's over, and we like where we're fixed. We've been very saddened by affairs at home. All the same, I've been in a good vein of work, and I've written some things I like. They want me out to lecture in Grand Rapids and of course I'll be in on you in Chicago on my way.

"I've read Masefield's *Enslaved* and I should like to talk with you about it. There's a fervour about some of the poems that sweeps me along. It's the idea in *Enslaved* and *The Hounds of Hell* that wins me."

There had been advantages in Harriet's enforced abandonment of Hollywood. Her first move was to hurry to Ithaca, where she was to meet the committee that was to choose a new president for Cornell. This duty prevented her from standing reverentially on the dock to meet the Tagores' incoming ship, but she went to New York as soon as possible, and another of those reunions with the Indian family, that in reality always seemed to exceed even Harriet's expectations, joyfully took place. It was, of course, arranged that the Tagores should come to Chicago, as, later on, they did.

Afterward, from Chicago, on November 20, Harriet wrote

to Charles Squire, whom she had left behind in California: "Mr. Tagore . . . . is truly wonderful at the present moment. He is here with a series of ideas to present on the possibility of establishing independent nationalism without violence. He also has a lecture on the relation of poetry to religion, which I have not heard. His nationalism lecture I did hear and it was very inspiring. Tagore's real mission, however, is to enlist western interest in the founding of a Pan-Asiatic University in which all western students of eastern affairs can be educated, as well as all easterners. His idea is very big and it seems to have been favorably received in Europe.

"I introduced him to Faggi and took him to Faggi's studio. He was quite bowled over by Faggi's work and is to allow Alfeo to make a bust of himself. This I feel to be an event of international importance."

To her old friend Dr. Martin Fischer, who was now taking his turn at dedicating a book to her, she wrote, on the same date:

DEAREST MARTIN,

I feel very happy, very much honored, and in every way overjoyed with the thought that you will inscribe your book to me. It is one of the things that can be done by one person in this world to enrich the life of another permanently, and I shall always cherish this from you.

Neither Hollywood nor anything else could really displace poetry from Harriet's life, but certain sacrifices were naturally entailed by the two California visits. One of these was the missing of a visit, in April, from Siegfried Sassoon, the English poet. Another was the forfeiting of her usual summer visit to Cummington, which nowadays included the hope of a glimpse of Robert Frost. Frost had written her in June from Franconia:

MY DEAR HARRIET MOODY:

I never forget old friends: so you needn't be so reproachfully silent about it. What keeps me from writing to them is that I forget their street numbers. Why don't you live decently in a small town where you don't need a street number to be found?

170

It goes against me to have to write a letter as I write this with-out knowing where it's going to and what's to come of it. I only do it to be able to say I have done my duty.

I wonder if you are wondering off there what I have decided about the farm at West Cummington. How shall I decide about anything at my age. I have kicked myself out of Amherst with some finality. But perhaps you haven't heard what I have been doing. For the moment I have ceased from teaching for-ever or until I shall begin to grow hungry again for food. Manly has asked if I will give a course in prosody some term at Chicago. That would be, not next year, but the year after, as I under-stand it, by which time I ought to grow hungry again for food (as distinguished from truth). So I shall probably take him up, though as yet I haven't given him his answer any more than I have you yours about the farm.

To be right, the farm at West Cummington would have to give us a summer and winter house of not less than nine rooms and a high school within two miles. I'm afraid it can't be made out or made to do either. And it seems a pity. I'm particularly sorry because I don't see but that it makes it necessary for you to sell there and buy a sugar orchard farm somewhere in New Hampshire or Vermont with us where we can all go into the fancy sugar business together.

If this seems to offend against friendship, please remember that I should probably see more of you in one term of lecturing at Chicago than in a cycle of farming at West Cummington. Really now, shouldn't I?

And if you are still unplaced, here are a few poems in manuscript enclosed to make a bad matter worse.

Are you coming this way this summer?

Always yours faithfully,
ROBERT FROST

This suggestion she had had, of course, to set aside.

In spite of her absences in California, Harriet had within the year admitted to her circle of friendship Yone Noguchi, the Jap-anese poet, who earlier had spent much time in this country

171

and had many literary and personal connections here. "We have liked him well," she reported at the close of his first visit. "He is an inspiration to me."

Now in December she was again busy securing engagements for another young English poet who had just paid her a visit— and who was to become a permanent resident of America— Theodore Maynard. In writing about him to various colleges she was able to describe him as "a poet of very rare gifts." In England, Mr. Maynard had been closely associated with Gilbert Chesterton and had had a connection with the *New Witness*. Harriet immediately adopted him.

Writing this new poet from Chicago on December 20, she speaks of having had a "marvellous three days in New York with Mr. Tagore. He is full of enthusiasm for his projected international university and spent what time we had together pointing out to me the reaction toward universal brotherhood that might be expected from it. His is a great personality. It always move me deeply."

In this letter, too, Harriet mentions that she has recently learned of Madame Curie's need of radium. It must, therefore, have been at this time that she was inspired to make her own suggestion (for which she has never been given public credit) that the money be obtained by making an appeal to the women of America.

Before making the promised visit to Chicago, Mr. Tagore sent her, no doubt as a Christmas observance, the following:

GAMA FARMS, NAPANOCH, NEW YORK
Dec. 23, 1920

DEAR FRIEND,

I am sending you, with the greeting of my love and good wishes, a translation of my poem as a gift of one who has carried home across the sea the memory of your friendship as one of the best boons that your country has given him.

Affectionately yours,
RABINDRANATH TAGORE

172

Give me the supreme courage of love,—that is my prayer,
 the courage to speak, to do, to suffer at Thy will,
 to leave all things or be left alone.
Strengthen me on errands of danger,
 honor me with pain, and help me to climb to that
 difficult mood which sacrifices daily to Thee.
Give me the supreme confidence of love, this is my prayer,—
 the confidence that belongs to life in death,
 to victory in defeat, to the power hidden in frailest beauty,
 to that dignity in pain which accepts hurt but disdains to
 return it.

RABINDRANATH TAGORE

The tantalizing fact that she had been obliged to miss seeing
Robert Frost all through the year was emphasized by a very
Frostian letter that came from him as the year closed.

SOUTH SHAFTSBURY, VERMONT
December 28, 1920

DEAR MRS. MOODY:

If some things seem providential, what have you to say to
the way we managed to miss each other in New York? Blas-
pheme not, you say, and I won't. But it is as permissible I hope
to see design in things when they go wrong as when they go
right.

I had fully meant to get round to Henry Holt's office before
I caught my train for Vermont. If I had got round and heard
that Padraic had been looking for me of course I wouldn't be
here now: I would have been staying on in New York to talk
over with you our apples not of discord but of harmony. I had
never a suspicion that you would be where I could see you. I
had tried twice to get the Torrences by telephone on the off
chance that they might be back from Ohio. Not having much
hope, I gave up too easily. And now look at how blank the
months stretch ahead of us before we can possibly meet.

True, I shall be in New York again toward the 20th of February, if that is anything to you.

173

I have half a mind to accept the invitation of the Press Club in Des Moines to read to it on a date in January for the chance it would give me to look in on you in passing through Chicago.

You want to talk about farms and I do, for all I have invested in a farm and old stone (palaeolithic) house of some charm here just out of Bennington. To you alone I will confess I am still looking for a home. I may settle down and like this place. My present agony may be homesickness for the home I've left behind me rather than for the home that never was on land or sea. Something unusual is the matter with me so that I can do nothing but write poems, plays and novels. I'm never so serious as when I'm in earnest. There must have been a reason for our missing each other so dramatically, and it may have been to keep me from saying anything against this farm which I may live to be sorry for. I never saw a solitary fault in anything I owned before. Such is my loyalty. And I shall not begin at this late day. Things I have disowned are another matter.

In witness that I haven't disowned you or your household permit me to sign myself

Yours respectfully,

ROBERT FROST

CHAPTER XVII

"PASTURES NEW"

ALMOST by accident, Harriet started, late in 1920, an entirely new enterprise. Some women interested in charitable affairs had rented a floor at 615 North Michigan Avenue for a bazaar and later, having no further use for this considerable space, suggested to Harriet that she take it over. She did so and immediately decided to test still further her creative energy and resourcefulness by bringing into being not the conventionally insipid "tearoom" through which women too often express themselves but a legitimate restaurant to which she gave the name of "Au Petit Gourmet." With the setting that she arranged and the incomparable food that she supplied, this became, and remained, a success.

For Harriet, a merely commercial triumph was an arid sort of gratification, tantalizingly incomplete. Straightway there was an urge within her to get some human satisfaction out of the place. She saw that by making use of its scene and its equipment she could provide a hearing, and perhaps cash as well, for even the lesser among her migrant poets. So began that series of poetry evenings which continued through several winters and in which there figured most American poets of note except those who, like E. A. Robinson, never left the Atlantic seaboard. Casting about for a name for her new forum, Harriet recalled the celebrated Jeux Floraux[1] of Provence. With the

[1] The Académie des Jeux Floraux was founded by troubadours at Toulouse in 1323. Yearly prizes in the form of gold and silver flowers—violet, eglantine, amaranth—were awarded to the best poems written in the langue d'oc. After the Jeux were reorganized in 1694, only poems written in French were allowed to compete. Suppressed in 1790, the Académie was re-established in 1806 and then reorganized as the oldest literary organization in Europe.

addition merely of a diminutive, the recitals were appropriately and charmingly known as "Les Petits Jeux Floraux."

On the appointed Sunday evenings, tables were removed from the largest room and chairs were set about an open fire. An admission fee of a dollar was charged, and all the money taken in was turned over to the poet who read. At the close of the reading there was informal talk in which the poet joined, while Harriet's irrepressible hospitality prompted her to serve coffee, chocolate, and accompaniments. These affairs turned out happily both for poets and for their audiences, and certain ones—Robert Frost, Vachel Lindsay, Carl Sandburg, and Padraic Colum—appeared every season. Other poets who read were: Maxwell Bodenheim, Countee Cullen, DuBose Heyward, Stanley Kimmell, Alfred Kreymborg, Maurice Leseman, Amy Lowell, Percy MacKaye, Theodore Maynard, Edna St. Vincent Millay, Harriet Monroe, Leonora Speyer, James Stephens, Margery Swett, Ridgely Torrence, and others.

The enforced inaction of the long months in Hollywood was more than made up for by the multiple demands that life made on Harriet in the following year. Though she spoke of the new restaurant as "exacting in its demands," this, after all, was but a single thread in her web of responsibilities. Another visit from Mr. Tagore and his retinue during February and a part of March satisfied her human needs but involved, as usual, no little effort and strain. There were frequent necessary excursions to New York, one of these (leaving the entire Tagore party behind) being made necessary by the death of Harriet's cousin and almost brother, Henry Lyman. Shortly afterward she went again, this time accompanied by the Tagores, who were about to sail for England. Harriet spread her protective wings over Mr. Tagore up to the moment of his departure and, as usual, was able to muster a distinguished group to join in the farewells. She well knew it was extremely probable that the Poet would not be seen again in this country, so that, although his comings and goings were always momentous affairs, this departure in particular seemed somberly final.

During the stormy crossing Mr. Tagore wrote her in the playfully wounded vein that becomes familiar in his correspondence—as of a person who was persistently imposed upon by the universe and whose dignity the churlish ocean notably failed to respect. But it must have been temptingly easy to address complaints of any sort whatever to the wellspring of sympathy and love as well as the buttress of efficient and comprehensive care that he had found in Harriet.

HOLLAND-AMERICAN LINE (EN ROUTE TO ENGLAND)
March 29, 1921

MY DEAR FRIEND,

Tomorrow the steamer will reach Plymouth and we shall be glad to get ashore. The sea has been exceedingly rough for the last few days, and violently shaking us day and night as a cat does its victim mouse. On the land where you dwell, you adjust your movements to your own purpose, but on the rough sea like this you have constantly to adjust your movements which are without purpose. When I am tossed about in this wretchedly undignified manner I feel that a steamer as an institution is a failure—it gives the fullest opportunity to the element which is alien to us, to treat us with utter humiliation. I am longing to reach the land in order to regain my erect posture and with it my self-respect. While frantically struggling to keep one's equilibrium it is difficult to write and therefore this letter of mine will show you some sign of my physical unsteadiness— but I must not allow this to prevent my thoughts from running towards you. I hastily write these lines only to prove to you that though the wind and the water have conspired to shake out from my mind the greater part of its contents, yet my remembrance of you remains unimpaired. Kindly remember me to my friends in your house who with their presence and helpful kindness have added grace to your hospitality.

With grateful love,

Ever yours,
RABINDRANATH TAGORE

One sacrifice which the Tagore visit had entailed was that she had been unable to join Robert and Elinor Frost in New York. Robert Frost had written her from South Shaftsbury (January 20, 1921):

DEAR HARRIET MOODY:

Elinor and I are to be in New York on and about the twentieth (20th) of next month (February). We want to see you for the fun of a good talk before we do or don't decide to take this step into Michigan. Whichever we decide we'll be right. That's why we find it impossible to treat anything as momentous. If you oppose the step too much we shall think you have some reason for not wanting us as near you and Chicago as the step would bring us. Maybe you think there are enough poets within the first postal zone from Chicago. We shall listen to you with respect and encouraging smiles.

One thing as a mere woman of no practical experience you may need to be told: our going to Michigan will not prevent our planting all outdoors with pines and apples. We could plant them in New England or in Michigan just the same.

Say (a little abruptly), you haven't seen this beautiful house that captivated us in passing last year. It is the easiest thing in the world for you to visit us here on your way to or from New York. We are on the main line from New York through Albany to Montreal and not more than two hours from Albany. If you can't be in New York in February when we are, will you agree to come here and see how you like this for the apple enterprise? This is important, though I will not have it momentous or even serious—we'll have to act soon.

Thank Theodore Maynard. I should be more pleased with your good opinion if you hadn't told me that time that I might be the best poet in America, but the best in America couldn't hope to come up to the worst in England. Have a little national pride. Don't you know it's provincial to look up to England? So it is to brag about America. What isn't provincial will be the question before the house at the next meeting.

Always yours,
ROBERT FROST

178

Two weeks later he wrote:

Did you mean that if you could be in New York for a few days on each side of February 23rd you could have Elinor and me at the apartment in Waverly Place? We should like that. We could come right there from Philadelphia where I shall have been teaching them a lesson in art, morals and agriculture on the 18th. Suppose we got there a little ahead of you; could we get in and wait a day or two for you? Is there anybody there? I take it, not, from what I hear from Ridgely. Could you send in a key now or tell us where to find a key?

I went to bed sick just after receiving the telegram from you and Ridgely. It would have made anybody sick to see the way the names of those poems you called for had got improved upon. And since I was going to be sick I decided to be very sick. I am just up around again today and feeling as cross as a last year's bird's nest. I had to give up the Iowa trip. Perhaps later, but I don't know.

You haven't actually forbidden me to go to Michigan, I notice.

And again, just before leaving Vermont.

We are off for Philadelphia on the 16th. Business over there on the 18th. We shall stop two days to say Hello right and left and then come up to the apartment in Waverly Place Monday morning. Ridgely has keyed us for getting in. I don't believe you are one little bit in earnest about being there to cook us Birds of Paradise. You're not a very serious-minded person, anyway. I wish I knew where to find ———. I'd like to talk you over with him.

Anyway you can't say I haven't let you know.

> Reservedly,
> ROBERT FROST

Mr. Frost knew very well, of course, that only the presence of the Tagores in her house would have prevented Harriet from meeting him in New York and offering—as she would so have delighted in doing—some succulent equivalent, in the material

179

or other sense, of the "Birds of Paradise" he pretended to demand of her.

Later, some weeks after Mr. Tagore's sailing, Mr. Frost produced the following explanation of his having missed the opportunity Harriet had offered him of meeting the Indian poet in New York. He wrote her:

DEAR HARRIET:

I had my instructions more than a month ago to write and tell you in simple language why I didn't get down to New York to see Mr. Tagore off. I have been all this time simplifying my language. I have got it down now to where I think I can safely say as follows:

I was in Utica or Rochester or Buffalo (I don't know one town from another west of Albany) with people who naturally wanted to keep me or who, if they let me go, wanted some assurance that they could have me back. I could promise them to come back, but I had no pledge to give them of my good faith except my word that I was leaving them for you most unwillingly. Couldn't they see it? I hated to go. But all the time I was saying this, I could see them thinking I was probably saying the opposite to you, namely, that I hated to stay. What were these Syracusans but a lot of Main Streeters anyhow? etc. You know how everybody always takes me. People love me because of rather than in spite of my insincerity. The Buffalonians (or whoever they are [you see I am trying right now with you to convey the impression that they are nothing to me: I can't tell them apart]) decided to look out for themselves and refused to let me go. They left me perfectly free to go and come as I pleased myself. But every time they caught me starting downstairs with suitcase, they kindly but firmly said, "Here you, where are you going with that?" and sent me back. They kept their tempers admirably and they could afford to, because they had their way. At times I was a little cross. But no one minded me. I was only a poet and very likely suffering from shellshock.

I have shown this to the instructress from whom I had my instruction and it does not meet with her approval. She says it

180

was undignified to go into the psychology of it all. She says
I don't know how I make myself look.

                    Always yours faithfully,
                              ROBERT FROST

Must send you copy of the new Mt. Interval. Be on the
lookout.

The stimulating pace at which Harriet had lived since she
came back from California is partly indicated in a letter that
she wrote to Charles Squire (who had remained in California)
early in March, 1921: "I have been at home very little some way
since I came back here in November. Committee work and
business interests in New York have taken me east four or
five times. Mr. Tagore and the children came to visit me in
February and have been with me since then. This is always
preoccupying, you know, because I have to seem idle in
the midst of any business demands that might come to the
front. . . . .

"We have had several visitors here since I wrote you last.
Ridgely Torrence spent a week with me, and Padraic has been
here for a few days. Theodore Maynard, a new star in the
horizon, spent a few days at a time with me several times."

It was in March of this busy year that Harriet opened her
arms and her house to her old friend Mrs. Martha Foote Crow,
who was in a low state of health and whose illness increased
with various ups and downs during the three years—the last
years of her life—that she spent there. At the same time, in
addition to the concern that she felt for Mrs. Crow and to the
anxiety occasioned by the coming and going of doctors, nurses,
and so on, she was beset by the further and more acute worry of
her brother Fred's uncertain condition. On his account she gave
up in May a trip to Europe which she would otherwise have
made.

Robert Frost wrote her from South Shaftsbury in June:

DEAR HARRIET:
Did you receive a copy of "Mountain Interval" from me?
Or did it get lost on the way? Or didn't I send it?

This is just for once in a way to be writing when I am not on the defensive and have nothing to explain.

With the best wishes in the world I'm

> *Always yours sincerely,*
> ROBERT FROST

When are you coming to see our apple farm?

The approach of summer always meant a trip, however brief, to Cummington and the farm. This year Harriet completed the plan she had cherished for some time of restoring the Bryant birthplace, an enterprise that she describes in a letter to Alice Corbin, written in August:

She writes: " .... in spite of your opinion I have amused myself by restoring the little cottage which was the birthplace of William Cullen Bryant. The old Bryant homestead happens to join my farm in Massachusetts.

"This little house was a gambrel-roof cottage of two rooms, always rather pretty in its drawing. It has been given to an old retainer of the Bryant house and moved down from the hills where it was built and became the property of Luther Shaw, our farmer, through the will of the owner. I moved it (to my farm) almost unpremeditatedly, because the decision to do it came about in a very unexpected way. It is now sufficiently restored so that it makes a cheery little place for two people to live."

As her own words prove, restoring the birthplace was far from being sheer antiquarianism on Harriet's part. What pleased her most was the fact that she had provided a charming extra home for a succession of artists.

In the same letter she joyously mentions, knowing that she is addressing a sympathetic ear: "You have heard of his [Tagore's] marvellous reception in various parts of Europe, including Germany. It seems he was fairly carried over the heads of the crowd, his birthday celebrated by gifts and many acknowledgments of his service to humanity, made wherever he went. He was gladly received in America this time, that is, in the northern part. His visit here resulted in a gift of $10,000 a year for five years for the endowment of chairs at the university, through an unknown benefactor.....

"A young Englishman named Leonard Elmhirst, on Mr. Tagore's invitation, will go out to be his secretary, personal and academic. He is a graduate of Cambridge, England, and also of the Agricultural College at Cornell, and has got together the funds to buy agricultural implements of the types needed in India, which he is taking over with him in October. He is to join Mr. Pearson October 15th, and they are going out together. A short line from Protima tells me they were just arriving at Port Said, so they have long since been home."

Another trip to the farm in August resulted in a happy encounter which Harriet describes as follows in a letter to Wilfrid Gibson: ".... I saw Robert Frost a few weeks ago for the better part of one day. We met in Pittsfield and he drove over with me to my farm. Then we drove him back again to his train for home. He lives only a short distance from Pittsfield. He is very well, stronger than I have ever seen him. You will perhaps have heard of his appointment to a position in the University of Michigan for the coming year, which is not fettered with any college responsibilities and for which he receives a good salary. He is going to be there with his whole family for one year at least. This is a new idea being advanced in America. It seems to me wonderful for the university, but not so extremely good for the poet. But this may not be true at all. He has written a great many very good things in the last few months and published them in magazines. I suppose you get them....."

Harriet must have been in Cummington, recovering from the strain of her hot Chicago summer, when the following appeal from Carl Sandburg reached her. Since she could and would supply almost anything on earth to a friend who needed it, it goes without saying that she lost little time in remedying the doglessness of the Sandburg family.

DEAR HARRIET:

We have lost our dog. If you get hold of a setter, sheep dog, collie, German police dog, mastiff, Danish bloodhound, or any dog spotted or unspotted that growls at strangers and is good to children—bring him along. Don't let dog thoughts interrupt your vacation. Of all the teeming millions in Chicago you deserve an uninterrupted vacation. But if anybody says to you, careless like, that they got a good dog you can have, and it does look to you like a good dog, call their bluff, copper the hund, nail the dog, sign a contract that there will be the best of care.

I am trying to get some final revised copies of some of those kid stories done next week and hope to send some on to you. Along about the last of October I hope your reading eyes will be in good form because there will be almost fifteen or twenty of these babies of literary destiny sent to you.

Your black-hearted renegade,

CARL

At about this time Lindsay had accomplished his "Johnny Appleseed" poems and Harriet wrote to him: ". . . . 'Johnny Appleseed' flashed before my eyes as an earnest of the fact that Lindsay was at work. I think you must have derived from me the hero-worship for Johnny—at least, I should like to think so. . . . . Ohio is a wonderful place for apples. The most delightful varieties I ever knew of in my life grew there, and as we ate them around the winter fire my mother used to tell me about good old rosy-cheeked Johnny and his sowing the seeds broadcast as he bent to the wind and traversed the noble state of Ohio. This was a tradition in her family, and as I am a little shaky in my dates, I think her father may have entertained him [Johnny] in his hospitable home. But of that I am uncertain."

Almost immediately afterward she heard from Lindsay that he was on the wing and that she would shortly see him. He wrote to her from Glacier National Park:

My dear Harriet Cordelia:

Stephen Graham and your humble servant have been travelling two or three weeks together, as you may have heard. I have told him a great deal about our mutual friendship, and I hope we may stop over to see you in Chicago on our way to Springfield, any time between Sept. 15, and Oct. 30. I am hoping to persuade Stephen to march to Kingdom Come and back, but he may think he must get back to England. I have not the least notion of stopping till he is tired. I am at last on the path I attempted when I called in Chicago for Carl Sandburg, in my corduroys, about 1915. I met Eleanor [Dougherty] instead, as you remember, since Carl did not find himself able to walk. That was all very darling and lovely, thanks to you, and I remember those games to this day, and will remember them always with a glad heart.

Nevertheless, I am now on the other track and I hope to stretch it out. We have been climbing like goats, away from the trail, by compass only, starting at Glacier Park Station, Montana, and making for the North-West through the park, and on toward Canada.

I have a vague notion we have just started on many adventures. At any rate, I know before I get to Chicago again, I will have had worlds of exercise, scenery, conversation, and stars. We carry our food on our backs, renewing the pack every week, and generally starving the last three days. It is wonderful.

In the whole literary world, Graham is the man who started out on lines most similar to mine, including beginning formal publication with books of tramp sketches. His legs are a foot longer than mine and he can climb much better and easier. At the same time, I can walk faster, so it is about a stand-off.

As I think it over this morning, I am hoping to persuade Stephen to march much farther than he at first planned. I have been waiting too long to see the world, to quit for frivolous reasons.

If you write soon, write to Cardston, Alberta, Canada.

I have not yet shuffled off this mortal coil. I still feel full of

185

dust and ashes. I want to come back new as the green pine, all
the way to my back-bone.

All my mail, first and second class, I am having stopped in
Springfield. It piles so high these days, it only makes a mess in
my mind. I will be glad to hear from you indeed.

My mother has a cottage-room at Charlevoix, Michigan, and
is with old friends.

With every good wish and with lifelong love,

VACHEL.

At the close of his journey Lindsay did appear in Chicago
with his companion. Stephen Graham, being delivered to
Harriet with warm personal recommendations from Lindsay,
became her guest for a week and, as she reported, "endeared
himself to us all." Of his writings she said merely at that time
that she had "read some of them with much interest."

Harriet never lost sight of anybody she was interested in.
She was now occupied with her usual multiple concerns, besides entertaining a series of friends and ministering to the invalid Martha Foote Crow. She took the risk of sending two
young men to see E. A. Robinson, at the same time suggesting
that, like her other friends, he address her by her first name. This
was a difficult plunge for Robinson to make, but he made it,
writing from Peterborough, New Hampshire:

. . . . I was glad to see the boys you sent, and liked them. The
world is undoubtedly better for your being in it. Let me hear
when you are in New York.

Yours always,

E. A. R.

A note that she sent at the same time to Dan and Isadora
Reed[2] has an extremely characteristic accent: "To ask me for
an address is like offering a feed of oats to a horse loose in a

[2] Harriet had become interested in Isadora Bennett when, at eighteen, this
young girl was the fiancée of Vachel Lindsay, whom she had known in Springfield, her own "home town." At that time she had both a job on a Chicago
newspaper and a scholarship at the University. Later, the engagement with
Lindsay was broken, and Miss Bennett married Daniel Reed, with whom she
afterward started and conducted a community theater in Columbia, N.C.

186

pasture. I can turn a deaf ear to friendship, tenderness, inspiration, but not to anyone's desire to know where another fellow mortal is. This I think is because I feel bound to keep the human link unbroken. Padraic Colum is to be reached through —————."

Meanwhile Robert Frost, with or without Harriet's approval, had established himself and his family at Ann Arbor, and as a natural sequence Harriet set to work to secure for him a group of engagements in and about Chicago, including, of course, an appearance at Les Petits Jeux Floraux.

Replying to a letter from her on this subject, Frost wrote:

ANN ARBOR, MICH.

DEAR HARRIET:

Just the few words you permit me.

My first engagement down your way will be at Oshkosh (do you get that?) on December 7 (Wednesday). You are welcome to me on the 4th, but if I come that early you must try to get me at least one more engagement to fill the gap between the 4th and the 7th. Percy Boynton might be spoken to, I think. Don't let me lie rusting two whole days. You know how I need action.

Mrs. Sherry has engagements to fill my time from the 8th to the 11th. I shall have to return for an engagement here on the 12th. Live absurdly is my motto.

Incidentally I mean to give you a glimpse of Elinor. She only partly knows it as yet.

Surely it is a beautiful thing Faggi has made of Yone Noguchi. I have the picture of it in Noguchi's book.

Ever yours,
ROBERT FROST

At the same time, she heard from E. A. Robinson, from Peterborough:

DEAR HARRIET:

There you are again. And here is your surprising remembrance in the shape of your admirable wares, which are gradu-

187

ally going out of existence—or rather going through a transformation into blank verse. Many thanks. Mr. Bois is a most engaging addition to this place, and is admired by all sorts and conditions of talented seekers after light. He can drop from heaven to earth with an ease that only a Frenchman could command. I hope very much to see you in New York sometime this winter.

Yours always sincerely,
E. A. ROBINSON

To Theodore Maynard (now settled with his young family in California), who had proposed dedicating a book to Harriet and who later fulfilled this intention, Harriet now wrote:

DEAR THEODORE:

First, let me say it is touching to me that you have thought of dedicating a book to me. You will know that I deeply appreciate it. And then, if you will pardon my thinking over what I feel in this matter, perhaps you will come to agree with me. I should be very happy to have you dedicate a book to me, but perhaps the time has not come yet; or if you think it has, would you be willing just to make a simple inscription without discussion of me or my qualities? I always think such inscriptions stand the test of time better, as for example, hereafter when my posthumous poetry is published, think how sad it would make you to have condemned it in advance. I throw out these suggestions. Let me know what you think of them.

To John Masefield at Oxford she had dispatched a young traveler. Not long afterwards she heard from him:

DEAR KIND MRS. MOODY,

I was so glad to have your letter and to see your friend the other day. He came up to Oxford specially, and we had a jolly talk together, and I hope presently to see more of him. It was charming to hear about so many old and lovely friends.

This just a brief word in the midst of rehearsals and turmoil, to thank you, and to send my greetings and tender thoughts to all your household, and the little girl, (now, I suppose, fast growing up)—and the sweet musicians who played to me.

Blessings on you all,

JOHN MASEFIELD

The Frosts, now at Ann Arbor, were within fairly easy reach of Chicago, and any member of the Frost family would at any time be eagerly welcomed at Harriet's house. Knowing this, Robert Frost wrote Harriet toward the end of the following February:

DEAR HARRIET:

I'm bringing Lesley instead of Elinor. Don't forget. I wouldn't have you take Lesley for Elinor. She calls for entirely different treatment. That is to say, she can be treated worse, though I shouldn't say there weren't bounds beyond which bad treatment ought not to go even in her case, young and tough as she is and of small account to her father.

If it could be arranged I should like to leave her a little while with you in Chicago for the good you would do her. The poor kid is rather sick of this institution and that through no fault of hers. She's had splendid marks and likes seventy-five per cent of her teachers. But my line of talk isn't calculated to make her like any institution. You know how I'm always at it against colleges, in a vain attempt to reconcile myself with them. The part of them which the youngsters are most free in or where they could be most free, their own so-called activities, they are the most slavish and conventional in. Self-sacrifice there must always be in religion and out of religion and with small people it seems to take the form of sacrificing their initiative and independence.

If you think they would like me at the Parker School Friday morning for whatever it was they said they would pay, I'm at their service.

We shall arrive at the 43rd St. station at 2:50 P.M., Thursday, Feb. 23. So if you don't want to meet us you'll know where not to be. But in any case I shall remain

Faithfully yours,
ROBERT FROST

This visit was particularly successful and was followed by a correspondence between Harriet and charming young Lesley Frost, who became excellent friends.

At the close of the preceding year Stephen Graham had written her from London:

DEAR HARRIET MOODY:

*My mind goes back tonight over the joyous year 1921.....
I think of Vachel and then of you and of the generous warmth
and kindness of America. Bless you for 1922! May it be very
happy! ....*

*I hope to go to Russia in March and then in July to America—
to visit Panama, to climb the Peak of Darien—to come through
Mexico to Santa Fé and then tramp perhaps with Vachel
through some more Rocky Mountain country.*

STEPHEN

Replying evidently to a letter written later than this, Harriet wrote Mr. Graham on March first: ".... It is a long time since you left us all bound to you by a deep sense of human kinship. It has been wonderful of you to drop these notes from time to time. We have all been rejoiced by them, and now it is a great piece of news that on your return to America you will stay at least two months in Chicago. I hope you will count on making your headquarters in my house, and if your wife is with you, that will be all the more acceptable. . . . .

"I am greatly excited by what you say about your forthcoming book on the great tramp in the northwest. Altogether it was a good day, that day in September, that brought you to our house."

Harriet and Vilhjalmur Stefansson had known each other from a time preceding Moody's death, Moody and Stefansson having met frequently in New York. The following letter from Harriet, written in May in response to a letter of inquiry from Stefansson, has significance partly because of Harriet's immense admiration for Mr. Stefansson and his achievements; she had

190

once said that she considered him one of the two most interesting men in the United States. She would, therefore, have been particularly gratified by his interest in any of her husband's poems, though she probably was unaware of a fact that Mr. Stefansson has since disclosed, namely, that, having in his youth cared greatly for poetry and written many poems of his own, he deliberately ceased writing them on the publication of Moody's poem, "Gloucester Moors." Its beauty revealed to him, he has modestly said, that poetry was a field he was not prepared to enter. His own path lay elsewhere.

DEAR MR. STEFANSSON:

Will's poem "Gloucester Moors" was written one summer while he was staying for a time at East Gloucester, which you will remember is on Cape Ann. He was very fond of it there, and I believe every local touch in it was a record of something written on his heart. The poem still remains one of the favorites among his readers. I know he would be glad that you had felt interest in it.

In May, also, the Pulitzer prizes were awarded, and E. A. Robinson received the poetry prize for his *Collected Poems.* Since Vachel Lindsay happened to be staying with Harriet when this news came, he joined her in a congratulatory telegram to Robinson. Reply came promptly from Peterborough in a tone that for Robinson was fairly jovial. He implies that he had been surprised at the award but admits that the surprise was agreeable.

One of the women poets in this country whose work Harriet genuinely admired was Lola Ridge. So, when writing Theodore Maynard, a few months later, apropos of *Broom,* she said:

DEAR THEODORE,

.... Do you see copies of Broom, and can't you find a bright angel there in your neighborhood to look after it financially? It seems to have a very good intention, namely, that of an uncompromising international magazine of all arts. It is good

looking, flattering to the eye and touch. It has a genius behind it in this country, in the case of Lola Ridge, who has done some impressive things. I find her latest book "Sun-Up" as interesting as her first one "Ghetto." Her tribute to Robinson is a masterpiece.

In the same letter she assures her correspondent:

The only thing that is absolutely reliable about me is my heart, which retains its allegiance unswervingly.

This complete allegiance to those her heart had chosen, which Harriet was so well justified in noting as her characteristic, was each year becoming stronger and tenderer in the case of nine-year-old Alice Harriet who, Harriet noted on September 25, 1922, "is a schoolgirl this year for the first time." Harriet's program for educating the little girl had so far been carried out. Already the child could play the piano a little and draw creditably. Harriet was enchanted.

"She will make all three years of primary education before this first is over," the delighted aunt wrote Mrs. Kennedy-Fraser. "I am anxious to take her to Europe but we are impeded by a chain of family influences. . . . . I am determined, however, not to let this . . . . prevent Alice Harriet's getting her wider education and knowledge of the world."

Twenty-one years after Harriet suffered the accident to her ankle—years during which she and Ferdinand Schevill had maintained a close and understanding friendship—he wrote her, while away from Chicago, in the light vein they both employed, bringing from her the following in reply: "No praise is too lavish for me, nor is there ever any such stimulant. . . . . Meantime, let me say if you were told to pause and declare which aspect of the many noble ones you have seen me in has most commanded appreciative wonder, I am sure your mind would quickly find its way back to that summer in 1901 in which I hung suspended between heaven and earth by four iron chains, while two of America's best men gave themselves up to diverting me. It is pleasant to contemplate one's own maximum."

192

CHAPTER XVIII

HOLLYWOOD AGAIN

FOR several years Harriet had guided her course with caution, fearing lest she be out of reach when her brother, whose health she knew to be precarious, might most critically need her. But it happened that she was at home after all when, in January, 1923, there befell her the crushing blow of his death. "The one I loved best on earth," she described him. "He was my best friend, you remember—brother, son and lover," she wrote her cousin Leila Hutchens.

Harriet grieved as intensely as she loved, as her friends well knew. Robert Frost knew it and sent her a brief letter that was like a warming handclasp:

DEAR HARRIET:

I'm heart-broken for you. You two had stayed brother and sister all these years against the world. Your hold was a match for everything but death. You know better than I what to say to death. I'm willing you should say it.

I had one of my great times with Ridgely last week. I always keep seeing a light as I talk with him—and of course losing it as quickly; the thing is the seeing it. He's some consolation. Nevertheless I am ready to say when you are that pretty nearly everything is vanity.*

> Affectionately,
> ROBERT

*Sometime I propose to make you a short list of the things that aren't.

Stricken as she was, she lost little time in taking the family situation masterfully in hand. Something should be done, she felt, for her brother's widow, and she herself longed for im-

193

mediate change. Fred had always wanted to see Honolulu. Why shouldn't they, all three—for the ten-year-old Alice Harriet was an indispensable figure in any adventure—embark on what might be considered a memorial expedition? Old friends of Harriet's were living in Honolulu, and the Colums for the time being were there also, Padraic Colum having a commission to study the local folklore. So in February they set forth.

Previously, Harriet had written to Mr. Tagore's secretary, W. W. Pearson, announcing her brother's death and making the revealing statement that, now that this separation had occurred, "the last reason for my dreading to leave home and to go to great distances is over, and if I regain my health, I think in another year I shall certainly go to India."

To anyone who knew Harriet, however, this remark should cause no surprise. Her imagination must have dwelt broodingly upon the Indian scene ever since her first meeting with Tagore, and the length and strangeness of the journey would in themselves have tempted her. Had she at any time been free to go, she would gaily have prepared herself at a day's notice.

To a woman contemplating, however hazily, a trip to the Orient, going to Honolulu was relatively a small matter, and little was made of it. The three travelers spent a week there, guests of Harriet's friends, the Butlers and the Rudolph Bukeleys, and they saw much of the Colums. Yet Harriet remained in a stunned condition, and on board ship, returning to California, she wrote home to Bessie O'Neill: ". . . . All the time I am profoundly wounded, cut to pieces, without Fred; unable to go on, and still going on, like a prisoner of war driven into exile."

But to Margaret Cuthbert, who had a post at Cornell University, she was able to send, after arriving in California, a lighter version of the experience.

". . . . Honolulu is altogether too hot for my taste, but it is a place with many and varied beauties. We were entertained by friends and saw many of the native specialties, such as the *luau*, a native feast, cooked in an improvised fireless cooker, the viands being variously tied up in broad leaves called *ti* leaves,

194

and then buried in a pit in the ground, previously heated. They are covered with hot stones and left there for a stipulated period. Out of this pit they come hot and succulent. The table is laid with a number of these little tied bundles placed in front of each person. You untie them at your own discretion, and eat almost in one and the same breath baked fish, baked bananas, baked suckling pig. These delicacies are supported by a curious porridgy kind of mush, called poi. You eat them all, fish, flesh, and fowl, with your fingers, and when you are put to it for something else to do you dip those same fingers in the poi and suck the poi audibly from them. Our feast of this kind was attended by island chanters and hula dancers. I did my living best to feel like a native, but the whole ceremonial seemed a little lacking in sincerity. I could not help thinking the natives would do it somewhat differently if it were prepared for them alone. I will tell you more of this when I see you. . . . .

"By all means have Sandburg.[1] He will be well liked, and is different from any one else. He not only recites his own and other people's poetry, but he also sings Negro blues in a telling minor voice to his own original strumming on a guitar."

Returning home on May 1, 1923, Harriet found herself in time for the end of the Jeux Floraux season. Her competent young friend Mary Fox had managed the evenings during her absence, and Amy Lowell's reading, in particular, had been a marked success. Now, Robert Frost came from Ann Arbor to spend a few days with Harriet and to appear also at the Jeux Floraux.

Meanwhile, Vachel Lindsay, after an illness, had been teaching at Gulf Park College, Gulfport, Mississippi. His subject was poetry, he reports to Harriet, but he was obliged to give to it only forty-five minutes a day. "The quietest and strictest regime I have had for years and years."

So Harriet wrote him in late May: "I am glad you sank into snug harbor after your sickness and for the rest of the winter. I am sure you needed the kind of personal friendly care that you speak of getting. Besides that, your presence there was

[1] To read at Cornell.

undoubtedly a great inspiration to the young students. I should not like you to become a teacher in the long run, for fear you might fall into the groove that you speak of..... Teaching is all right for a sick poet, but I doubt if it is for a well one, and I hope the spring will see you in the retreat you have thought of so much, vigorously enjoying your own unique life and thought. Remember always that sick or well you can stay at my house as long as you like at any time."

Later in the summer Lindsay sent her his *Golden Book of Springfield,* and she wrote him in characteristic vein: "I am always thanking you in my heart for your splendid great book. People that handle it and read from it here in the house admire it very much. They envy me the friendly inscription on the first page. I have, however, to call you to account for the number of my volume of the limited edition. I need to know where you began these numbers, and why, if you began at 1, I should be 335. Whereas I should have expected to be 3 at the least, and I should not have been any too much surprised if I had had the first volume of the series."

At about the same time she discovered a young poet, Schuyler Jackson, of whose work she thought well and upon whom she bestowed many kindnesses. She described him as: "living in a Ford truck with a Russian painter, Vladimir Perfilieff, and on his way south to see Lindsay and others. He is a boy about 22 years old, with an English education, but a native American, and full of interest in America."

Some time afterward Mr. Jackson wrote her from New York:

Dear Mrs. Moody—

Vachel Lindsay and I walked up and down the beach at Gulfport, read poetry together, laughed, listened and stared; and I love him. He stands always on a stump, and is the tallest man in the United States..... In a sense, I am born again in you; and what I once hoped for I work for now. It's like harvesting in May.....

Your letters mean a great deal to me. You have my admiration and love always, from the roots of my being.

Schuyler Jackson

Vachel Lindsay was well and happy. I recited some of my poems to his class; and afterwards one of the girls came up and asked me for "Sunday in Chicago.". . . . Her eyes were full of tears.

Meanwhile, Lindsay had written her from Memphis:

My dearest Harriet:

I think I enjoy the human race most when I am walking unknown in a town, or sitting unknown in a hotel lobby. I really love everybody and I love to see them going by, and I am happy when the crowd looks happy.

This often is far more fun than an audience, and I truly love them all.

Often and often I think of changing my name and plunging in and disappearing awhile. Every time I did something like it before, I was too conscious of all those I left behind me. But now I have no ties that would forbid it, or make it wrong to disappear completely awhile, and once my books are cleared up and presentable, I may do this. I remember the last time I seriously tried it you stopped me. . . . . Well, I will have to try harder next time! I may deceive myself, but it seems to me I have now the necessary philosophy. And I have now no literary itch to tempt me to return. Only very bad health could do it. Of course, if sick, I will crawl back!

More later,

With love,
Vachel

And again, from Gulfport:

My dear Cordelia:

This is to say I am thinking of you this evening, that I am very thankful to have you to write to, and to think about—you are the good gift indeed. This is no letter. It is just a sort of dream-note to say you are well-beloved, that you were made with great care in the first place, and you have nobly built upon the start God gave you. I will write a letter some other time. This is just to say—"God bless you."

From
Vachel

197

All this time Harriet had heard nothing from Mr. Tagore since her brother died in January. But now he wrote her from Santiniketan, on October 10, 1923, and the letter was a compensation for his silence:

DEAR FRIEND,

When I heard the sad news of your brother's death I wished that I were near you to be able to offer you some consolation from my store of experience. For I have suffered and have learnt my lessons from death's hands. But I know that you have the power and have had opportunity to think deeply and have reaped the rich harvest of a life mature in wisdom that can bring you help from your own inner resources.

You know how often I boasted of my gift of inexhaustible youth and how I had determined not to die old. But I have been humbled and in the course of the last two or three years I have grown more and more conscious of the burden of existence which is the sure sign of old age. All that I owe to the incessant grasping after material means for my institution, which leaves me with a meager result tragically inadequate to the sacrifice it claims from me. Lately I have received a letter from ——— containing hints of liberal help from your country about which I shall know in definite details when he comes to India in November.

I do not know if you have read in the papers about the sudden death of Pearson through some accident in Italy where he was traveling lately. It is a very great shock to me and it has given an intensely painful shock to our ashram people who always adored him.

In November of 1923 Harriet had what was for her a red-letter experience in the production of *The Faith Healer* at the Theatre of the College of Fine Arts at the Carnegie Institute of Technology in Pittsburgh.

The uncommon degree of satisfaction that this gave her is shown in the letters she wrote after returning home.

To Mrs. Thomas Wood Stevens, wife of the director, she wrote:

198

Dear Mrs. Stevens,

As I look back on my stay in Pittsburgh I am deeply impressed with the pleasure that it gave me. I feel inclined to say with Rhoda,[2] "I had not been so happy before." It was wonderful thing to see your large and powerful group working together in such perfect harmony. Why don't we always realize that this is the only way to do big things? I suppose it is because harmony is the crowning human virtue, and few people have attained to it.

I think of those young men and women too with the greatest of affection. They were kind to me. They took me so completely into their group. If this never happens to me again, as it does seldom now, I shall rejoice in it indefinitely and have it as a thing to refer my thoughts to in less harmonious moments.

And to Dan Reed, always himself immersed in stage matters: "I have just been over to Carnegie Institute in Pittsburgh to see their school's production of 'The Faith Healer.' It was very good, and brought me in contact with a tremendously interesting group of young actors, who spread down the purple and crimson garments of their imagination before me and let me sit enthroned in their affection. I think Carnegie Institute is the best school I have ever seen. It is a place where the young growing human things disport themselves in a free sunshiny atmosphere on equal terms with the older people with whom they are associated and whom they don't know by the deadly name of professor."

Since this living experience in Pittsburgh was the very opposite of the dreary blankness that she had lived through in California, Harriet felt correspondingly refreshed. Her mood of elation was sustained by a bit of news that she mentions in a letter to Padraic Colum written on December 3: "This morning I am bowled over with happiness at the word that Duse is coming to Chicago. The Lord be praised! My fidelity has been rewarded!"

Mrs. Martha Foote Crow, Harriet's old friend who had been ill in her house for more than three years (this being one of

[2] Heroine of The Faith Healer.

many conspicuous instances of the extraordinary range of Harriet's conception—and practice—of friendship), died on the first day of the new year, 1924. Harriet wrote of her: "I cannot let my imagination run back beyond the time when I first met Mrs. Crow on a train going from Chicago to Lake Forest in the year 1892, when we were going out to spend the night at the country home of a common friend. I shall never forget the charm of her manner, nor the grace and beauty of her bearing as she stood there in the aisle of the train, with her close-fitting little mourning bonnet that she was still wearing because of the death a year before of her husband and child."

A friend of them both, Mrs. Elia W. Peattie, the writer, wrote from "Dunwandrin," Tryon, North Carolina:

The Poetry Society Bulletin brings me word of Martha's going, and through tears I rejoice at her release from dragging illness, and your honorable discharge from heavy, tho' willing service. She was a sweet friend, was Martha; a devoted lover of beauty, and one who asked nothing better than to hold high the lamp of idealism. That life should have been hard for her was something to which I found it hard to reconcile myself. But those last, suffering years found every material want supplied by your generosity. It must have been very hard for you. The heavy financial drain, and still more, the constant pull upon your sympathies, were, we all knew, very severe, and at times almost unendurable. It was a great chance to be beautiful in service, and you profited by it to the utmost. It cannot fail to bring you rich returns. There will be an added beauty to your nights and days because of it.

. . . . Of course, the most enjoyable thing of all is the deep, steady flow of consciousness. So long as we live, we shall have that. Nor have I ever known it to be deeper or richer with anyone than with you. . . . .

Affectionately always,
ELIA W. PEATTIE

A figure who was to be personally important to Harriet entered her world when, a few weeks later, Frank Swinnerton, the English novelist, was urgently committed to her charge by Mary Colum.

Mr. Swinnerton, a most disarming correspondent, sent from Battle Creek, Michigan, on January 14, 1924, his first delicate announcement that he was on the way:

DEAR MRS. MOODY:

I have a letter from Mrs. Padraic Colum saying that you very kindly invite me to stay with you while I am in Chicago. Do you realize what that means? I shall most probably arrive in the city on Wednesday, January 23, and not depart until Wednesday, January 30. Just imagine if you should take a violent dislike to me at sight! It is also true that I am bound to have a good many engagements in Chicago, which makes me rather hesitate to plank myself down in your house for a week when you don't know me at all. I think the best thing will be for me to show myself, and, if you find me a nuisance, for you to say so, when I will make a move. Does that seem to you fair? When I am more certain of the date and time of my arrival, I will send you a telegram, as Mrs. Colum says you have offered to meet me. Will you please let me say how very greatly I appreciate your generous kindness? Thank you much indeed for it. I really do not make myself a boisterous nuisance in any house, and will do my best in Chicago not to make you feel your kindness abused.

From Detroit, a week later, came a second letter that Harriet must have found equally winning. Mr. Swinnerton wrote:

Thank you very much indeed for your kind letter. I am at this moment suffering from cold and bad throat (relaxed—no longer sore!) and any home at all would be a Paradise to me. But Mrs. Colum was so urgent in her determination that when I came to Chicago it was to stay with you, that I am looking forward very eagerly to meeting you. I propose travelling to Chicago tomorrow night, arriving on Wednesday morning; and although I shall telegraph tomorrow morning the time of the train, I think it will be best if you let me take a taxi from the station to your house. I am not recognizable from my photographs, as I am ginger and they are dark; and the train is likely to be late. So I shall come along after breakfasting at the railway station, and will then secrete myself somewhere out of your way until you are ready to spare me a short time.

With all good wishes, and real appreciation of your brave and kind hospitality,

Sincerely yours,
FRANK SWINNERTON

Arriving according to schedule, Mr. Swinnerton seems immediately to have overcome the handicap (from Harriet's point of view) of not being a poet and to have established an extremely satisfactory relationship with his hostess. Indeed, writing her afterward, with proper courtesy, from Texas, he signs himself, Englishman though he was and after a week's acquaintance only, "very affectionately," and assures her that he is "looking forward very much indeed to arriving all over again on February 18th."

Just as he was boarding his ship to return to England, he wrote: "I can't leave—though the Berengaria waits—without sending you a note of *au revoir*. I have sent you a copy of 'September,' inscribed, and also have asked that a copy of a new photograph of me, taken by Pirie MacDonald, should be sent. Hope you will like both. Please let me say that I think my week in Chicago saved my life. I believe I should have been ill if you had not looked after me so perfectly. And it was a very great delight to me to be with you. . . . ."

Indeed a genuine and rewarding friendship had been formed.

Earlier, Harriet had made her own report to Ridgely Torrence: "We have had an amusing week with Frank Swinnerton as a house guest. He is a person of devilish perspicacity and remorseless humor. I wish I might be in New York when Mr. Swinnerton is there. . . . . He is anxious to meet you and E. A. Of course Molly Colum can give him the look-in anywhere. She is a great friend of his. I like him very much, but, as I say, he is a dangerously humorous person."

202

Replying, in January, to Mr. Tagore's recent letter, Harriet wrote him of an event by which she had been deeply stirred.

DEARLY BELOVED POET,

I have just been a joyful witness to the most wonderful confirmation of your belief in art as the one influence for creating a consciousness of human brotherhood. You perhaps are not even aware of the terrible racial antipathy which throughout my entire lifetime and longer still has existed between the blacks and the whites in America. It is almost a matter of daily experience to see white people spring indignantly up from their seats because a colored person has sat down by their side. As I say, all my life I have seen this antipathy manifested in every possible manner. You know how people move out of houses because Negroes are their neighbors, and so on.

A few nights ago I went to a song recital given by a Negro, Roland Hayes, who has had fine European training and not only is an artist but also carries with his singing a higher spiritual influence that is unclassifiable. His recital was in Orchestra Hall. The hall was filled and the audience was made up of alternate blacks and whites, sitting close to each other without any hesitation and joining in sympathetic applause at the end of each song. I don't know that any but an American could realize what a transformation this was, nor how deeply moving it was to one who had felt sorrow through her whole life because of this bitter inter-racial opposition.

My people were strong abolitionists and Negro sympathizers, so that I was brought up to feel a great protest against the treatment of the Negroes.

As I sat in that concert hall I thought constantly of you, of your lifelong dedication to the cause of human harmony, and of the joy it would give you to see your loving conviction so marvelously exemplified. . . . .

I am going to write a letter to this young Negro musician and I shall tell him how sincerely I felt he had made practically realizable the most important modern humanizing belief. . . . .

203

Sometimes it is rumored that you are coming here again. I wonder. It would be a great delight to see you.....

> Always devotedly yours.

At the same time, in a letter to Mrs. Heyward, DuBose Heyward's mother, Harriet says: "This amazing tenor singer Roland Hayes suggests a kind of superman, developed by racial suffering into something akin to prophecy."

Of this year, 1924, Harriet was, unwillingly, to spend a large share in California. In May the Metro-Goldwyn-Mayer firm, with whom she had a year previously signed a contract for the second screen production of *The Great Divide*, sent for her to come to Hollywood, as the production was scheduled to take place immediately. Harriet protested to no purpose. So she, Mrs. Fred Tilden, and Alice Harriet moved into a Los Angeles bungalow, and Harriet placed herself at the disposal of the producers, with the hope of protecting the character of the play to some extent.

But matters proceeded precisely as in the case of *The Faith Healer*, so that by the middle of May she had come to the point (in a letter to Bessie O'Neill) of the following delicious outburst: ".... I hate bungalows, flowers, moving-pictures, little leaky-handed dried-up old women-servants, the sun, and everything but the low growl of the sea..... I don't think I'll come to California again after this picture is made. I'd rather any rusty corner of Europe."

A week later, in the same mood, she wailed: "I continue a waif on the surface of life, needing leisure, rest, elegance of surroundings and lacking all these."

Indeed, two months after her arrival the scenario had not been finished. No cast had been chosen, no photographing done. Nothing in the world was so exhausting to Harriet as inaction. She was in despair.

She did, however, in June, steal away for a ten-day business trip to Chicago. A letter that she wrote during the return trip, to Bessie O'Neill, always in charge of the Groveland Avenue house during her absence, is but a single instance of her detailed thoughtfulness, this time in behalf of Charlotte Moody, who had not been well during an Eastern visit: ".... If Charlotte should come home now any time, try to arrange it that she only goes downstairs and up again once each day; that she has her breakfast in her room, stays there till she wants to come down, and that she goes out to drive whenever she wishes to, and as long as she wishes to; and so back to her room at her discretion whenever she feels like it. Charlotte will have her own room, but I presume while there are no guests she will wish to sleep on the porch."

There was no possibility of becoming reconciled either to the heat of a California summer or to the dulness of Hollywood. In July, Harriet wrote Evelyn Matz: "Your praise of my letter heartened me immensely. I meant to answer it that very day so as to provide myself with more praise as soon as possible.....

"We here are having a very hot and arid time. I never believed before that human beings would dwindle on top of baked earth the same as trees do. But I can tell you that is the case. Look out on the luscious green all around you and the ground dripping with water if you dig a little place in it. Here I feel like a cactus growing in the desert with thirsty earth under my feet, a heavy hot blanket over my head, and a life devoid of imagination, social opportunity, music, poetry,— most of all devoid of anything inside of me.

".... The *Great Divide* is undoubtedly going to be one of the most stupid screen pictures ever made."

There was a considerable solace in the presence of Alice Harriet, who, as it happened, had with her a young companion. Of this child Harriet could write to Chicago: "Ethel is full of wonder at the glory of the world. She is a most satisfactory child to take for a holiday..... *You know how seldom I find enthusiasm enough to comrade my own.*"

The last sentence, not italicized by Harriet, is packed with significance.

Also, poets had a way of appearing wherever Harriet was.

So she recorded, in a letter to a Chicago correspondent: "Just now we have had a visit from two delightful young people, a young poet and his still younger wife, not yet married a year, who have come all the way across from New York in a Ford truck, camping on the roadside, cooking their meals, sleeping in a truck bed, rejoicing in good roads and defying poor ones, encountering grizzly bears and coming triumphant out of their encounters. They are very enthusiastic, very charming young things. The man is Schuyler Jackson."

And there were poets at a distance to be looked after. When September came, Mrs. Edward MacDowell, whom Harriet greatly admired and whose lifework in the creation of the Mac-Dowell Colony bore a kinship to Harriet's own preferred concerns, wrote asking her to take in for a week or so a young poet in need of hospitality, James A. Daly. Harriet responded with the utmost warmth, making arrangements to have the young man taken care of in Chicago and writing to Mrs. MacDowell, in the course of a cordial letter: "You know how sympathetic I am in regard to your great enterprise and your spirit of sacrifice."

In Chicago, Harriet had known the poet Ivor Winters. The best service one could render Harriet was to bring to her attention a new, original, and, if possible, a needy worker in any of the arts. So Harriet set forth in a letter to Bessie O'Neill: "Ivor Winters has introduced a young painter to me who is pouring the oil of sincerity on my troubled waters. His name is Hunter. He brought five or six water-colors over to show me and after he took them home I was lonesome; decorative studies of human beings and out-door life; some of them carrying the story of relation to environment after the Asiatic fashion. He has humor and love. I only write of him because he is the spark of life out of the unquickened dust that I have found here. I am meaning to write Mr. Daly again to say how glad I am to have a real poet once more (for such I hear he is) in Will Moody's old rooms. I wrote him to Peterboro."

To Mr. Winters she wrote that she would give an exhibition of Vernon Hunter's pictures in Chicago, either at the Petit

Gourmet or in an office with good light at 152 East Ontario Street. She herself, she promised, would have the pictures hung and would send out lists and announcements. "I have been looking for something really new and good to start occasional artists' displays with."

At the same time she wrote to Kathleen Foster Campbell, asking her to take over Mary Fox's work in conducting Les Petits Jeux Floraux, as Miss Fox was obliged to leave Chicago for New York. Later she suggested to Mrs. Campbell that the first meeting of the year—as had been done before—should be given over to the young Chicago poets.

In the same letter she said: "Congratulations on your friendship with AE as he is one of the most important men alive. It will certainly be a source of illumination to you to know him."

The long season in Hollywood did not end until the first of December. Harriet's own belief was that she had for the most part been forced to waste her time. " 'My work,' " she had written to Chicago, "always seems to me most insecure and is in fact no work at all but idle waiting around." In another letter, after a variety of domestic directions, she says, characteristically: "This letter has a very business-like sound; but my heart is as soft as a late melon.

"I will write Mr. Daly today or tomorrow. Please give him my greetings, and tell him I shall be quite desolate if I find he has left the house before I get back. I wish I could think of some favorable opening for him; but first off I must know him before I can think of the things that it would contribute to his happiness to do."

As always, there were a hundred matters to be considered and written about. Her brother-in-law, Frank Moody, with whom she does not seem to have had any close connection, died. "The unbreakable persistence [after death] is the truth," she wrote.

She congratulated Mrs. Kennedy-Fraser that her "long continued devotion to the Hebridean cause has received its just recognition at the hands of the British government and that you should have had your decoration at the hands of the British king."

The six months and more that she had spent away from home were summed up in a letter that she wrote to Frank Swinnerton when she was finally en route to Chicago:

"This entire summer I have spent in California, as I may say, for my sins. It has been hot and heartless there, and I have been dominated by nothing short of a madness, which has induced me to stay day after day and week after week waiting summons from the Metro studio, and so foregoing all possible diversion.

". . . . They kept me on and on at the studio, apparently for no other purpose than humiliating me by the knowledge of my own uselessness. From time to time I was called to a conference, and in these conferences I remonstrated with all my might and main against the worst liberties they were taking with 'The Great Divide.' I can only remember one suggestion of mine, found weighty enough for them to consider. I said on one occasion, 'This scene is so vulgar I am sure it will be censored,' and the director, looking at me for a moment said, 'Do you think so?' Then turning to the cutter he said, 'Cut that down somewhat. It might be censored.' There is so much to say against the methods employed in the studios that it would be worth the effort of some honest soul to say it. But a revolution will come of itself in time. The photoplay is a tremendous force and it is capable of being made into real art when an artist feels the call of the cold curtain as the sculptor feels the call of the cold clay. . . . .

"I am now hurrying across this wonderful stretch of mountain and prairie back to my home. . . . . We take this journey calmly—not with amazement as you were obliged to—and so we suffer less from exposure in changing within the space of three days from something over 90° to something under 20°. I am getting in tomorrow morning."

It was a comfort to be at home again. There was her work that needed her, though this had nowadays, and increasingly, its corollary of anxiety. There was her familiar circle. There were the maturing poets in whose careers she could now take quiet pride and the younger ones whom she could helpfully encourage, upon whom she could build exciting hopes. It was the life she had spiritedly made for herself, that she could live with zest and, to some degree now, with happiness.

But her family of friends and protegés was too large to keep within reach. The younger ones in particular had a way of following destinies that led them away from her. Harriet allowed no cessation of friendship to occur, keeping an eye on her young men and women wherever they might choose to perch. Yet, hard though this may be to believe of anyone who was almost never alone, she was a lonely woman. There were times when she felt a sense almost of bereavement. On one of these days she wrote to Nelson Rowley and Harold Triggs, two promising young musicians who had gone to New York to live: "It is lonely without you. In fact personally I don't find it easy to bear. Even a mother eagle, I suppose, has a momentary pang when she pushes her young over the cliff. My heart is a little softer than hers."

CHAPTER XIX

JAMES STEPHENS

For Harriet, the principal event of the following year was the forming of a link with James Stephens, the Irish poet and teller of tales, who, during the rest of her life, was to delight and tantalize her by turns.

Early in January, 1925, she wrote that her plans for Les Petits Jeux Floraux were as follows: "Padraic Colum will be here in Janary, DuBose Heyward in March and James Stephens toward the end of March. DuBose Heyward is a poet in whom I am quite deeply interested." Also, "it is part of my plan to try to get Ridgely Torrence here to read one of his Negro plays."

To Theodore Maynard, at that time teaching in California, she wrote: "There is the glad news that James Stephens is . . . . to give some readings here. This to me seems almost too good to be true." In the same letter—reaching out, as usual, beyond her own ever widening circle—she asked: "Do you happen to know Robinson Jeffers, a poet of considerable power who interests me? They say he lives at Carmel. You probably know him personally. If you do, commend me to him."

In advance of these happenings, she had to hurry on to New York to confer with moving-picture magnates, as well as with who shall say how many poets, and to hear, in a week's time, four plays and three concerts.

But none of the multiple currents of her busy life could ever really distract her from one constant inner preoccupation. Isadora Bennett Reed had another baby. Harriet wrote her, repeating the paean that with her sprang from so deep and real a source:

"What a wonderful thing a baby is! The words are empty

but the fact is enormous. I marvel at the treasure and at you for owning it. How desolate it is to live without children! and how wonderful to have them! I reach out toward the youngest things that sweep across my path; but no detaining hand will arrest them. They pass on. The stream is continuous, but so also is the feeling of lack of relationship to it."

It was a few years later than this, her own life almost lived, that she wrote, calmly and unsentimentally, in a private letter: "Motherhood is the experience that completes a woman's life. I who have never had a child realize this profoundly. Without having borne a child a woman has no realization of what life truly is."[1]

In March, James Stephens and his wife Cynthia, introduced by the Colums, made the anticipated visit. Harriet had feared before they came that, because of an eye difficulty she was undergoing, she would be unable to make any social engagements for these guests. But when they proved to be even more winning than she had foreseen—when, in fact, they seemed to have cast an actual Celtic spell upon her—she must immediately have forgotten every physical handicap. And when Mr. Stephens, shortly after his arrival, betrayed an interest in the Negro, his hostess decided that this race, of whose capacity as artists she herself happened to have a liberal estimate (the Negro poet, Countee Cullen, winner of a Guggenheim prize, had recently read from his writings at Les Petits Jeux Floraux), must be presented for the foreign poet to behold. Harriet's letter to Rabindranath Tagore about Roland Hayes would sufficiently acquit her—even to anyone who failed to understand her complete sincerity—of any tendency toward sensationalism. She had none. But now, through the mediation of an acquaintance of hers, a colored professional woman, she made herself known to a number of colored artists in various fields and invited them to dinner so that they and the Stephens might meet each other. Harriet was always so simple and direct that she was able to carry this through naturally, even without

[1] Letter to an unknown woman.

211

a previous acquaintance with her guests, who included, besides a number of musicians, a newspaper editor, a young doctor who had studied in London and Paris and who spoke French and German fluently, and an actress or two.

It had been proposed to the dinner guests that they invite certain of their friends to come in during the evening. So there was much movement and animation. Charles Squire, who also had been asked to come in after dinner, recalls the program of songs, recitation, piano music, and dancing, all of superior quality. He remembers—all but the names—an accomplished young pianist-composer and a singer who sang in Russian, French, and English. A brilliant party, he thought it. It is a pity that nobody knows what Mr. Stephens' comments were. "Harriet never had quite such an evening again," Mr. Squire says, "but it shows how she could pull the rabbit out of the hat."

James Stephens made a profound impression upon Harriet from the first. She writes of him as "a wonderful reader, sometimes half chanting his poetry, but in a most unaffected way." "A very great man," she described him to Jules-Bois. "He has a great hold on the human affections," she artlessly wrote Padraic Colum. Moreover, he was a success publicly, drawing large audiences wherever he spoke. "An incomparable person," she says of him, in concluding the arrangement for him to speak at Cornell.

Greatly stimulated by the discovery of this new personality that was also the sheath of a poetic gift, Harriet by the end of April, 1925, was able to write to the poet Leonora Speyer, with whom she was by this time pursuing a friendship that yielded her much satisfaction: "The winter has been rather hard for me, but it seems to me on the other hand that I have never felt more joyous."

Stephens himself wrote her in May from New York:

My dear Harriet:

From running up and down the earth and the American spaces thereof, greetings. I have been thinking of you every blessed day of the days, and wishing that I could see you every

212

second minute of the minutes, and dodging the writing of a
letter, for I come to a pen as another comes to a toothache.
And here I am still, safe and sound and lecturing fit to break
the heart, and all one disgruntled pup of a man, and never
more forever a poet by virtue of the bloody lecturing, and the
pink blobs that are the faces of an audience everywhere and
anywhere, and I saying my pieces. I Princetoned a few days
ago, and I Cornelled yesterday night in poorish form, and got to
the train on the heels of the lecture, and thus to here, and to a
dumps that makes me want to write to you, for barring the
dumps I can't write a letter. I, I, I—and so forth, and so on.
I am sending you on, with this, a book[2] that I treasure as a
priest treasures the host, and will write you again in a few days.
Remember me affectionately to —— and to all those whom
you care for, and to yourself I enclose an hundred hugs.

JAMES STEPHENS

Meanwhile she had written to Vachel Lindsay that "James
Stephens went over these United States saying that the outstanding poets in the English language at the present moment
were Ralph Hodgson and Vachel Lindsay. He announced your
name from every platform. I was glad to hear it."

Such news, at this moment, seemed to mean little to the
perverse Lindsay. He was practically renouncing poetry, he
wrote. Now that his parents were dead he seemed to ask who
cared whether he continued to pursue the "colossally artificial"
occupation of writing books.

At some length he assured Harriet that "one thing .... has
never failed me, and that is the highroad. It is just the side of
me that you like least, and never understood. But if you really
want to know what I think about, day and night, it is the highroad. .... Three times I turned to it, and in vain, each time
dreaming I would some day make it permanent. I really believe
I will make it permanent before the year is over."

Whether or not Harriet took this seriously, she was totally

[2] *The Divine Pymander of Hermes Mercurius Trismegistus; In XVII Books;
Translated .... into English, by that Learned Divine Doctor Everard* (London,
1650).

unprepared for the complete reversal of the highroad program that Lindsay announced less than two months later. On May 22, 1925, he wrote Harriet from Spokane, where he had been living, to tell her of his sudden marriage:

My dear Cordelia:

.... *This letter is just to announce news so sweet my pen seems to get paralyzed when it starts to tell you. I was married May 19, here in my room, to Elizabeth Conner, whose name I have changed to Elizabeth Locust-Blossom Conner, because on our walk next day we found nothing but locust trees in full flower, the town bursting with them. We were not engaged, but married by spontaneous combustion the minute we got acquainted, which was somewhere around May 18, though we had of course met a good many times in a decidedly pleasant way before.*

I am wanting you to write to Elizabeth and Elizabeth to you, and I am reading her this epistle.

Alice Corbin always boasted of being your brightest pupil, follower and disciple when you were more definitely a teacher of English down by the University. I fancy Elizabeth had a similar relation to that remarkable Statue of Liberty, President Reinhardt of Mills College, California. There—perhaps—she has had a great pacemaker and inspirer, and forcer of her mental flowering.

Well, I am not going to write you an essay on my lovely bride, for doubtless it will sound much like other bridegroom songs, and this lady, of course, is different. What is far more important, we start life with a clean slate, with no heavy obligations, no unpaid debts and no promises, and the future is indeed the future. We are both in excellent health, both fond of hiking, both walk fast and hard, but she is one jump ahead of me in adoring a Latin Poet called Catullus, and I can't pass on his merits, not being able to read Latin. Maybe you can have a Catullus picnic with her some day, when I'm asleep as usual upstairs. Catullus is just about your line, I guess!

214

Certainly, dear Cordelia, the world has begun anew for me and all disasters have fled away.

Our wedding was sudden, but there was not one hitch or spoiled event in the pageantry. We tried to have it sudden and secret, but it was at least sudden and private, with all our friends wildly enthusiastic the next day, and the little wedding party in this room the most beautifully reverent and intimate of all wedding-parties.

As a matter of fact we wanted a secret wedding with only witnesses sworn to secrecy—two, I suppose. I was so sick of publicity and having my heart poked into by dirty fingers for the last few years, I wanted privacy at all costs. So our guests in the end just came in at the last minute as it were, also by spontaneous combustion, and it all turned out dewy as Milton's Eden dawn.

Well, why do I go babbling about this wedding and skipping the essential matter—the Bride. I am in no state of mind to describe this Bride to you, so I must needs refer to the classics. Let's see: there's Juliet. She is like Juliet. She is 23 and acts 13. Then there's the wonderful girl Rosalind who put on boy's pants and went on a toot through the Forest of Arden. She is like Rosalind. Then John Milton has written some nice poems. She is like the heroines in some of Milton's nicest poems.

Of course my letters about the road came from a desperate heart. They were 1,000,000 years ago. With Elizabeth Locust-Blossom Conner Lindsay wild to take the road with me, I may yet do it, but I do not see the gigantic and rebellious hikes I previously planned in my defiance. If you think the little seduction whose pictures I enclose is capable of walking to Halifax and back, why maybe we will. I have every intention of being as brave and as feeble, as smart and as stupid, as this little lady. She is the head of the firm and my gratitude to her for being so kind to me can never be told. I was going all to pieces for lack of a young governor, a young ruler, a brave young dreamer, and here she is, with a firm hand and a very tender and absolute devotion. I have been physically and mentally well a long time, but the mere weight of such praise as that James Stephens

215

has heaped upon me, for instance, has isolated me from natural life and from mankind. She has bravely broken the spell and taken the whole curse away. The beauty, secrecy and suddenness of our wedding was part of it. It went through with glory, yet as an act of God, not a device of man. Surely I shall obey this girl as I would an angel from the skies, as surely I shall pray for an obedient heart, for she is youth and poetry itself, with no patent devices.

With love indeed,
VACHEL

Harriet loved Lindsay and believed in him. She heartily approved of marriage. So she bestowed her blessing forthwith.

In the summer she made her usual happy trip to Cummington, where she was occupied with plans for a trip to Europe in the fall, the object of which was to further Alice Harriet's education by immersing her for the winter in a French atmosphere. This project was carried out. Early in October, 1925, Harriet, her sister-in-law (Alice Harriet's mother), Edith Kellogg, and the little girl herself sailed on the "Cleveland." Harriet particularly enjoyed the voyage. The spirited young niece was always a fresh delight, and she records that highly agreeable adult companionship was supplied by the painter Carl Lindin and his family.

To Ferdinand and Clara Schevill she wrote, on shipboard: "I find myself forced to an unnatural restraint in writing letters, because of my passionate enthusiasm for the sea, which leads me to an all too excessive expression when I try to write. The blue of the sky and the ocean, the soft play of light-running waves, touched with white at the edges, and this sublime expression of being, all carry me beyond myself."

Admitting, however, in a letter home, written before landing, that she still felt deficient in energy, she added, "but as Edith so pertinently or impertinently, says, a little excitement would make me all right for a while."

This she found, in various forms, in Europe.

216

Having arrived in Paris, it was incumbent upon Harriet to make certain professional investigations, in which the members of her party can scarcely have been loath to join her. Her technical discoveries, extremely mouth-watering in character, she dispatched promptly to Miss Scott, manager of the Home Delicacies Association's kitchen:

DEAR LUCY,

At Rumpelmeyer's the special thing that was worthy of notice was the fact that they had a great many small cakes, fairly in the group of our petits fours, but very different in shape. Some of them were about the size of the bottom of a teacup, made of two thin layers of delicious cake, with almond paste, or marron filling, and various kinds of fillings, set between, frosted with elegant smoothness—a thin frosting that made them most delightful to eat, and not at all too sweet, sticky, or heavy. Others were bars about a good inch wide and 2½ inches long, set together in the same way, and frosted only on top, very light tube work of Parisian meringue. Various kinds of delicious fillings were set between these bars. The whole object of this show seemed to be to make the things look tempting to eat rather than exciting through their artistic decoration. I saw little paste shells, very shallow, made in something about the size of our (individual) pie plates, Marshall Field type, but not so high, and these had just a spread of delicious apple slices in them, one thickness only, and over them a very thin piece of pie crust, rolled so thin it was almost transparent, and so put on that it pulled and broke away a little bit from the edges and over the apples. I make sure Bordeaux would know how that was.

They are serving here as an entrée a large pie-shaped thing, probably 14 inches across, and made, I should think, somewhat like this: Take very thin bacon and crisp it. Cover a broad shallow pie plate with ordinary pie crust. Lay over it the crisp bacon and pour in on this an unsweetened custard made without corn starch, the custard not too thick, and the whole baked in the oven. This was good, and to me new.

217

Will you recommend for your Thanksgiving pumpkin pies honey in the comb to be served with the pie? They say this changes the pumpkin pie into an exquisite sweet.

However, meringues and maroons occasioned but a twenty-four-hour delay, and the travelers were shortly en route to the Riviera, "establishing," as Harriet afterward wrote, "a new record for movement." Hurrying to Cannes by an uncomfortable train, Alice Harriet must have surprised her elders by the discovery on arriving there that she was "lonesome" and could not eat. Harriet herself, however, was content. "Never did the breezes from the four points finger my cheek so lightly . . . . never was I so exquisitely wrapped around with transparent color. Ah well! I have seen it at any rate." The entire party returning to Paris, they there decided that, after all, a reconciliation might be effected between Alice Harriet and Cannes, and the second journey south was accomplished by motor, "over roads not repaired since the war trucks ruined them." Parting finally with the Tildens in Cannes, Harriet sped to London.

Here James and Cynthia Stephens, "who have the most wonderful cordiality and are altogether among the most friendly people I know," as Harriet described them, took her to see the Irish players in Sean O'Casey's *Juno and the Paycock*, and Harriet gave a dinner party at the Tour d'Eiffel, a French restaurant in Percy Street, for both the Stephens and the Swinnertons, who had not previously known each other. This proved to be a gratifying success, Frank Swinnerton writing immediately afterward:

My dear Harriet:

Your dinner-party was delightful. It was a great treat for both Mary and me, and we thank you most warmly. I don't know whether James Stephens was at his best, as I never saw him before; but he seemed to me to be magnificent. I don't think I've enjoyed talk so much for ever so long; and only wished that I wasn't so tired. When we got home, and to bed, I fell asleep instantly. But it had been lovely, and everything as nice as could be; and I wish it was all to do over again. Are you really

218

off on Saturday? If so, we'll wish you bon voyage, and a safe return; with very soon, another, and longer visit. You see we want you to see Old Tokefield. In fact if you could possibly spare time to come even now we should love to have you there. It is for you to say. We go back tomorrow (Thursday) evening. What about a snatched visit on Friday? Any chance? If not, come back in May. It is glorious then, with the flowers coming, and sunshine. Whatever you do, believe that you will always be welcome and that Mary and I will always be grateful to you for your kindness, and always

Yours affectionately,
FRANK

The short, busy winter in Chicago, each day thickly filled with new people and new experiences, was, after all, but a gap between two European journeys. Harriet, since she was responsible for Alice Harriet's being in Europe, felt that she must herself return to Cannes. With the lordly capriciousness of childhood, the little girl had at last made a certain surrender to Europe and now rather more than tolerated the Mediterranean shore but was waiting, nevertheless, to be brought home again. And this in no routine fashion but in the dramatic way in which her remarkable aunt always traveled, with all its lively unexpectedness and with scores, it seemed, of unusual people always surrounding her wherever she was, on trains, in cities, or on the ocean, and with Alice Harriet herself never by any chance overlooked but always drawn lovingly into the very heart of whatever might be going on.

To this greatly loved young person Harriet herself wrote in January, incidentally picturing a state of things with which the child had been familiar from babyhood, since she had always spent so much time at 2970 that one almost thought of her as part of the household: ". . . . Everything has been happening to me. . . . . I have had so many visitors, some of them coming quite unexpectedly. Mr. and Mrs. Stephens are in the house now, and Mr. and Mrs. Beckhard [Arthur Beckhard, the theatrical producer, and his wife, Esther Dale, the singer]. Last week

we had Mr. [Harold] Vinal and Mr. [Edward] Davison. . . . .
I have tried to write a letter with my own hand several times,
but never succeeded. I think now very soon this group will be
gone and everything will settle down quietly.

"I know just how delighted you are with Walter Scott, and
that delight will never stop. When I come I will read to you
as much as ever you want me to."

Also there had been a welcome visit from Robert Frost. And
a new poet, Lynn Riggs, came to see Harriet. "He is a very interesting fellow," Harriet wrote, "and I am glad to put him on the
list of young friends." Mr. Riggs afterward read from his poems
at one of Les Petits Jeux Floraux evenings. At the same time,
the young English poet Edward Davison had been sent to her
by Leonora Speyer, to whom she wrote, protesting against her
poem, "Farewell to the Fiddle"—"because I cannot bear the
idea of your striking off any side of your vivid life.

"Again there is your gift of Edward Davison, which is priceless. He is a 'braw gallant,' and a gifted; and he was driven away
from us all too soon. He cut a broad swath in Chicago.

"I pray you may be in New York when I go through to
Europe. It is more than a year since we have met."

James and Cynthia Stephens continued to be among the
most eagerly welcomed of Harriet's inner circle and during this
winter, in the course of a lecture tour, visited her twice. In
between visits Mr. Stephens wrote her from New Orleans on
February 5, 1926:

DEAR HARRIET:
This is but a note to say we are still alive, and like Felix,
walking still. I begin to feel I should be developing some kind
of wheel-system where my legs are, we have wheeled so much
and so far. It was curious to waken up from Chicago into Texas,
and to find our vanished summer. The population of Fort
Worth were all sauntering about in their shirt-sleeves, and the
sun was doing itself proud. Naturally, and, of course, I caught
a fifty-sneeze-power cold. I have been sneezing myself into and
away from lectures ever since. Very miserable this person was,

220

and very frightened that he wouldn't be able to talk in loud and rotund noises, and very desirous of being back in Chicago, and very much better now. Now we are away, far away by the Gulf of Mexico, a name I have seen before on a map and maps, but never dreamed I should neighbor. 'Tis an un-American-looking city and 'tis dressing itself for the Mardi-Gras. Bunting in the streets, and congregations in the ten-cent stores; and all the neighboring territories are sending in hourly contingents to swell the crowds. On the 16th (I think) all of these people will clamp red-plaster noses over their own noses, and will blow blasts on tin whistles. But we, thank God, will be back in Chicago by then, unwhistled and un-nosed. I think that public happiness is about the unhappiest. But that is to carp, which the Lord forever save me from. I talk here on the 8th and we hope to quit these parts on the 9th and be on the straight route for Chicago. We will wire you as to this.

I talked to all kinds of reviewers about your Léonie Adams, and hope that some of them will give her a mention. But when I get back you must read the Fire-Bringer to me—we will make a special evening for that. It will be good to be with you again. Love to you from us both, and twice from me.

But when James Stephens did arrive, it was to face a month's illness, spent partly at Harriet's house and partly at a hospital. This was diagnosed as pleurisy, involved a lung operation, and caused great anxiety, as well as the canceling of Mr. Stephens' remaining lecture engagements. Harriet's departure for Europe was thereby delayed, as was the Stephens' own. With the journey more or less immediately in view, however, it was pleasant, as March arrived, to have the following friendly letter from the Swinnertons, written at Var, France. There had been talk of Harriet's joining them on the Continent.

Dear Harriet:

Your very welcome letter does not say when you are arriving in the South of France, but I fear you are bound to miss us. Our allotted two months is nearly up, and we go home a week today—Feb. 26—according to plan. We are bound to go. We don't want to, but our return accommodation was taken before we started, and there are many calls for us. For one thing, both Mary and I have mothers, who depend much upon periodical glimpses of us. For another, I'm really troubled about the badness of my new novel, and I fear that I shall not be able even to begin to put it right until we are home. And as our well-being, and our trip to America, and every other promised joy, depend upon my pen I am bound to give early heed to these matters. Otherwise we should stay, for though it is blowing ferociously at this moment we've had lovely summer weather at intervals for seven weeks, and we're as well and as cheerful as can be. And it would have been so lovely to see you here, among all these beauties of mimosa and pine, blue skies, blue seas, and marvelous sunrises and sunsets. We shall no doubt be longing, even at Tokefield, to be a part of your delightful company. Alas!

I said "even at Tokefield." If you have a chance, do come to Tokefield. We've had it all dolled up while we've been away— new whitewash, old beams uncovered, and a lot of other things. Secretly, we're pining for Tokefield; but we want Tokefield here, if you know what I mean. We don't want to go, and we want to be home, and the thought of going back makes us gloomy, and elates us—well, what can be done? We dislike the English visitors at this hotel, and scowl at them as deeply as they scowl at us. We resent their loud, self-important conversation. And we've got no defense against them. Neither Mary nor I can talk loud, and we couldn't think of anything to say if we could. But on the other hand all the people on the hotel staff are very pleasant and very kind to us, and we like them, extremely. We'll have to go back. We shall miss the great pleasure of seeing you. Do try and come to Toke. Mary would be so proud to show you her devices and comforts.

Do not trouble to read "The Elder Sister." It is already forgotten. We came on a Tauchnitz edition of it the other day, outside a shop in Saint Raphael. It gave us quite a shock. We didn't buy one, though I afterwards thought I ought to have done so. We have been once to Nice, and twice to Cannes (which we like). We think Cannes and Ste. Maxime are the most interesting and attractive places we have seen along the coast, from Hyères to Nice. But we've been no further than Nice, and some of the towns on the Italian side of the border (which you must visit) ought to be charming.

Well, now, we send you our best love. We wish you the happiest possible time here in the south. We hope to see you at Tokefield. And we wish you to know how very much indeed we desire that you should go on liking us and keeping close to us. It is a great disappointment to us that we are to miss your stay here, and it has clouded our pleasure in your splendid letters, which otherwise gave us both great joy.

For us both, I am

Yours affectionately,

FRANK AND MARY

Later in the month she writes Mrs. Speyer that her new book of poems has arrived and praises Kahlil Gibran's drawing of the author.

"I am putting a little frame on mine and am going to hang it on the wall in my poets' corner; the first woman there. . . . . I am glad of the book with your writing on the flypage. My own looked rather pathetic with 'Harriet from Harriet' inscribed on its blank leaf. I shall keep it, as a token of how cruelty can be healed by kindness. . . . .

"I have been trying to get off to Europe for several weeks. . . . . I am delighted at the sea prospect. That is where I am face to face with the inscrutable. I am hoping by this means to get back my old endurance."

By April 19, Harriet had achieved her departure and was on board the "Olympic" bound for Europe, Edith Kellogg with her. In mid-ocean she wrote for Bessie O'Neill in Chicago a brief sketch of the few hours she had spent at a New York hotel before sailing. This sounds like a hundred other of Harriet's hasty dramatic pauses in New York. In the evening before the ship sailed she had gone with Mrs. Speyer, Padraic Colum, and others to see Ben Ami in Werfel's play, Schweiger. Earlier, at teatime, the same group had surrounded her in the hotel.

"Marguerite d'Alvarez[3] came in while Leonora was there. I placed her by my side, turned Leonora over to Padraic, and talked exclusively with d'Alvarez. We planned to meet in London. (She is singing, it seems, in London in June.) We made the grand gesture in every direction. She stayed on awhile and then said she was sorry but she had to keep an engagement. I urged her to stay; but she said it was impossible. So we parted tearfully and effusively. Later on Edith came in and found her sitting in another part of the hotel." . . . .

This time the weeks Harriet spent in Europe were considerably more of a tumultuous whirl than her stay had been the preceding autumn. Alice Harriet was supposed by this time to have gained an idea of the way French is actually spoken. Before returning, she was to be given an impressionistic view of the main capitals of Europe. This was accomplished, but at the cost of what difficulty Harriet herself suggests in a letter written late in June at Ste Gervaise, France, to a young California friend of hers, Harriet Morris. She says: "One circumstance of my stay here I am sure you will find explanatory of my whole life. While I was still in Chicago I argued it out with the most competent of my financial advisers in the H.D.A. that it would be a real economy to buy a motor car, hire a chauffeur over here, and motor everywhere. It was easy to show that it would be simpler to do this than to take my own car, and less racking to the nerves at the same time, because my own chauffeur will only go to the places he wants to see. So we bought a Ford like the one I have in Los Angeles, agreeing that it should be sold at a slightly advanced price after I was through with it. In Paris I ultimately got this car. It had a French top, far inferior to those made in America, and a few other slight defects, but still it was a very good operating machine. A Russian painter (Vladimir Perfilieff), whom I know in Paris and like, said with the flash of a Knight's Templar that he would get me a perfect chauffeur, which he did, and incontinently produced him, a man endearing to look at, with a most useful

[3] The singer, a relatively new friend of Harriet's—"the nearest to a child of nature I have ever seen," as Harriet described her.

and attractive click to his heels when he made his bow, an ex-naval officer, who in his time had commanded the flagship of his admiral.

"So we began our lives together, each trying to impress the other as belonging to the supreme group. In France it worked perfectly, but when I came to try to escape from France on any of its borders I found that there was a definite embargo on ingress and egress so far as Russians were concerned. So I had an expensive Russian on my hands. After using, first, my own certainty that nothing can withstand me and that I could overcome the difficulty, and secondly, that nothing can resist the little old U.S.A., and that I could therefore get past the regulations, I had to leave him, as it were, marking time on the border, and have now been traveling for three weeks, doing the best I can without him. He is, however, taking a summer vacation with my car in Cannes."

Harriet and her companions reached Rome early in June. It is interesting that she found the imperial city, which she had not seen before, completely satisfying. "I never saw anything so wonderful as Rome," she exclaimed afterward. It was even "more serious, more magnificent, more inspiring," than she had imagined—a fit background, she must have thought it, for the supreme poet of his age. To her immense delight, Rabindranath Tagore was in Rome also, a guest of the Italian government.

"On the moment of my arrival," Harriet wrote later to Mrs. Arthur Seymour, of Urbana, Illinois, "I learned to my great delight that Rabindranath Tagore was at the Grand Hotel, and that he was asking for me. I saw him at once and found him looking as noble and beautiful as ever, with perhaps a touch of fatigue owing to the strenuous exertion he was making to keep up with the hospitality offered him. Rathi and Protima were very well and the little child was with them. They had also a considerable escort of Indian men and women.

"Feeling that Mr. Tagore was needing, more than anything else, time when he could snatch a chance to rest, I left him with the agreement that we should meet in London later on.

This we afterwards did, and there I had two or three more absorbing opportunities to hear his well-loved voice and sit in the presence of his profound wisdom.

"In London Mr. Tagore had a portrait bust made by Epstein. I did not see it finished, but I went with him to look at it in a transition stage and it promised to have abundant strength, though at the moment when I saw it, it did not express his supreme and masterly beauty. Mr. Epstein was very cordial to me, and seemed to be on the best of terms with Mr. Tagore, as who is not."

After all, seeing Mr. Tagore in London was a fragmentary affair at best. By this time he was thoroughly accepted in Europe as a personage. Being a personage takes up a great deal of one's time, but during that last decade the philosopher seemed to have reconciled himself more or less to that. So all this would have been very well if Mr. Tagore had but regarded London as a stepping-stone to America. It seemed that this time he regarded it as nothing of the sort. He did not intend to cross the Atlantic. There would be no seeing him in Chicago. There would be no seeing him .... perhaps ever. A dark cloud hung over Harriet's departure from England.

Before leaving, however, she had the refreshment of a meeting with the Swinnertons, this time on their own territory. This she speaks of in a letter that she wrote them from New York, in August, on her way home.

DEAR FRANK AND MARY,

My afternoon with you was wonderful. We praised it all the way home. The charming sincerity of your house, the ingenious insincerities, your wonderful study, your garden, but most of all the atmosphere of quiet peace, and the imminent presence of understanding companionship. It is a great experience to have a home like that to plunge back to in one's thought and to know that if that thought should become reality there would be added to it a real welcome. I cannot say that my own home is either in any sense as interesting or as clean as yours,

226

but I will not yield to any one in the royalty of welcome it will offer you two when you appear there in the fall.

But Harriet did not readily recover from what seemed to her Mr. Tagore's rejection of this country. Months afterward she wrote to their common friend, Mrs. Seymour: "I am always grateful to you for keeping me so closely in touch with the plans and occupations of the Tagores. It is a disappointment to me that the Poet did not come to America. . . . .

"I don't know whether you feel as I do, but to me it always seems that Robi Babu's absolute severance from his exterior environment unfits him for getting the real quality of American life or from knowing the deeper truth about his friends and our outstanding leaders, although his own magnificent initiative is of course invaluable. But I feel that it is somewhat defeating to have it so coupled with misapprehension about others. Nothing but his settled conviction that America is hostile, mediocre and commercial has prevented his coming back here this time. . . . ."

These may have been the first or perhaps the only almost-critical words that ever came from this most constant of the philosopher's disciples. But her devotion to him was by no means lessened.

CHAPTER XX

MADAME CURIE

Harriet may have become somewhat fainthearted about going to India, though it had been her supreme hope. Yet she never admitted this and even in 1931 wrote to young Protima Tagore of "those Hindu princes whom I have met in your company and whom I should like to know if fortune ever takes me to your country."

Now, newly returned from a lively but, of course, exhausting European jaunt, she seems to have leaned eagerly toward scenes more attainable than India and to have imagined not only visiting them but abiding in them. If it is the human tendency as one grows older to hug the illusion of safety, to cling to the most familiar spot, there are striking exceptions to this rule, and Harriet was one of them. In a letter to James Stephens and his wife, written in February, 1927, she confides: "I want .... to build a cottage on my farm, one that is winterproof, so that I may be able to get into the country in the cold weather."

And, in the next paragraph: "I hear in a random way that you are building a house in France. If it is true, it is too wonderful. My mind turns with the utmost eagerness and frequency to the thought of having homes in several countries."

Subsequently, she wrote to Francis and Jessica Brett Young: "Many congratulations on the English home. I have often longed to have one for myself. In fact, if my husband had lived, we should have bought something in Devonshire or else on some one of the islands."

It had been early in this year, 1927, that she had had the agreeable distraction of a visit from the English writer Francis Brett Young (then on a lecture tour) and his wife. Their hostess described them as "very interesting, both of them. . . . . She is a very good raconteur. . . . . He is a man of quiet speech and with the deep nature of a true artist." Later, she wrote of Brett Young: "He is a tremendous force, one of the most vital people I have ever known." And, after hearing a public talk that he gave, she praised his humanity and his "fearless idealism."

After leaving Chicago, Mr. Brett Young sent Harriet from New York a letter that emphasizes her extraordinary gift for arousing a stranger's admiring loyalty in a minimum of time. The too familiar tradition as to British reserve and surface chilliness would seem to be forcibly gainsaid. He wrote:

MY VERY DEAR MRS. MOODY:

I know that you haven't been expecting an orthodox "bread and butter" letter from me: first of all, because you gave us so much more than bread and butter—I speak figuratively as well as literally—and next because I think there is very little need for words among people of feeling. You know, as well as I do, that our short contact in Chicago wasn't one that can be measured in time (if there be such a thing) and that it remains one of the rarest and most beautiful of my American experiences. From the first moment I felt entirely at home with you, and even if we never met again—which God forbid!—I should feel that something valuable, in the best sense of the word, had been added to my experience and that I had made a friend of whom I should always think with tenderness and affection. This is the first "declaration" that I have ever made by typewriter but you, as a busines woman, will approve it.

Just one thing more. . . . . I could not bear your thinking (if you did think it) that I had any shadow of reservation about J. M. Synge's stick.[1] I was deeply moved, but do not let us think of wills when both of us are so happily and beautifully alive. . . . .

Always yours affectionately,
FRANCIS BRETT YOUNG

The Brett Youngs lived in Anacapri in a house that they had had built, and thence, in May, Mr. Brett Young wrote

[1] Which happened to be in Mrs. Moody's possession.

229

to Harriet, acknowledging her gift of Moody's prose plays which, he says, "I have read with eagerness and intense satisfaction—partly because I think they throw quite a lot of light upon yourself."

To various of her friends Harriet had expressed a hope that she could return to Europe in the summer of this year. Next she thought of going in October—then, for the winter. Her sense of the transiency of life was becoming more and more acute. She longed to share in all its movement, absorb all its significance, while it was still possible.

From Paris, on the first of May, 1927, Jules-Bois, her friend of many years, affectionately summoned her:

TRÈS CHÈRE AMIE,

Here I am in my dear France whom you love also. I left on the steamer with Paul Claudel, the great poet-Ambassador. You have to come at once so that I can be your guide and "cicerone." I wait for your letter with a real impatience. Write me please.

Mr. and Mrs. Speyer were on the same boat. We talked about your and remembered you with a warm heart.

I will explain the things when I see you. They—all of them —were very nice to me during the voyage, and my colleagues in Paris plan many receptions and banquets in my honor. But what imports is what comes from the heart and this has consoled me for many sorrows.

Come, I pray. Do not be slow. It is not in your character. You are a spiritual flame with wings and all the blessings of God surround you. I kiss your hands with respect and love.

JULES-BOIS

But, instead, for this year Harriet was doomed to remain in Chicago—a summer of heat, of decreasing energy, and of foreboding as well.

James Stephens had evidently expected to see her in London and wrote her from there on August 3 in rather a curious vein:

230

DEAR HARRIET:

This is only a note to give you my love—& to embrace you. .... I have been worried and wouldn't, couldn't write, but I'm as mad as a hatter because, 'Skers, you don't write. Alas! I don't believe you're coming over this year, & 'tis thus, a rotten year, a rainy years, full of holes and blanks, not-muchness. I carry, religiously, your Thunderbird.[2] It has never once left me since the day it came, & I think of you, & at you via it every day. Remember me to all your nice people, & to William[3] & the big dog, if they are still with you. Write me that you are coming soon, even if you aren't.

Replying, in early September, Harriet wrote: "I did hope to get to Europe this fall and perhaps I may do it yet. .... In spite of being captains of our souls we are swept along all too much by an unswerving destiny. You know I am not a fatalist, but how solid the embankment of external obstacles seems to be and how incessant the strain to make of one's perfect circle a parabola. I will tell you privately it was never intended that I should seriously wear and persistently tug at the harness of a business woman. You know as well as I that I am not in any sense a business woman at all. ....

"Do tell me if you are well and what your plans are for the winter. I may turn up in London or in Paris. I sadly need a new spiritual stimulus. I had a delightful letter from your young rival[4] all too long ago. I shall answer it soon. I am proud of his affection."

The Schevills, whose companionship meant much to her, were also in Europe. At about this time she wrote to Ferdinand Schevill, then in Munich: "How I envy you the fact that you are free! They say the modern dance known as the Black Bottom gets its name from the fact that it is shuffled through by skilled dancers in spite of their feet being held in heavy mud. My own feet are caught in a black substratum too deep to permit my even dreaming of dancing, yet I think I shall pull them

[2] A small piece of jewelry made by the American Indians.
[3] A pleasant young colored boy.
[4] James Stephens' son and namesake.

free. I am reminded of many conversations with my mother. She would say, 'Why do you continue to let yourself be burdened in this way?' And it was my custom to answer, 'I do it because I know I can shake myself free whenever I desire.' This present grip is a little tighter than I am easily able to shake off. Yet it will let go and I shall escape some time somehow. I hope it only may be in time to play about with you and Clara in Munich."[5]

And she closes with a laughing sentence that shows how irrepressible life had found her and in what powerful waves her youth, her vitality, her girlish coquetry, even, at times returned to her: "It is safe to say that Diogenes himself, even if equipped with a modern electric flashlight, would at present not be able to discover one man, honest or otherwise, who had the slightest interest in me."

Meanwhile, there were repeated suggestions that she return to Europe, as in the following letter from Francis Brett Young, in Anacapri, written on September 9, 1927:

My dear Harriet Moody:

.... I have often thought of you as I stood up to my waist in the Welsh salmon-river—of you and all your household, not forgetting Brother,[6] and relatively inanimate objects—such as the deplorable gas-fitting in your guest's bathroom and the adorable AE picture at the angle of the stairs. As a matter of fact, now that the high-speed film of my multifarious American experience has run through, I often find myself repeating little sections of it in slow-motion pictures; and America "slowed up" is far more remarkable, I assure you, than America whizzing by at its usual phenomenal rate. My slow motion places are a great delight to me, who worship, as you know, all subtle atmospheres of place; and my slow-motion people have revealed to me innumerable and lovable aspects in a vast number of new friends. They say the world is small: I wish to

[5] Munich, she explained in another letter, was always for her the "cité desirée because Will was so fond of it."

[6] One of the succession of Irish setters.

232

God that it were smaller, or at least that life were long enough for one to compass a millionth part of its loveliness.

This letter leaves me in the act of approximating my nose to the grindstone once more, completing, at the moment, the translation of an Italian friend's book, and conscious, all the time, of the moment when I shall begin by own. You will be glad to hear that Clare has had an enormous succès d'estime, and sorry to know that the other kind of success remains still in the background. It has sold, in America, 8,000 copies; in England approximately 7,000. It isn't, however, quite dead, and should, with luck, drag slowly on till Xmas in both countries. It has rewarded me with a lot of intelligent and sympathetic correspondence from my anonymous audience, but hasn't given me (and won't) the material security for which I have been waiting so long. However, both my publishers assure me that better times are coming; and if they do come, it will be a great relief—for if I have to go on pouring out a third of a million words a year, I shall soon have said all that I have to say and shall be forced to set up a shop for Home Delicacies in Capri. Luckily when that time comes, I shall be able to rely on your experience! As to the immediate future, Knopf will publish in the spring a book called "The Key of Life"; its setting is Egypt, and its theme my detestation of those dead things called museums, and of man's preoccupation with the dead past rather than with the living present. Incidentally it will convey a fairly vivid picture of Egyptian excavation. In the meantime I am ashamed to say that my American visit and the time that we took to recover from its excitements have swallowed a whole year; it is more than twelve months since I wrote an original line. I hope to begin to make up for this leeway on October 1st. Is there any hope of seeing you in Capri this winter? It would be a great joy to

Your affectionate friend,
FRANCES BRETT YOUNG

A little later, autumn at last fairly upon her, Harriet wrote again to Ferdinand Schevill, her unfailing affection gently tinged with irony:

Dear Ferdinand,

With your far-reaching historical researches you have doubt-less heard of a certain quicksand in Mexico where the aborigines deposited all treasure they could secure in any way, either by honest toil or by cutting off the heads of grandees. These articles, thrown into the sacred spot, disappeared forever from human knowledge, you remember. I feel that I myself am standing on the edge of such a quicksand and throwing my letters to you, priceless treasures, into its capacious depths. I have never written you so much, it seems to me, when you have been aberrating, as I have been doing this summer, and so far I have not heard of the arrival of one of my letters. Now only a month in the fiction called time separates us. Just long enough for this note to get to you, but not long enough for you to send back an answer. So my writing at present is philanthropic.

Soon came another letter from James Stephens, written on October 2, 1927, from London:

Dear Harriet:

I was delighted to get your letter, and to know you are all right. About the Paris flat which someone has lent you for the winter—I do hope that you will be able to come over and use it: if not immediately and in the winter, at least in the spring.

You tell just the bare truth when you say that time and chance and fate and the devil did not really intend you to be a business woman. There are lots to do that, but there are not lots to be you. Naturally I (or we) have nothing against business. 'Tis only when we enquire how deeply it can interest a person (like you) that we see that it has much of poverty. 'Tis great to initiate and to bring to its success, and to quit; and that I hope you'll be able to do.

I see you have been reading "Beasts, Men and Gods." What a singular book! And what a singular author! He is an adept at personal evasion. After reading his book one has undergone many physical and mental adventures; but the sense of intimacy that should subsist between a writer and a reader has not been

234

given. One knows nothing at the end of the book about Ossendowsky—if he is dark or fair, or amorous or gluttonous or timid or not—or anything. This only comes, and it comes without being "given," that he is more determinedly and darkly, and (perhaps) fretfully, hunting God than any other modern we know of. God seems to be less his hope than his quarry. He consorts with "miracles," the sign always of a man whose God is power. I'm not blaming, not even criticising. We all go for what we want, and we all want what we can; and we all get what we are equal to. I am prepared to hope for every creature that it gets what it wants to the limit.

Anyhow, you write that you may be able to come over; it will brighten the winter. You like winter, God bless you. That do not I. Climatically—I am a Mr. Facing-Both-Ways. I rejoice in the summer when winter's in it; and I laud the winter when summer is here. Padraic and Mary Colum are here, and I have been seeing something of them this week.

It was during this month of October, 1927, that Harriet, almost incomprehensibly, agreed to increase her existing burdens by opening another restaurant.

"Just now, hag-ridden as it were," she wrote to the Schevills, "I have allowed myself to be made an accomplice with Mrs. Sturges in the opening of another restaurant on the North Side, 180 Delaware Place, called . . . . Au Grand Gourmet."

E. A. Robinson's *Tristram*, which proved to be the culminating point of his career, was published in 1927, and the author saw to it that Harriet's copy promptly reached her. But she was obliged to delay reading it, and it was on the last day of November, and facing the blankest winter she had ever known, that at last she wrote him:

DEAR E. A.:

When your new book "Tristram" reached me, I had a great feeling of gratitude toward you and enthusiasm for your gift; but I was in one of the moods of life when I could not read—

235

I suppose you must have had these yourself. I looked to see if your writing was on the first page, and seeing it there, I sank back into peaceful postponement.

I rallied in my mind to the invitation to attend the reading of your poem in New York,[7] thought of going, and wished to go; but the truth is, I have been enmeshed in business responsibilities for a whole year now, and the part of me that is a poetry and art lover has been denied almost out of existence. . . . .

Nevertheless, now that I have just finished reading your "Tristram," I am moved by gratitude to write and tell you how much I have enjoyed it. Another thing that has moved me has been the fact that —— has written a commentary upon the book, and as I am always driven to despair by ——'s literary criticism, and feared I should read it before I wrote to you, I am sending off this letter now. . . . .

What I didn't know about you is the tremendous understanding you have of the all-sufficing power of love, between two who are really capable of it. . . . . James Stephens says, "We all go for what we want, and we all want what we can; and we all get what we are equal to." I am prepared to hope for every creature that it gets what it wants to the limit; you have given all and more than all to these lovers, and they are equal to taking it.

I feel that I can give you the highest praise for your profound entering into this illuminated dedication, each to each, of these two lovers.

I can just hear you say, as you always do to me—"O no, not at all. That isn't it."

But this and much more is in your poem for me.

Stupid critics are sometimes perhaps betrayed by the fact that a poet uses old legends as a background for passionate modern stories; but to me these critics are as dull as those who proclaimed Will Moody Miltonic and Shelleyesque.

[7] The Literary Guild chose *Tristram* (Macmillan Co.) for a book-of-the-month and launched it at a reception held at the Little Theatre. Mrs. August Belmont (Eleanor Robson) read passages from the book. Hermann Hagedorn, in his biography of Robinson, says: "All that was distinguished in New York in art and letters was there to greet him."

By 1928, fifteen years after Rabindranath Tagore had first trailed his hierophantic robes across her threshold, Harriet's house had ceased to be a gathering-place for followers of the arts.

In the winter of that year she wrote that she had practically closed her house to visitors. This meant, not that her unyielded enthusiasms spurred her any less acutely, but that she was too exhausted by work and worry to have many house guests or to meet the usual throng of strangers. She had, however, by no means become a recluse.

The desire that she had long felt to see and know the poet George Russell (AE) was revived by a letter that James Stephens sent her in January, 1928.

"I wrote AE," he said, "lauding Chicago and you, but he could not come to London, and I don't know if he had already made his plans. You will see him anyhow. Tell him to let me know the date of his return to Dublin, so that I can run over there, and hear his stories of the States. I do hope he will be able to stay with you, and for a long time, and that he will love William and the big dog, and the see-saw bed in the dining-room. I would give a lot to be able to trot myself into that dining-room this mortal minute, and to see you cuddling the telephone on your chest, and beaming wild or wicked or wonderful beams according as the bloke or blokeen at the other end of the phone deserved or evoked these.

"All my thanks for Sandburg's big book,[8] and for the cake that weighed a ton but tasted feathery. There is none of it left. There is not any whatever. 'Twas a vast and satisfying *gateau*, but liable to time, diminution and disappearance. Alas! It was! It ain't! It won't again.

"I'm doing a tiny Anthology from Spenser. Lovely! And another from Byron. Lovely. These two chaps are more wonderful than ink can tell, saving it's ink used by themselves. I'll send you the booklets when they appear. I've another thing to send you, but will say naught of it till I send it. Meanwhile, come over to Macedonia. Don't come until you send me that

[8] *The American Song Bag.* New York: Harcourt, Brace & Co., 1927.

237

guitar thing[9]—but come that same minute. All good wishes to ——— and ———. Tell me how AE strikes you, and how he seems to others, and if he does and doesn't succeed, and how greatly he does or doesn't and everything."

To Padraic Colum she wrote in early February, 1928, expressing her satisfaction that he and Mollie had returned to America.

"I had another gorgeous letter from James Stephens the other day," she tells him. "Your letter about him was an absolute godsend because only a few days before I had heard . . . . that James was not well at all, and in my sorrow I contemplated starting right off to England to look him over. But your letter speaks of him as well and joyous, and his own letter has a gladsome ring into the bargain. I hope . . . . I need not waste my all too scanty energies in being sad about him.

"It is a grand prospect to think of seeing AE. This for me will be either here or in New York. I have been straining every nerve to get away in March—to Europe, Mexico or New Zealand, perhaps. Probably I shall be tied here, but if I thought there was danger of my not being in Chicago when Mr. Russell is here, I should make a special trip to New York to see him. . . . .

"Percy MacKaye came in on his way from somewhere to somewhere. He was looking marvelously handsome and pouring out his expansive human love in every direction. Percy might be cited as the incarnation of brotherhood. He has finished his life of his father—a pious but passionate undertaking —and is now thrusting his arms out vigorously into the air and with each motion freeing himself from a sense of duty which hitherto has somewhat impeded his creative work. . . . ."

And to James Stephens she wrote, with all her old fervor: "A great rumble of delighted astonishment is traversing this continent, proceeding from New York where George Russell is talking to audiences overwhelmed by his eloquence and by his vision. I am looking forward to seeing and hearing him. He is coming here in March."

Before this happened, she had to face an ordeal that boded

---

[9] *Modern Album for Guitar*, by Vahdah Olcott Bickford.

far more than she, in speaking of it to her friends, confessed—a prolonged and painful situation centering in the personnel of the Home Delicacies Association.

To Padraic Colum she described it in this light fashion: "There have been disruptions in the business due to the usual forming of cliques for underground work, and I finally had a strike, and shots fired, but my own unparalleled courage and decision brought me through with secret qualms disguised by smiles. Enough of this. . . . ."

It was, of course, a shattering experience, but this proud woman saw it through, pulled herself together, and turned from the treacherous morasses that her business now seemed to rest on to firmer ground. Sanity, honesty, health—when had she more cruelly needed the assurance that such qualities existed? And what, it seemed, could be more opportune than the coming arrival of the inspired Irishman in whose bardic wisdom she had placed such faith? Confident, almost happy, she waited the day that should bring him.

Rarely had Harriet's human encounters miscarried. She had every reason to be quietly sure of herself. So many times, all through her life, offering her own genuineness, her own gracious sympathy, she had, even in the face of indifference, of misunderstanding, disarmed and conquered. . . . .

Nevertheless, Mr. Russell's coming proved to be—in contrast with what Harriet had hoped for—almost tragically devoid of significance. He came to dine with her. A pianist who was a close friend dined also with Harriet that night, but unexpectedly. Afterward she played, though this was not at all what had been planned. At a suitable hour, the poet went away. No understanding word had been spoken.

Afterward, Harriet wrote to Padraic Colum, who she knew would be particularly interested: "I did see AE . . . . but I never got into his century nor he into mine. It was too bad. . . . .

"You know I have always thought my meeting with him would be one of life's real meetings. But it was like the search for the grail. You, the father of all mythologies, remember that the searcher often entered the chamber where the chalice was,

239

but never was prepared to see it until the proper moment arrived. He [AE] is, as I have always surmised, far greater than his formal expression of himself in prose or verse, but my meeting him didn't pull off."

Of James Stephens she writes, in the same letter: "My affection for him in unbounded. He is a crotchety tyrant but a divine spirit."

To Stephens himself she wrote of the book he had sent her, *Etched in Moonlight:* "It seems to me that it must be written for me, it gives me such extraordinary pleasure."

All through the winter she had wearily longed and planned for a European journey—her last one, as it proved—and in June, 1928, her plans took shape. For companion she had her lifelong friend, Evelyn Matz. Even as she sailed, she coolly prophesied that cables in regard to the far-from-settled situation in here business would call her back; and they did. But not before she and Miss Matz had been motored by friends through Austria and Switzerland, pausing, after a final dash through France, in Paris. Afterward they flew to London and spent ten days in England.

Here, though she no doubt felt it beyond her powers to attempt to make connection with her scattered group of English friends, she did reach out for Wilfrid Gibson, whose family included a godchild of hers whom she would have been glad to see. That she failed to do so was explained in a letter from Gowan Bank, Letchworth, that reached her as soon as she got home, saying that Gibson had been at that time "lying on his back in a nursing home."

The event of the summer, however, was Harriet's association with Mme Curie, whom she saw repeatedly during July and August.

There was excellent reason for their meeting, since, as has already been noted, it was Harriet Moody herself, though this has never been generally known, who first suggested the idea of inviting the women of America to contribute a fund whereby Mme Curie could acquire her needed radium and who was later one of the committee formed to carry out this purpose.

240

Now it was in her mind to act as an instrument in securing further help for this great woman for whom, as she characteristically put it, "my heart aches with admiration and respect." With Harriet, it was always the heart that was the motive power; and it was a reliable one.

To her Chicago household she wrote after having made her first call, by invitation, on Mme Curie: "She is a human being on whom the unimportant influences of life do not impinge. She asked to see me again and she will breakfast with me at one o'clock on Wednesday. . . . .

"The luncheon with Mme Curie [at Foyot's] was most interesting. She is as sweet and simple as Aunt Minnie. We sat from 12:30 to nearly three and talked." A week later Harriet reports that, the heat being extreme, she had taken Mme Curie for an ice in the afternoon and had invited her to drive in the Bois in the evening, at nine. Later: "We drove to the 'Ile de France' last night to the home of Madame Curie. She brought her young daughter[10] to drive with us, a charming beautiful, intelligent girl, a student of music. Evelyn went up to the flat to get her. I did not undertake it. Evelyn said her flat was severe and distinguished. We drove in the cool Bois for an hour—a very pleasant hour—and we got home at half past ten. . . . ."

A month afterward, in late August, Harriet continued this report. She speaks of motoring from Paris to Chartres, spending the night there, thence going on to see Madame Curie at Paimpol in Brittany.

"We saw her for a few minutes, accepted an invitation for lunch Thursday, arranged with her to dine with us, and went back to have our dinner at 9:30. The place is very rugged and beautiful [with a] rock-filled harbor and wonderful trees and skies. Part of it is very old. It reminded me much of Carmel-by-the-Sea. For lunch the most remarkable thing in a simple but distinguished meal was the crayfish, about the size of sardines, white instead of red, and delicious. Mme Curie was very gracious. We enjoyed her and her married daughter, the younger one was not there. We left about four and drove to Caen."

[10] Mlle Eve Curie.

The purpose of these meetings was clearly set forth by Harriet in a letter that she wrote after returning to Chicago and sent, with slight variations, to various persons of substantial means:

CHICAGO, October 9, 1928
————

When I was in Paris this summer I spent a number of hours with Madame Curie, the discoverer of radium. You are well informed, I am sure, concerning her work. She is a pure scientist, dedicated to the advancement of knowledge and is, I suppose, the most important woman in modern science in the world.

I found her exquisitely delicate, simple, and most moving in her dedication to the things she is doing. She had a readiness to talk with me about her work because by a lucky chance I was instrumental in getting her the radium which she received as a gift from America. Several years ago Mrs. Meloney, the editor of the Delineator, had spent some time with Madame Curie in Paris. She was enthusiastic about her work and had come back to America with the idea of helping Madame Curie buy the radium she so sadly needed. She asked me to breakfast with her to talk over a method of getting this radium, and I happened to suggest to her that she should put it to the American Women as the need of the greatest living woman scientist. This she did and with great rapidity collected the sum of $125,000 to buy the modicum of radium that was needed.

I asked Madame Curie what I could do to help along in her work. She said that her most serious need at the present time was the gift of a few thousand dollars to support the special students who were scientifically trained and very helpfully engaged in her studies.

I wonder if you would feel interested in getting a few of your friends to combine in making up a sum for this purpose. I am never able to do very much in the way of giving money, but .... I do feel that the discovery of radium, which was all hers, has been and promises to be a marvelous extension of human knowledge.

242

Home again; Chicago still feverish from summer heat; in the Home Delicacies Association, a disturbed and disturbing atmosphere.

To Miss Josephine Plows-Day, whose apartment she had occupied in London, she wrote early in September: "I so inadequately accomplished my purpose of getting a rest in Europe that my mind wanders back to the idea of completing my plan by returning, but I make sure I shall not be able to do that this year. I find myself quite unwilling to work, but crowded with more responsibilities than ever. I want to be a porpoise, a turtle, or a whale, but instead I am again become a dromedary."

The rest that she believed herself perpetually in search of eluded her, partly because her desperate anxieties stood always in the way and also because she depended more than ever upon the stimulus of human associations. Indeed, rest in the stern strict sense would have been for Harriet as dire a thing as death itself.

She was genuinely glad to hear, therefore, that the Francis Brett Youngs were about to make another American visit. She wrote cordially urging them to come to her but adding: "It troubles me . . . . to think that I have so little to offer you, outside of my own friendship, as I have practically cut myself off, you may remember, from the social life of the city."

During all the years that he had lived in Spokane, Harriet had not seen Vachel Lindsay. But in June of this year, 1928, he had written her that he and his young family were coming back to Illinois to live—coming home. He assured her:

This is but to say you are loved as of old. I am thinking of you, and Elizabeth and I do speak of you ever and ever. We count on you as a forever friend. . . . .

Everything is favorable in our universe. I have three Macmillan books coming out this year, so by next Christmas we may be able to make new plans. We ardently desire to live in Springfield, as of old, and to study a bit in the University of Chicago. I will do the living, Elizabeth the studying. Do you want two nice babies to raise? There is Nicholas Cave who can

243

crawl like a steam tractor, and Susan Montjoy Doniphan Frazee Lindsay, who acts with more flourishes than her name, can really dance poetry and is the boss of this end of the state.

Whatever our future, it involves Illinois and Harriet Cordelia and—we hope, Springfield. To pull up stakes is not easy, but be sure we are looking Eastward. Tell us everything. We want to know, and we love you.

Most eternally,
VACHEL

In December he came alone, on a lecture tour, by way of preliminary and, of course, stayed with Harriet in Chicago. It was a different Lindsay now. He was a no less sincerely devoted friend to Harriet. He was deeply absorbed both in his poetry and in his charming wife and children. But a new restraint had gripped him. Harriet saw that for telling her what he thought and felt he seemed no longer to need an eager torrent of picturesque expression. Had life asked too much of this strange gifted creature, all individualist, half recluse?

What gaiety there was in the holiday season this year emanated from the vigorous and charming figure of young Alice Harriet, who, alternately rejecting study and then reveling in it, was almost ready for college. Like Harriet, whom she resembled, she was a lover of life and a dispenser of it, with a warm human power of drawing people to her. Harriet's letters, now and always, have much to say of her: "A sweet, dear little girl." She is praised by her teachers. "We are very pleased at the progress she is making. . . . . I think she is going to be a fine woman." Harriet adored her, clinging to her presence and to all she signified—this last of the race of Tildens—with an intensity of which the young girl herself could have had no knowledge.

Also, there were enheartening letters from distant places; Mrs. Kennedy-Fraser had recently written in a happy vein from Edinburgh, recording new triumphs and announcing that she would shortly send as a Christmas greeting her own autobiography, "A Life of Song," then on the eve of being published. "I almost think I may try to cross the Atlantic for the last time next winter. . . . . I am as strong and well as when I was with you twelve years ago."

Timed to reach her exactly at Christmas, came one of Frank Swinnerton's letters which, written always in his extraordinarily careful and beautiful script, had almost the look—except for missing touches of gold—of a missal containing precious knowledge not to be hastily or irreverently conveyed. From Old Tokefield he wrote:

DEAR HARRIET,

I have been an unconscionable time in writing to you, and I expect that if you remember me at all it will be with loathing and execration. But at this season of the year I insist upon writing to send our best wishes to you and all our friends in your household. We have been thinking a great deal about you all, for we have followed with concern the passing of time, and have been recalling how it is not much more than a few days over the anniversary of our return from the United States two years ago. We have said "At this time, two years ago, we were at Harriet's"; and "On this day, two years ago, we saw Harriet in New York." Such memories, for us, keep the vision of 2970 Ellis very bright, because we never forget kindness. In this, it seems to me, we are deserving of forgiveness for any otherwise indefensible failures in the matter of correspondence. I have written very few letters this year, largely owing to the trouble with my arm, which has reduced me to the typewriter, a horrible means of conducting really intimate correspondence. Nor have I written much otherwise, for I have had some jobs on hand which have forced me to read a great deal—to little clear purpose—and these jobs have taken up the time, so that the year has rushed away. Well, it is nearly over now, and with the new year I am determined to regain my self-respect.

We are well and still as happy as ever. We are, at the moment, in a terrible pickle, as we decided that we must have some artificial heating in this cottage, so that when visitors come to us from the United States, they will not have to crouch over the fire in their fur coats, shivering. All will be different for the future. When next you come you will find "a home from home" as they say, all as warm as toast—unless, of course, the heating apparatus does not work. I do not know if this is a possibility, but I do know that while the job is in progress we have been having what for us is extremely cold weather—twenty or more degrees of frost. To you, such cold will seem child's play, but in the midst of brick dust and banking, draughts and open doors and holes in the roof, etc. it has seemed very much like Hell (which I insist upon regarding as a place of eternal cold). We should have fled to the South of France, where we are going as soon as the job is finished, but our little cat, Bogey, is the most timid and easily panic-stricken cat that ever lived, and we have felt compelled to stay here and supply him with moral stamina. He has grasped the situation, and each morning, after his breakfast, he now walks into the one room in the house where the men do not go with their hammers and pipes, and seats himself in an armchair, where he remains for the whole day, until the house is silent, when he miaows to come out, and sits purring in front of the fire on his cushion until it is time for his tea and his nocturnal prowl. Then farewell until the morning, when he calls at our bedroom window to be admitted. We hope this program will continue until the place is clear of men, but as, when the pipes are in, other men are coming to install the electric light, I fear we are not at the end of our troubles, or Bogey at the end of his apprehensiveness.

However, you may think our concern with a little cat a very trivial matter, and I must not take up the whole of my letter with such details. . . . . As soon as the job is done, we are going to skip across the Channel and hasten to the South for the coldest weeks of the year. We shall then return and take up the English Spring. Shall we see you then? . . . .

Yours affectionately.

It was from New York that Vachel Lindsay wrote her two days after Christmas:

DEAREST HARRIET CORDELIA:

.... I hope all is well with you, that your energy has returned full force. I profoundly appreciate your kindness while I was in Chicago this time. So many times you sat up and smiled bravely and I know it hurt.....

I am one of the many, dear Cordelia, who send to you a grateful heart. And let me hasten to say that I am most practically grateful for the Christmas box for my loved ones, and the prospect of a welcoming hand to Illinois to my trembling Elizabeth. She knows not Illinois! ....

With all my heart,

VACHEL

CHAPTER XXI

AUTHORSHIP

IN HARRIET'S secret ear the threat of oncoming disaster was all this time distinctly audible, but she referred to it only remotely, while admitting that for nearly a year her business had kept her closely tied to Chicago without even a jaunt to New York. "My spirit gallivants," she wrote, and we may well believe her, "but I have been tied to the stake."

Lamentable, too, was the circumstance she briefly recorded in late April of 1929:

"The great Rabindranath Tagore got as far as California this spring, coming across the Pacific. He was said not to be well, and only stayed a short time, going back as he came."

Mr. Tagore had, as a matter of course, urged her to join him on the Pacific Coast. Quite naturally, he could by this time scarcely think of an American visit that failed to include her. It is true that, as Harriet had herself perceived and pointed out, the fastidious Oriental didn't, after all, particularly care for American ways. But Harriet's ways—which included an intense concentration on his well-being—were something different. And he had a sincerely affectionate regard for Harriet herself.

She had been obliged to write him early in May:

MY DEAR POET,

.... you cannot know how sadly disappointed I was not to be able to fly to Vancouver to greet you on your arrival, and so to be in California during your stay there.

Only the most imperative restraints kept me from doing this. .... I have had a most distressing lameness on me all the winter and spring. .... However, I should have ventured upon going, for the great happiness of seeing you again, and of possibly being

248

able to make your stay in California a little pleasanter or easier by reason of many facilities I have there, but my business has undergone a great strain, and is in rather a precarious condition, and I may not safely leave it, fearing I might come back to find it entirely disrupted.

There was a faint solace in the letter that Mr. Tagore sent her after returning to India, with its proposal that they meet in Europe the following year, but, as matters now stood, even Harriet's undiscouraged heart can have attached scant substance to such a hope. He wrote on July 10, 1929:

DEAR FRIEND,

I cannot tell you how deeply I regret to have come away from your gate without seeing you. I hope that this lost opportunity is not a final one, though I feel that my days being limited now, I should economize my energy for giving my sole attention to all my works that still remain unfinished.

I am glad to know that you have been kind to your Datta[1] and that you liked him. I am told that he has enjoyed his travels in America and is hoping to have a good time in Europe also.

Rathi is helping me in my institution and is working hard. Protima is also working among my girls here. I have been cherishing a great desire in my mind for founding a Women's University in my country, making it an ideal one for our girls. I was encouraged by a bishop from your country to hope to raise a sufficient fund in America for this purpose. But knowing that I have not the power of appeal or the requisite talent for this kind of work I shrank from making an attempt and have come back to my own proper vocation. I think Andrews has a better chance of success and I leave this mission to him.

Next year there is some likelihood of my visiting Europe if in the meanwhile I have the time to write my Hibbert Lectures. I hope that you may also come there at the same time and that we may meet. With loving regards,

Yours affectionately,
RABINDRANATH TAGORE

[1] An Indian poet who had crossed the Pacific with Tagore. He came to Chicago and to Mrs. Moody and thence went on his way around the world.

Some months earlier, having missed Tagore, Harriet had written with complete sincerity to James Stephens, who had sent her his newest volume inscribed in words that keenly pleased her: "Do believe that the best thing that has come to me in this year 1929 has been my reassurance from you and my gratitude for your lovely manifestation of it in your book."

Such reassurances were what Harriet now most deeply needed. And one of them came to her in the form of a visit from Robert Frost in April. Earlier she had written him, after he had sent her his most recent book: "I don't know when anything has seemed so much a gift as it did."

In the way of significant if brief encounters, she was able to record: "We have just now had John Dewey for a good long call—a brilliant man, who is also most tender and human. Roelvaag, the Norwegian Minnesota writer, was here and spent an evening also."

She had satisfaction in the fact that E. A. Robinson had dedicated his *Cavender's House*, which appeared at this time, to Moody, his long-dead friend, and, on receiving the book, Harriet wrote him. He replied, writing from Boston in early June:

DEAR HARRIET,

It is a great pleasure for me to hear that you were pleased with the dedication—and with the book. . . . . I am sending today a copy of the large paper edition of Cavender's House, which I have been keeping until I knew for certain where to send it. You may like to have it. As for Cavender's wife, I don't know just what she did. I'm rather inclined to agree with you in your hope that she found something more attractive than his complacent ownership of her attractions—which I hope was made evident, though she is never there. I wish people wouldn't call her a ghost, especially when I have gone perhaps beyond the bounds of good art to say that she is only what he has brought with him. Of course this does not apply to you, for you evidently see what I meant.

250

Meanwhile, month after month Harriet stuck faithfully to Chicago and to the Home Delicacies, smiling grimly to herself, no doubt, in her knowledge of the futility of it. Yet she could write in a moment of self-delusion to Esther Dale: "I have now got a promising new manager into my business, and I have started on a course of conduct that will lead to permanent ease, although there is nothing in my past history that would encourage me to believe I should find it. If, however, this does work out and the business gets exactly into balance the way that I can see it may, I shall have much freedom after the immediate present, which I intend to use for seeing the world, if there is enough of me left to take it in."

But, as everybody remembers, 1929 was the year of the general debacle, the year when American business proved to be to so great an extent a financial house of cards. To those familiar not with its always admirable output but with the untrustworthiness of persons whom Harriet injudiciously placed in control of its finances, there can have seemed to be no reason to suppose that her business—her lifework—would survive. . . . .

In October, as a matter of fact, the storm broke. The Home Delicacies Association passed into the hands of its creditors.

Upon Harriet herself the effect of this thoroughgoing catastrophe was precisely what might have been expected by anyone who really knew her.

There are many women, and men likewise, who, in the economic position in which she now found herself and with impaired health into the bargain, would have adopted a pose of self-pitying helplessness. Nor would anyone have wondered at their doing so. This heroic figure neither relaxed nor mourned except in swift secret flashes. Instead, she held her head high, insisted that she could recover control of her business, and, gently protecting the sensibilities of her friends, wrote them one after another that they must not be sorry for her.

"I must relieve any possible anxiety," she wrote Ridgely Torrence, "by telling you that unless I should happen to be carried off before the conclusion of this episode, I shall be

251

re-established in an entirely satisfactory manner. But the things that I have been going through are hostile to life."

"I am terribly sorry for your struggle," Harriet told an unknown correspondent, whose trials were doubtless petty in comparison with her own. "I have often found under hardship that a radical right-about-face and determination to enjoy every possible enjoyable feature in a difficult and monotonous routine gave me more relief than anything else—that I was, in fact, able to get the upper hand of my difficulties in that way."

And to Wilfrid Gibson she expressed an almost incredible degree of steadiness and calm:

"I am so to speak sitting like Watts' *Hope* with my finger on the last string on my lyre. But I have been brought up by my father in a school where, facing a complete loss of all assets, one took a deep breath and began to reassemble one's fortune. I think myself that I am acting very much like a child, but I always feel, as Mr. Tagore says, if you can see any escape, you can bear any confinement; but if you can see no escape, you can bear no confinement. I seem at present to find my plan for escape."

If recovery of her business was her ultimate aim—and this was a possibility she forced herself to believe in—she did not dream of waiting for this solution of her troubles to come about. Instead, and without any loss of time, she applied her energy and native resourcefulness to devising expedients that might relieve her need. Most promising among these was a project that now first enters into her story—preparation of a volume that was to be known as *Mrs. William Vaughn Moody's Cookbook*. This was her last completed creative enterprise.

Perhaps there is nothing more remarkable in Harriet Moody's entire story than the fact that, even after the complete collapse of her fortunes and the disappointments and humiliations that this entailed, life came to have no bitter taste for her. From first to last her great love was for life itself, the supreme gift that is forever sweet and of which one can never drink too deeply.

Some months earlier, when she could already foresee the

252

catastrophe, she had written her friend Elizabeth Wallace (former professor of Romance languages at the University of Chicago): "I think it would be well for me to take to the lecture platform, advising all women to keep out of business. I suppose you remember Daudet's little story of the lamb in the mountain, and its pathetic conclusion, 'but in the morning he was eaten.' This seems for the moment to be the curtain on my own life."

Nevertheless in the same letter she made this spirited declaration: "However, you see our friends the scientists are working for us. In a few years, hopefully within the scope of our appointed number, they are going to turn the trick and make it possible for us to live on indefinitely. I shall rejoice at this. A great-uncle of mine at the age of 93 replied to a friend who said, 'I suppose, Mr. Tilden, you are ready to pass on to another form of experience,'—'No, no. I would rather stay here. *I am acquainted here.*' I myself like this old world so well that I would sign a thousand-year contract, even with a broken ankle."

To Ridgely Torrence she wrote: "I am crazy about everything I read in connection with modern science, and I am building my hopes very high of enjoying a normal expectancy of 300 years."

Harriet had never cared to write a cookbook. Often as the project had been urged upon her, she had replied always by smiling, half-assenting but failing to take the first practical step. Her art, for such it was and as such she regarded it, she ranked high. Yet there were other arts, having no connection with her livelihood, that more deeply engaged her. So, until the crisis came, her instinctive urge had no doubt been to salvage for poetry's sake as much time as she could from the "world of bread, pie, and cake" that she once ruefully spoke of herself as living in.

But during one of James Stephens' visits somebody happened to broach the matter of the unwritten cookbook with especial importunacy. Stephens listened, asked a question or two, brooded a moment, then supplied to Harriet in a flash the motive power, the enthusiasm, that she had always needed for launching this affair and that she had always lacked. There must be a composite introduction to the book, Stephens explained. This must consist of short disquisitions on food, on the cooking, perhaps, or, more likely, on the eating of it, written by such of Harriet's friends as happened to be poets or writers of note. Each contributor must be given the utmost latitude, so that he might be as gay or as serious as he pleased. The result would be a book with a strong double appeal, enchanting the lovers both of delicate food and of sound literature.

Harriet needed no persuasion to accept this beguiling idea but by the next day was already at work upon it, inviting sixteen poet friends each to contribute to her book some essay or whatever it might be on the vast and delightful subject of epicureanism. It was inspiriting that Vachel Lindsay and a number of others sent her immediate assurance that they would comply. Before long the actual essays began to come in. E. A. Robinson sent her a charming one, which has since been published.[2]

Thus, even before the hour of her extremest need, Harriet was devoting herself, though never with eagerness or real pleasure so far as her own share in the necessary labor went—for, instead, she looked forward to the lustrous part that her fellow-contributors would play—to preparation of the much-talked-of volume.

"As far as I can see," she wrote Nelson Rowley, then in London, "my cookbook will be the most unimportant of its kind ever presented to the public. . . . . I am sure you will testify that I can produce good food. Like everything else about me it is always done in a dramatic interest. By this I mean that the person who is to eat the food—even an unknown and never to be encountered gourmet—inspires me to think of combinations—but not in the least to talk about food. . . . . A chafing dish, a few condiments, and a spoon are all to the good with me. But this is about as far as it goes. I can remember only one incident in my life when I was sufficiently hungry to talk about food as an artist should."

² In the quarterly issue of *Colophon*, III (winter, 1938), 92–99.

It goes without saying that to supply technical information about cookery she had rich reserves to draw upon. Her many years of successful experience, her knowledge of foreign, especially of French, cooking, gained both at first hand in France and also through the French chefs she employed, supplied her with such abundant material that the only real problem was one of selection. The delightful recipes thus assembled are precious to anyone who already knows good food from bad or who even hopes to learn to do so. They are not addressed to profane stirrers-up of hasty meals whose main object is time-saving, nor, it must be confessed, do they in the least consider the question of economy. If you are hard up or in a hurry, Harriet would have counseled, take a sandwich and a glass of milk. But if you are seriously attempting to cook, do not violate this art by buying inferior materials, by immorally subtracting eggs, butter, cream, or wine from the stipulated list of ingredients, or by curtailing the required length of time.

Also, it is apparent that not a single passage in the book could have been set down by any hack-writing "ghost." Harriet's own unmistakable touch is everywhere. You can hear her voice and watch her slow smile as she describes what she terms in capitals, THE RENOWNED CHICKEN IN CREAM OF BOURG, FRANCE. And this, in addition to the necessary technicalities, is what she tells you:

"In most countries a hen takes her chance, looking about her with her single-eyed vision. Not so in Bourg! In Bourg there are no inferior hens. White of breast, and tender in the heart-wing, the Bourg hen goes her proud way, preparing for an awaiting paradise. This is the way I knew her, after she had achieved this paradise; after the high chef had laid his hands upon her, and the white-filleted acolyte had set her down before me."

Besides, the author prefaces each separate section of the book with an earnest and charming essay of her own, whether on soups, on salads, or on desserts, each being politely but warningly addressed to the culinary philistine. She also writes a general preface, which anyone—perhaps particularly any woman not interested in her dinner—will do well to read. Herein she persuasively sets forth that, although overeating is, of course, a sin and undereating a stupid form of suicide, intelligent and joyful consumption of proper food is not only a tribute to an art and the artists practicing it—but a positive virtue. The case for eating the right things—that is, dishes both authentically compounded and agreeable to the palate—could scarcely be better presented. Eating for medical or hygienic reasons, with a cautious eye on the calorie and the vitamin, was always magnificently disregarded by Harriet, if not by implication actually condemned.

A friend of hers (though a fellow-Ohioan and a participant, therefore, in the Johnny Appleseed tradition) wailed recently that he had never eaten apple pie with the proper relish while Harriet was alive, even at her own table. This had not only seemed to her a lack of good sense and a shocking waste of opportunity, it had, in fact, wounded her; for, rising above all prejudices to the contrary, Harriet always extolled a properly made pie, tender, juicy, and flavorsome, as one of the most excellent of foods. So that now, having to a certain degree entered into her wisdom, this tardy convert longed desperately, in piety and remorse, to consume a succulent pie or two before her forgiving eyes and thus win her belated approval.

By March, 1930, the cookbook was finished. Harriet went to New York to consult publishers. Almost immediately the New York Herald Tribune agreed to run sections of the book during a period of sixteen weeks. In June the book was accepted by Scribner's. At that time, though the group of contributions from poets, which had been promised almost to a man, was not yet complete enough to include with the manuscript, Harriet thought it "a foregone conclusion that Scribner will decide to use them."

But the publishers unfortunately thought otherwise, and the essays were excluded.

It was not easy for Harriet to reconcile herself to the view that her design for a cookbook was "too literary." She disdained the idea of a volume of mere facts, inclosed in an oilcloth cover.

She herself, she said in writing to a friend, could "point out the aesthetic values of foods and perceive the fusion of poetry, music, sculpture and painting . . . . where a little kettle bubbles on the hearth and two birds are to be found sizzling in a casserole, waiting for the men or women who shall enjoy them." But she could not work herself into a frenzy over the compounding of flour, sugar, eggs, and whatnot, serious matter though this was.

As it finally appeared, this book is not of a sort to be kept in the kitchen (unless the kitchen is the private province of an epicure) upon however immaculate a shelf. It belongs rather to the library, in the section devoted to the arts. It is, to be sure, a priceless book of reference, if you wish to settle a fine point of soup-making or sauce-concocting. But what more charming book could there be for reading aloud in the country, by the fire, to a small group, at a time when dinner is not too far distant and the listeners are not too uncontrollably hungry to enjoy Harriet's delightful phrase-making? This certainly is a use for her book that would gratify its modest author.

During this disturbed interval Harriet found a lively interest in the following letter from her friend Vilhaljmur Stefansson.

New York, November 19, 1929

Dear Mrs. Moody:

Believe it or not, there is being written in Canada a biography of me. The author is D. M. LeBourdais, of 103 St. George St., Toronto. He is secretary of the Canadian National Committee for Mental Hygiene but is not (as far as I know) treating me from that point of view. Yesterday there arose a situation pertinent to you which is most easily explained by giving you extracts from a letter which I am writing LeBourdais in this mail.

When LeBourdais started his biographical investigations, I thought the ideal way was for him to approach people directly without any intervention from me. But he soon discovered that some of my friends would not tell him even creditable things about me fearing that he might put them to some bad use. This, no doubt, partly because of the current biographical fashion which is to strip from the subject every shred of respectability if he had previously been supposed by the public to be a good man, or to explain away as of little account all his achievements if he had previously been supposed to be a great or merely an able man. . . . . At any rate, I found it necessary to intervene on LeBourdais' behalf with many of my friends, at least to the extent of urging them to write him as fully and as frankly as time and inclination permit. I have suggested that even the most unfavorable things about me had better be known to LeBourdais for I am a controversial subject in Canada and any peccadillos not brought out in the original biography will be emphatically brought out in reviews and comments at the time of publication, producing not only publicity of a kind hurtful to me but also creating the impression that the LeBourdais biography was an attempt at a whitewash and unreliable.

I hope very much that you will write Mr. LeBourdais as fully as time and opportunity permit.

V. Stefansson

From the Japanese poet Yone Noguchi, in Tokyo, came the following, early in the year 1930:

Dear Harriet,

How often I write you in spirit! It is true that my spirit flows, but my pen does not follow. I had almost forgotten how to write in English. My work in Japanese presses me all the time; and I have scarcely a time to enjoy myself in English.

Your friend-sculptor, a Chicago lady,[3] came to see me sometime ago, and I knew how you had been lately.

Yes, time passes so fast—so it is about ten years ago that I saw you last—or perhaps more than ten years ago. I forget. But I trust you are the same in both spirit and health.

I am sending you a book of a Japanese color-print artist, Haronobu, which I brought out just now by subscription. Of course you cannot have interest in the text, since it is written

[3] Lucile Swan Blum.

in Japanese, but the pictures talk an universal language. I hope that you will have interest in them. Of course you will.

With greetings for the new year,

I am yours,
YONE NOGUCHI

Oh, how I wish you could read my Japanese essays.

And from England, Wilfrid Gibson sent assurance of sympathy:

DEAR HARRIET,

Though it was lovely to have a letter from you, we are terribly distressed to hear of your difficulties. It is dreadful to think of this happening to you who have never spared yourself but have laboured for others and have acted as the good angel to so many. I cannot tell you how passionately we wish we could do anything to help; but, as you know, we live always on the edge, perilously balanced over the abyss . . . . and now it would seem that any sort of success is out of my reach. Of course, I really have everything worth having—having a happy home, and the children; and a feeling of security might prove a soul-destroying thing; but when one hears of distress happening to dear friends and one can do nothing to help, then, indeed, one wishes for more of the world's goods! I realize how bad things must be with you for you to have said anything about it—you with your indomitable courage! And we can do nothing but send you a word of sympathy! We, who have always lived from hand to mouth, can realize your position without any exercise of the imagination, dear Harriet!

How ardently we hope to hear that things are already taking a turn for the better. Our loving thoughts are now with you, brave heart!

Yours affectionately,
WILFRID

In the latter part of 1930 there was a wretchedly tantalizing correspondence with Tagore, who was spending several months in America but remaining in the East. It was bitter indeed to

Harriet to realize that the pilgrimage to New York, of which she formerly would have thought less than nothing, was now impossible to her.

From Williamstown, Massachusetts, on October 12, the Poet wrote:

DEAR FRIEND,

After a long wandering I have come at last to your gate. But your dear face is not yet seen.

Ever yours,
RABINDRANATH TAGORE

Harriet must have made an immediate response, for he wrote her again, a few days later:

DEAR FRIEND,

I shall be whirling in an eddy of movement round New Haven, New York, Boston, Philadelphia and other centers till I find myself in my own corner across the sea. I shall try my best to come to your neighborhood if I survive the strain. My fixed address is American Express, New York. I shall never forgive my fate if I ever go away without seeing you—but fate remains unperturbed however fiercely we may revile her. She is not nearly as sensitive as the poet who so often has the provocation to execrate her.

Ever yours
RABINDRANATH TAGORE

I hope to be in New York about the time that you are there.

The meeting that would have been so great a joy was now impossible to the fettered woman. With New York scarcely more than a day's journey away, with the prince of poets and of friends awaiting her, there was no alternative to the sacrifice that Harriet was obliged to make.

So Mr. Tagore wrote her on December 5, 1930:

MY DEAR FRIEND,

I understand your difficulties and it will cause me pain if I know that you have strained your resources too much in order to come to see me. In any case I am sure of your affection and I am deeply satisfied. I am arranging to leave New York for England on the 16th of this month. My experience has not been favorable but failure is a trial that has its own value for wisdom. . . . .

And ten days later came his final message:

DEAR FRIEND,
  Good bye.

With love and kind wishes,
RABINDRANATH TAGORE

CHAPTER XXII

"ON EVIL DAYS THOUGH FALLEN...."

HER book was to be published in January, 1931. If it should have a large and immediate sale, Harriet could breathe freely again. That this was a very considerable "if," nobody knew better than she. Yet she spoke hopefully.

As it proved, publication was delayed three months. When the book did appear, the sale was good but not phenomenal, as indeed it scarcely could have been. This was no volume for the average housewife, particularly in the lax and lazy age of the can opener. And it had been shorn of the poets' prefaces, which would have been a recommendation to the elect.....
So, after a few months' interval, Harriet relaxed the intensity of her hope and turned her attention to other matters.

The greater part of Harriet Moody's life had been spent in helping other people. Thus nothing could have been more suitable or more just than that, after the catastrophe of 1929, she should herself have been helped in certain welcome ways by various persons who saw her need, who were attached to her, and who were happily able to lend a hand. That one of her former pupils, now anonymous by his own wish, should acquire her Ellis Avenue house and invite her to live in it, was a generous and graceful action that must have warmed Harriet's aching heart. Another loyal former pupil, Mr. Charles Hayes, author of the play, *The Natural Law*, placed his New York apartment at her disposal whenever she might care to use it. But in neither habitation was she able to spend restful leisure. There was so much to be done, such imperative urgency as to the doing of it. It was clear that the greatly needed financial miracle was not to come to pass, now that the cookbook bubble had burst. Yet an immediate regular income, however modest, had to be conjured into being.

Various possibilities presented themselves. An opportunity that Harriet seized upon was writing advertisements for certain articles of food. It was while she was doing this that a visit from Robert and Elinor Frost greatly enlivened her. Mr. Frost had a friendly interest in this new occupation of hers, and they consulted together. . . . . At this same time, however, she wrote to Padraic Colum, in an especially candid moment: "If any of your friends of the old mythology had been set to write these things, I think it would have been a just punishment for any misdemeanor they might have been guilty of."

Then somebody asked her to design for a flat-pursed academic clientele meals which were to be sold at impossibly low figures. This would have meant the denial of every principle her work had been built on. It would have meant using her name and prestige to confer an undeserved respectability on inferior foods. To such a proposal she could say nothing. It was the final irony. . . . .

Her chief interest from now on and her chief reliance were to be centered in a second volume, a cooking manual, which was to be a severely practical affair. Incidentally, like all cookbooks, it was designed for the untutored bride of legend. But primarily it was to be a textbook for use in high schools and normal schools. It had the indorsement, even before it was finished, of the Illinois Board of Education, and its plan was devised after close consultation with Harriet's friends Miss Rose and Miss Van Rensselaer of Cornell. Here was a book that should be indispensable, a book that ought to sell.

Harriet could not forget, after all, and did not wish to forget that she was dealing with an art—an art that is of primary importance to the human race and about which countless wise writers have said memorable things. Although she had vowed that this second project should have no literary taint, as publishers might consider it, she persuaded herself that a few bits of happy phrasing, deftly slipped in, could not possibly prejudice its fortunes. So she wrote to Nelson Rowley who, though first of all a musician, had, she knew, a sophisticated outlook that included the very field she had in mind. ". . . . I am telling you of a thing I want you, of all people in the world, to do for me. I want excerpts from the writings of those sensitive to 'gourmandise,' to make a little section of my *Manual*. . . . . You are just the person to find and select them for me. . . . . What I most want is modern stuff, but I should like some old bits too. I can offer no guide."

Mr. Rowley responded promptly with some paragraphs from Proust, and the assemblage of quotations was under way.

There could be no waiting until the manual should be completed and published. So, while still working on it, but desperately pursued by her urgent need, Harriet again became a teacher, this time in a very special field. What she now undertook was to teach cooking to a class of girls both deaf and dumb, with the idea of preparing them to earn a living. This, of course, wasn't too easy a matter. But as she had long ago proved, Harriet had the teacher's passion, and, as effectively as she had once imparted to her English classes a love of the great writers, she now inspired these handicapped students with an enthusiasm for making good bread. Coming to them with no training for communication with the deaf, she was nevertheless able to teach them through lip reading. "I am convinced that Helen Keller was right when she said that the defect of one sense intensifies the value of the others," Harriet wrote.

Her young friend Kathleen Campbell, who watched some of the sessions, now recalls her own amazement as she saw how far from perfunctory Harriet's work with these girls was—how patient, how charming, how stimulating, they found her. And they actually did learn to cook, while the fact that the hours were exacting was no new experience to Harriet, even though it was a strain her friends would have wished to spare her.

Writing to Nelson Rowley at the beginning of May, in the midst of these busy, anxiety-ridden weeks, Harriet made a particularly interesting revelation. More fully aware than anyone else could be of the dramatic material at her disposal, she confided that she had it in mind to write her autobiography. "If only," she said, "I could get a little freedom from this persistent 'hammer, hammer and the hard, hard road,' and could absent myself from the racking details of my everyday life, I would finish my Manual—which will be much better than this book[1] both as regards interest and also originality—and then I think I am going to do the one thing that everybody has told me would make money in sufficient quantity—write a semibiographic sketch of my victorious life. If only I could induce that imp who has traveled with me for all these years to be as good as he is at his best, I think I could turn him right into cash."

But at the very height of her valiant effort to become, as she said, "once more in the class of independent people," anything short of which must have been inconceivably bitter to this proud spirit, destiny inflicted upon Harriet a further and, this time, a personal blow from which there could be no recovering.

It was arranged that Alice Harriet should go to live permanently in California.

For the first time in her life Harriet was helpless. This particular helplessness was surely far bitterer to her than the sacrifice of her material fortunes. To Mr. and Mrs. Brett Young she wrote in late May: "My heart is .... broken by the fact that my niece, Alice Harriet, whom I have been so fond of all these years, is going away to live and take her college course in California, and this is a thing I can hardly bear. Milton's lament applies particularly well to me:—

> .... though fallen on evil days,
> On evil days though fallen ...."

In June, 1931, feeling herself in a state both of physical and temperamental collapse and understanding only too clearly how

[1] The *Cookbook*.

265

this had come about, she wrote to another friend: "This departure of Alice Harriet from my life, and especially as I had so eagerly planned many important things for her education, seems to have been one of the causes of my complete knockout."

Harriet's well-grounded attachment for Cornell had been, as we have seen, lifelong. She had preserved an intimate connection with the university, and her own standing there, as alumna and trustee, was of the highest. Thus, it was natural for her to wish that Alice Harriet, who was ready for college, should enter Cornell. But now, without warning, the long-cherished hope was killed. The girl herself knew little of the East, though she knew and loved California. Indeed, she and Harriet had often been there together. There could be no violence—it would seem to her—in exchanging the bleakness of Chicago for that bright, glowing region. She was deeply devoted to Harriet. Yet who could think of Harriet as a stationary person? Surely they would meet soon .... meet often.....
Harriet herself said nothing.

It happened that at this very time Harriet had a reason, perhaps not too pressing, for making, herself, the trip to Ithaca. She decided to start immediately and proposed that Alice Harriet should drive her there. This may have been only for the sake of the girl's precious companionship. But she must also have had the idea that, if Alice Harriet could only see the university, what might not happen, even now, at this next to the last moment?

So the two set forth and spent three days at Cornell, deliciously happy ones that were a comfort to Harriet all the rest of her life.

To her friends and collaborators at Cornell she wrote after her return: "Alice Harriet and I got home on Saturday. We looked back to our visit in Ithaca with rapture. I think A. H. enjoyed herself more than she ever did before."

The trip had been a great success, but that was all. There was no question, it seemed, of any change of plan. And a few days later the beloved young creature was out of Harriet's life forever.

266

At about this time Arnold Bennett died. Harriet had never met him but had wanted to. Frank Swinnerton, who knew this, wrote her from his home in England:

The loss of Arnold Bennett has been one of the greatest blows of my life. I could tell you a long story about this, but it must be for when we meet. Mary and I went to lunch with him and with the Wellses [not H. G., but T.B., of Harper's] in London just before Christmas. He was then going to France. He was away perhaps just over a fortnight, came back tired and ill, and went to bed. The day after his return, he called his secretary, and said, "I want to see Mr. Swinnerton." But when next I was in town I had a luncheon engagement, and the following week, although we had an appointment, he was too ill to come. I offered to go and see him, but in vain. It was not until he was unconscious that I was allowed to see him, and then, though he gripped my hands in his, and talked, he was really only delirious. Terrible. Nobody who knew him really can believe that we shall not see him again in our midst. That strong personality was too strong to fade quickly from life. I shall not say more now. But it is significant that a number of people felt that they had to tell somebody how deeply they felt of his death, and so wrote to me. I was reminded of the very old lady in America, who said to me, "Mr. Swinnerton, I've always wanted to shake hands with Mr. Arnold Bennett. I never shall. I reckon you're the next best thing." I told A. B. that, and he liked it tremendously.

Yours affectionately,
FRANK

This year there was no respite for Harriet when the choking sultriness of July and August beset Chicago. Her cooking classes had a summer session, so she kept on day after day.

In this last summer of her life she admitted: "What with the heat . . . . and what with my little deaf girls, who take up much time and strength, I sometimes find it slightly hard to keep up my courage."

Yet to Theodore Maynard, who that summer dropped in,

in the old way, her buoyancy seemed unlessened. Such it could be, no doubt, when the talk was with a poet and of poetry rather than of the grim topics that life now forced on her.

The truth was that now, when her strength was deserting her, when poetry itself seemed to flutter unattainably in fields just beyond her own, and when the adored young Alice Harriet was, as she must have known, never to be seen again, she worked harder and more unremittingly—and with infinitely less reward —than at any other time in her life.

Alice Harriet, two thousand miles away, was not forgetful. College was enthralling but bewildering. So many decisions must be made. There was the matter of sororities—for it seemed she had a choice. Touchingly, she turned to Harriet. Couldn't they be sisters?

Deeply moved, Harriet wrote that at Cornell she had not joined a sorority. Her democratic sentiments had stood in the way. "But when I hear that you would have considered my sorority on my account, I cannot regret enough that I was not a member."

There was comfort in the fact that another gracious hand had reached out to help her. A younger woman of large means, not a personal friend but an admirer of the selfless liberality of Harriet's life, now made over to her a yearly income, which Harriet, undefeated in spirit, insisted on regarding as a loan. This greatly eased the hardest stretches.

As the weather became cooler, she could say of her daily work, more confidently: ".... I am making a 'Vocational Kitchen' for these girls of subnormal hearing to run as a business..... Last Tuesday we filled an order for a mass meeting from various western states."

But life had lost all pretense to serenity. Early in December there came to her the severe shock of Vachel Lindsay's death in Springfield. This brought forth from Harriet the strange revelation of a thing she may never have confessed before.

Writing Elizabeth Lindsay on January 24, she said: "In the first hours after I heard of Vachel's death a kind of terror seized me which I struggled against almost in vain. I tried to go on with the things I was doing in a natural and commonplace way, but the *terrible musical accompaniment that so often with me goes with any tragic occurrence*[2] finally overwhelmed me, and when I wrote you I hardly felt myself to be in a state of mental balance. . . . . As Mrs. Browning says:

" 'Death struck sharp on life makes awful music.' "

She pulled herself together and a month later was able to declare: "I have had a beautiful Christmas, with loving and reinforcing words from many cherished friends. . . . ." And also: "My class in the Normal School goes on famously."

But bold and desperate swimmer though she was, Harriet was struggling beyond her strength in the effort to span her sea of troubles. In February, 1932, almost without warning, she was swiftly overthrown by the enemy she had never been willing to recognize. "I won't have asthma!" she had protested, half seriously, over and over again. Even this she met with serene courage. The gallant life had a heroic ending.

[2] Italics not Mrs. Moody's.

ACKNOWLEDGMENTS

ACKNOWLEDGMENTS

THE writer wishes to record that for such biographical material as did not come through her own personal friendship with Mrs. Moody she is glad to acknowledge her indebtedness, first of all, to Miss Edith S. Kellogg, for many years Mrs. Moody's friend and secretary, who supplied the greater number of the letters to and from Mrs. Moody and who patiently answered countless questions as to dates and other important details. She is also indebted to Miss Elizabeth O'Neill, long a member of Mrs. Moody's household, who generously offered letters and memories, and to Miss Katharine Lyle for similar help. She is especially grateful, for sharing their recollections, to Mrs. Alice Corbin Henderson and to the late Mrs. Leila Kennedy Hutchens; as well as to Mrs. Kathleen Foster Campbell, Mrs. Edith Foster Flint, the late Mrs. Teresina Peck Rowell, Mr. Nelson Rowley, Mrs. Theodore Sheldon, Mrs. Leonora Speyer, Mr. Charles Squire, and Miss Helen Tilden.

INDEX

INDEX

Adams, Léonie, 221
Addams, Jane, 42
AE; see Russell, George
Agricultural College (Cornell University), 183
Albany, New York, 65, 178, 180
Alps, French, 101
Alvarez, Marguerite d', 224
America, 15, 78, 129, 131, 133, 143, 144, 145, 152, 155, 157, 172, 178, 182, 190, 192, 196, 203, 222, 224, 226, 227, 232, 233, 238, 240, 242, 249, 259
American Song Bag, The; see Sandburg, Carl
Amherst College, 136, 137, 149, 153, 157, 170
Anacapri, Italy, 232
Andersen, Hans Christian, 168
Andrews, 249
Anglin, Margaret, 113, 124
Angora cats, 166
Ann Arbor, Michigan, 187, 189
Anthology from Bryon; see Stephens, James
Anthology from Spenser; see Stephens, James
Arden, Forest of, 215
Arizona, 64
Arnold, Matthew, 145
Art Institute (Chicago), 11
Atlantic Monthly, 64
Atlantic Ocean, 7, 144, 175, 226, 245
Aunt Minnie, 241
Austria, 240
Ayres, Mrs. Ella, 166

Bad Lands, South Dakota, 15
Baltimore, Maryland, 82
Battle Creek, Michigan, 201
Beasts, Men and Gods; see Ossendowsky
"Beau Brocade," setter dog, 125
Beckford, Vahdah Olcott, 238
Beckhard, Arthur, 219
Beckhard, Mrs. Arthur; see Dale, Esther

Belgium, 140
Belmont, Mrs. August, 236
Ben Ami, Jacob, 223
Bengal, 96, 104
Bennett, Arnold, 267
Bennett, Isadora, 186
Bennington, Vermont, 174
Benson, Arthur, 100
"Berengaria," S.S., 202
Berkshires, 6, 36, 156
"Birds of Paradise," 180
Birthplace, William Cullen Bryant's, 5, 182
Björnson, Professor Björnsterne, 22
Black Hills, South Dakota, 15
Blavatsky, Helena, 22, 24, 25
Blue Bird, The (Maeterlinck), 79
Blum, Lucile Swan, 131, 258
Boar's Hill (Oxford), 167
Board of Trade (Chicago), 17
Bodenheim, Maxwell, 176
"Bogey," a cat, 246
Bois de Boulogne, 241
Bolpur (India), 105
Bonchurch (Isle of Wight), 75
Booker Washington Trilogy; see Lindsay, Vachel
Bordeaux, 217
Boston, 97, 250, 260
"Boul' Mich' " (Michigan Boulevard, Chicago), 18
Bouley Bay (Jersey), 78
Bourg, France, 255
Box Hill, George Meredith's estate in England, 46
Boy Apprenticed to an Enchanter, The; see Colum, Padraic
Boynton, Percy, 187
Brainard, Dr. Daniel, 30
Brainard, Edwin, 30, 31
Brainard, Mrs. Edwin: divorce, 31; begins teaching, 35; founds Home Delicacies Association (see Home Delicacies Association); meets and forms friendship with William Vaughn Moody, 47, 48 ff.; her accident, 55, 56; gives up teaching, 59;

277

interest in music, 60; marriage to William Vaughn Moody, 71; *see also* Tilden, Harriet Converse; and Moody, Mrs. William Vaughn
Brett Young, Francis, 228, 229, 243, 265; *Clare*, 233; *The Key of Life*, 233; letter from, 232
Brett Young, Jessica, 228, 229, 243, 265
Briton, 128, 152
Brittany, 241
Broadway (New York), 166
Broom (magazine), 191
"Brother," setter dog, 232
Browning, Elizabeth Barrett, 139, 269
Browning, Robert, 23
Bryan, William Jennings, 122
Bryant, William Cullen, 5; *see also* Birthplace
Buffalo, New York, 180
Bukeleys, the Rudolph, 194
Bull, Dr. William, 63
Butlers, the, 194

Caen (France), 141
Calcutta, 103, 105, 125, 155
California, 43, 69, 82, 84, 87, 88, 93, 97, 98, 131, 161, 168, 169, 170, 181, 188, 194, 199, 204, 205, 208, 210, 214, 248, 249, 265, 266
Cambridge, England, 49, 183
Cambridge, Massachusetts, 62, 63, 96
Campbell, Donald, 156
Campbell, Mrs. Donald, 156; *see also* Foster, Kathleen
Campbell, Harriet Moody, 156
Canada, 71, 186, 257, 258
"Canada Maru," S.S., 131
Canadian National Committee for Mental Hygiene, 257
"Candida," 51
Cannes, France, 218, 219, 222, 225
Cape Ann, Massachusetts, 191
Cape Henry, Virginia, 63
Capri, 233
Captain Craig; see Robinson, Edwin Arlington
Cardston (Alberta, Canada), 185
Carmel, California, 210, 241
Carnegie Hall, 112
Carnegie Institute of Technology, 198, 199
Catholic church, 98, 123
Catonsville, Maryland, 82

Catullus, 214
Cavender's House; see Robinson, Edwin Arlington
Charlevoix, Michigan, 186
Chaucer, 23
Chautauqua, 123
Chelsea (London), 100
Chesterton, Gilbert, 172
Cheyne Walk, Chelsea, London, S.W., 100
Chicago, 4, 7, 15, 21, 23, 26, 28, 31, 39, 44, 46, 51, 54, 55, 56, 57, 59, 60, 62, 64, 65, 68, 69, 71, 81, 83, 85, 86, 87, 88, 89, 93, 95, 97, 98, 101, 116, 121, 122, 123, 128, 129, 131, 132, 135, 136, 137, 143, 149, 153, 154, 157, 158, 159, 160, 163, 168, 169, 171, 172, 174, 178, 184, 185, 186, 187, 189, 190, 192, 199, 200, 201, 202, 204, 205, 206, 207, 208, 219, 220, 221, 223, 224, 226, 229, 230, 237, 238, 242, 243, 244, 247, 248, 249, 251, 258, 267
Chicago clubs, 122
Chicago Daily News, 184
Chicago home, 144
Chicago household, 82, 101
Chicago life, 161
China, 119, 120, 147, 155, 160
"Chinese Nightingale, The"; *see* Lindsay, Vachel
Chinese Palaces, 120
Chitra; see Tagore, Rabindranath
"City of Lahore," S.S., 103
Clare; see Brett Young, Francis
"Clarence," a carriage, 41
Claudel, Paul, 230
Cleveland, Ohio, 134, 216
Clinton, Illinois, 128
Collected Poems; see Robinson, Edwin Arlington
Colophon (quarterly magazine), 254
Colorado Springs, 85, 86, 120, 159
Colum, Mary, 9, 121, 122, 126, 127, 129, 158, 159, 201, 202, 211, 235, 238
Colum, Padraic, 6, 9, 13, 121, 122, 126, 127, 129, 133, 136, 158, 159, 161, 168, 173, 176, 181, 187, 194, 199, 210, 211, 212, 223, 235, 238, 239, 263; *The Boy Apprenticed to an Enchanter*, 169; *The Eddas* (with dedication to Harriet C. Moody), 169; *The King of the Cats*,

282

283

her "salon," 150; continued friendship with John Masefield and other poets, 150–58; two Hollywood sojourns in connection with filming of *The Great Divide*, 161–68; starts restaurant, Au Petit Gourmet, 175; also starts series of poetry readings, Les Petits Jeux Floraux, 175; correspondence with poets, 177–92; Hollywood again in the interest of *The Great Divide*, 204–8; friendship with James Stephens begun, 210; takes Alice Harriet to France, 216; makes a second trip to bring Alice Harriet home, 224–26; goes to France and makes personal connection with Mme Curie, 240–42; collapse of Home Delicacies Association, 251; begins preparation of *Cookbook*, 253; *Cookbook* published, 262; begins writing a cooking Manual, 263; writes advertisements, 263; teaches cooking to deaf and dumb girls, 264; final parting with Alice Harriet, on the latter's departure for California, 266; brief illness and death, 269; see also Tilden, Harriet Converse; and Brainard, Mrs. Edwin

"Moon-Moth, The"; see Moody, William Vaughn

More's Garden (London), 99, 103

Morell, 51

Morris, Harriet, 224

Mount Orgueil (Jersey), 77

Mount Posilippo (Italy), 67

Mountain Interval; see Frost, Robert

Munich, 231, 232

Murray, Gilbert, 108

Mythology, Greek, 65

Napanoch, New York, 172

Naples, 67

Nashville, Tennessee, 128

Nation (London), 102, 159

Natural Law, The; see Hayes, Charles

Negro, the, 166, 203, 211

Negro blues, 195

New England, 16, 63, 178

New Haven, Connecticut, 260

New Orleans, 69, 220

New Witness, 112

New York, 34, 36, 63, 64, 69, 70, 85, 89, 96, 97, 102, 108, 111, 112, 113, 121, 123, 133, 134

New York City, 133, 134, 138, 151, 158, 161, 164, 168, 169, 172, 173, 176, 178, 179, 180, 186, 188, 190, 202, 207, 209, 210, 212, 220, 223, 226, 229, 236, 238, 245, 246, 248, 256, 257, 260

New York Herald Tribune, 256

New Yorkers, 112

New Zealand, 238

Ney, Elly, 13

Nichols, Robert, 150, 156, 157, 160, 167; letter to Harriet C. Moody, 157

Nielsen, Mme Oda, 168

Ninety-first Psalm, 89

Ninety-three (Victor Hugo), 84

Nobel prize, 96, 104, 105

Noguchi, Yone, 8, 171, 187, 258, 259; letter from, 258

Normal School (Chicago), 269

North of Boston; see Frost, Robert

North Michigan Avenue (Chicago), 170

North Star, 118

Oakhampton, England, 79

O'Casey, Sean, 218

Occidentals, 95

"Ode in Time of Hesitation"; see Moody, William Vaughn

Offner, Richard, 163

Ohio, 15, 154, 173, 184

Okakura, Mr., 97

Old Tokefield (England), 219, 222, 223, 245

"Olympic," S.S., 90, 223

Omaha, Nebraska, 146

One Hundred and Fifty-fifth Street (New York), 71

O'Neill, Elizabeth (Bessie), 39, 46, 59, 62, 63, 65, 67, 69, 70, 71, 75, 79, 84, 86, 128, 168, 194, 204, 206, 223

Orchestra Hall, Chicago, 203

Orient, 194

Oriental, the, 95, 248

Oshkosh, Wisconsin, 187

Ossendowsky, author of *Beasts, Men and Gods,* 234

Oxford (England), 145, 148, 167, 188

Oxford Book of Verse, 153

284

Pacific Ocean, 131, 248, 249
Paimpol (Brittany), 241
Panama, 190
Pan-Asiatic University, a, 170
Paradise, 301
Paris, 21, 75, 119, 212, 217, 218, 224, 230, 231, 234, 240, 241, 242
Parker, Sir Gilbert, 79
Parker School (Chicago), 189
Parkman, Hannah Breck, 15
Parkman, Ohio, 16, 17, 41, 67, 101
Parnassus, Mount, 63
Patrick, Dr. Hugh, 81
Pearson, W. W., 146, 183, 194; death of, 198
Peattie, Elia W., 200; letter to Harriet C. Moody, 200
Peck, Teresina (Mrs. Wilfred A. Rowell), 22
Pennsylvania Station, 89
Percy Street (London), 218
Perfilieff, Vladimir, 196, 224
Peterborough, New Hampshire, 111, 186, 187, 191, 206
Petits Jeux Floraux, Les, 175, 176, 187, 195, 207, 210, 211, 220
Philadelphia, 27, 179, 260
Philpotts, Eden, 79, 80
Pinafore, 45
Pittsburgh, Pennsylvania, 157, 198, 199
Pittsfield, Massachusetts, 183
Players, The Irish, 99
Plows, Gladys, 46, 48
Plymouth (England), 177
Poems and Poetic Dramas; see Moody, William Vaughn
Poetry: A Magazine of Verse, 3, 96, 107, 109, 111, 112, 135
Poetry Society Bulletin, 200
Pond, James B., Lecture Bureau, 130
Porcupine, The; see Robinson, Edwin Arlington
Portchester, New York, 69
Port Said, 183
Post Office, The; see Tagore, Rabindranath
"Pott's compound fracture," 55
Potter, Hotel (Santa Barbara, California), 84
"Prairie Ride, A"; see Moody, William Vaughn
Press Club, Des Moines, 174
Prince Town (England), 79

"Princetoned," 213
Prometheus, 63
Proust, Marcel, 264
Provence, 175
Pulitzer prizes, 191
Pymander, The Divine, 213

Quaker meeting, 122
Quebec, 65, 71
Queenstown, Ireland, 21

Rachel (heroine of The Porcupine), 114, 123
Randolph, Vermont, 15
Reed, Daniel A., 186, 199
Reed, Isadora, 210; see also Bennett, Isadora
Reedy, William Marion, 124
Reedy's Mirror, 124
Reinhardt, President Aurelia H., 214
Rhoda (heroine of The Faith Healer), 199
Rhymes To Be Traded for Bread; see Lindsay, Vachel
Rider of Dreams, The; see Torrence, Ridgely
Ridge, Lola, 191; Sun-Up, 192; The Ghetto, 192
Riggs, Lynn, 220
Riverside, California, 84
Riviera, 218
Robi Babu (familiar name), 227, 131; see also Tagore, Rabindranath
Robinson Crusoe, 84
Robinson, Edwin Arlington, 3, 14, 49, 107, 109, 111, 113, 114, 175, 186, 187, 188, 191; wins Pulitzer prize for Collected Poems, 91, 192, 254; Captain Craig, 124; Cavender's House, 250; Eros Turannos, 108; The Porcupine, 108; Tristram, 235; Van Zorn, 111, 112, 113, 124; letters to Harriet C. Moody, 108, 111, 113, 186, 187, 250; letter from Harriet C. Moody, 235
Robson, Eleanor; see Belmont, Mrs. August
Rochester, New York, 180
Rockies, Canadian, 15
Rocky Mountain country, 190
Roelvaag, 250
Romance languages, 253
Rome, Italy, 225
Roosevelt, President Theodore, 140
Rosalind (Shakespeare's), 215